When God Comes to Town

Culture and Politics / Politics and Culture

General Editors:
Laura Nader, *University of California, Berkeley*
Rik Pinxten, *Ghent University, Belgium*
Ellen Preckler, *Ghent University, Belgium*

Cultural Identity, whether real or imagined, has become an important marker of societal differentiation. This series focuses on the interplay of politics and culture and offers a forum for analysis and discussion of such key issues as multiculturalism, racism and human rights.

Volume 1
Europe's New Racism: Causes, Manifestations and Solutions
Edited by **The Evens Foundation**

Volume 2
Culture and Politics: Identity and Conflict in a Multicultural World
Edited by **Rik Pinxten**, **Ghislain Verstraete** and **Chia Longman**

Volume 3
Racism in Metropolitan Areas
Edited by **Rik Pinxten** and **Ellen Preckler**

Volume 4
When God Comes to Town: Religious Traditions in Urban Contexts
Edited by **Rik Pinxten** and **Lisa Dikomitis**

Volume 5
The Mirage of China: Anti-Humanism, Narcissism, and Corporeality of the Contemporary World
By **Xin Liu**

WHEN GOD COMES TO TOWN

Religious Traditions in Urban Contexts

Edited by

Rik Pinxten & Lisa Dikomitis

Berghahn Books
New York • Oxford

First published in 2009 by

Berghahn Books
www.BerghahnBooks.com

© 2009, 2012 Rik Pinxten and Lisa Dikomitis
First paperback edition published in 2012

All rights reserved.
Except for the quotation of short passages
for the purposes of criticism and review, no part of this book
may be reproduced in any form or by any means, electronic or
mechanical, including photocopying, recording, or any information
storage and retrieval system now known or to be invented,
without the written permission of the publisher.

Library of Congress Cataloging-in-Publication Data

When God comes to town : religious traditions in urban contexts / edited by Rik Pinxten and Lisa Dikomitis.
   p. cm. -- (Culture and politics/politics and culture series ; v. 4)
   Includes bibliographical references and index.
   ISBN 978-1-84545-554-5 (hbk.)--ISBN 978-0-85745-807-0 (pbk.)
   1. Religion and sociology. 2. Cities and towns--Religious aspects. I. Pinxten, Rik. II. Dikomitis, Lisa.
   BL60.W49 2009
   200.9173'2--dc22

2008053757

British Library Cataloguing in Publication Data
A catalogue record for this book is available from the British Library.

Printed in the United States on acid-free paper.

ISBN: 978-0-85745-807-0 (paperback)   ISBN: 978-0-85745-823-0 (ebook)

Contents

List of Figures	vii
Introduction: When God Comes to Town *Rik Pinxten and Lisa Dikomitis*	ix
Part One: Nation Versus State	
1. Religion and Nationality: The Tangled Greek Case *Renée Hirschon*	3
2. A Church Lost in the Maze of a City without References *Bruno Drweski*	17
Part Two: Urban Transformations	
3. The Protestant Ethic and the Spirit of Urbanism *Simon Coleman*	33
4. The Ecology and Economy of Urban Religious Space: A Socio-Historical Account of Quakers in Town *Peter Collins*	45
Part Three: Urban Migration	
5. Rural Immigrants and Official Religion in an Urban Religious Festival in Greece *Giorgos Vozikas*	65
6. From the City to the Village and Back: Greek Cypriot Refugees Engaging in 'Pilgrimages' across the Border *Lisa Dikomitis*	79

Part Four: Impact of Modernity

7. Reading the City Religious: Urban Transformations and Social
Reconstruction in Recife, Brazil 97
Marjo de Theije

8. Modernity Contra Tradition? *Taijiquan*'s Struggle for Survival:
A Chinese Case Study 114
Dan Vercammen

Notes on Contributors 145

Index 147

Figures

Figure 1.1. An Eighteenth-Century Church Near the Main Square of Athens — 5

Figure 4.1. Slaughterford (West Country, before 1673) — 51
Figure 4.2. Strickland (Lake District, 1668) — 51
Figure 4.3. Coalbrookedale (1808, country meeting house) — 52
Figure 4.4. York (1817, town meeting house) — 52
Figure 4.5. Tipping Street Meeting House (Bolton, 1825) — 53
Figure 4.6. Manchester Mount Street Meeting House (1830) — 54
Figure 4.7. Silverwell Street Meeting House (Bolton, 1970) — 57
Figure 4.8. Canterbury (1772 and 1956) — 58
Figure 4.9. Maidstone (1956) — 59

Figure 6.1. A Political Banner as a *Tama* — 89
Figure 6.2. Refugees Conducting a Service — 90

Introduction:
When God Comes to Town

Rik Pinxten and Lisa Dikomitis

This volume in the series *Culture and Politics* investigates the way the city context and increasing urbanisation influence the styles of conversion, the social processes and the panorama of religions and life stance groups today. The book poses a deep philosophical problem: how does the 'transfer of recipes on the meaning of life' change with the global urbanisation of living conditions? Rather than philosophical generalisations, our approach is based on ethnographic and historical detail: how do people cope with this shift at a grassroots level? Examples from the Mediterranean area and elsewhere are elaborated by an interdisciplinary group of historians, scholars and anthropologists.

Humans Will Be Urbanites

Around 1800 a rough 3 per cent of the human population lived in urban areas. The prognosis is that by 2030 some 70 per cent of humankind will be urbanites (Castells 2002). Contemporary urban areas are not (or not only) the well ordered historical cities we know from the old world, but primarily the rapidly expanding and semi-ordered complexes such as Sao Paolo in Brazil, Cairo in Egypt or Kinshasa in Congo.

Traditional religions offered perspectives on life, explanations on customs and the meaning of life and ritual practices in society within the constraints of small groups (bands, clans, etc.) or villages. Even the ancient Greek and Roman or the early Christian cities Augustine was thinking about never held more than tens of thousands of citizens. We wonder in this book about the possible appeal of these old religious traditions in the urban predicament we are witnessing now. What could be the impact of global urbanisation on learning practices and on the contents of what is learnt and transferred on the meaning of life, on what ritual to perform and on belief and faith? Our presupposition is that the traditional religions we know about (including the religions of the book: Judaism, Christianity and Islam) used two foci of relatedness in order to appeal to their followers. On the one hand, some religious traditions offer a common ancestry or a lineage of descent to the followers: we are all children of Abraham (for Judaism, and in a slightly different way for Christianity and Islam), or we are all Navajo because that is the 'way of the People (Diné)' since the time of emergence (Wyman 1970). On the other hand, the peer group can be emphasised to represent the basic social reference group: through face-to-face relationships of a deep and continuous nature followers are reared as religious persons. A parish, a small synagogue school or a particular praying group are cases in point. Although both these references will probably continue to be relevant, they seem to be losing power in the context of a vast and anonymous context of the big city. That is to say, it becomes increasingly difficult to uphold that the insights gained from the peer level experiences will still be relevant for the questions of sense and meaning of life in the new conditions. In the new context, a great variety of religious traditions will be encountered and the historical uniformity of the nation-state (one religion, one language, one nation) will be hard to keep up: especially the religions of the book seem to confront this issue in their attempts to redefine their relationship with a state or a government (see Drweski, this volume). Another shift might be occasioned by the mere numbers of the new context, yielding a change in strategy to reach and serve the following by drawing on new media techniques or looking for mass demonstrations to supplement or substitute for the peer relationships. Some denominations (like the Evangelical Church, but also the Roman Catholic Church) explore this road. Our point of departure in this volume is that the urbanisation trends should be scrutinised as possible causes, or at the very least important factors of impact, to understand the evolution on the ground.

These are the macro questions addressed in this book. They were the focus of an interdisciplinary symposium 'Making Sense in the City' (December 2006), which we organised on the topic, by drawing in and confronting the competences on these issues from academics, artists and specialists from life stance organisations. In this volume we gathered some of the expertise we saw in this field that has special relevance. The focus here is on the changes in existing religious traditions, when they try to cope with a rather sudden shift towards urban life. That yields, typically for anthropologists and historians we believe, a microlevel analysis.

A phenomenal change is taking place right under our eyes: in two generations, or fifty years, the urban population in the world doubled. In that same period concepts shifted from 'city' to 'megapolis' and now to 'conurban complex', to denote the multimillion concentrations of people that are rapidly growing, especially in the Third World (Davis 2007). Where towns or cities number a few hundred thousand inhabitants, conurban complexes see concentrations of 20 and possibly up to 50 million people (the latter number being mentioned for the Shanghai area of the near future). Not only is this a new situation, it also poses the question of how people live and organise their lives in this type of interdependent complex. Davis's argument is that most of the Third World megapolises harbour the largest slums and semi-ordered masses of the world, on top of the mere numbers mentioned.

In this book we want to focus on some of the factors that accompany this tremendous and rapid evolution of the urban phenomenon: How do people cope in terms of life changes, of quality of life and of learning trajectories about values and meaning of life? In what way do the traditional religions offer answers or to what extent are they trying to adapt in order to cope with these shifts in the urbanisation patterns? Of course, no single book can map the issues at hand. That is why we focus on in-depth studies of particular religious groups, and analyse how they change and adapt within or notwithstanding the long tradition they represent. Moreover, by emphasising the in-depth or 'thick' description here we want to reach a better understanding of the ways they deal with the microsocial changes in their constituency, the existential dimension of their message or practice and the shifts in competences and discourse of their personnel. In other words, we want to ask: what does it entail for a parish or for the local believers to be situated in a rapidly and vastly expanding urban context? And how do the relationships between local, national and international levels of one's organisation change? Examples from different traditions will offer insights of a wide variety, based on which views theorists of religious studies will use to reach a more encompassing model on the impact of global urbanisation on the religious and life stance offer.

Structure of the Volume

The volume distinguishes between a set of relevant dimensions of the problem area. These dimensions do not represent an exhaustive view on the matter, but they are all relevant to the issues at hand.

The book structures the field of study according to four dimensions:

1. Nations versus church

In Europe, North America, China, India-Pakistan and – in a different way – Latin America, churches have been positioning themselves vis-à-vis national political structures. Not only did this yield 'national churches' – the Orthodox Christian churches can be mentioned, but also the Polish Catholic Church. With the shifts pointed at in the perspective of this book, the ties between church and nation-state now sometimes turn into a handicap rather than a blessing. Or, perhaps more often, the relationships between church and nation have to be explored again and redefined in a way that allows for a pluri-religious landscape that is politically viable, rather than a 'national church' option.

2. Urban transformations

The tremendous growth of cities and the transformations of tasks and impact of the city level on matters of social, economic and political coexistence are such that churches sometimes feel driven to change their own rules of conduct or practices because of the shifts in the urban context. With this dimension we want to offer some examples of the impact at the urban level.

3. Urban migration

Urbanisation equals immigration, as some politicians would argue. We singled out this issue of the impact of immigration, as intrinsic and relevant feature of the large cities in particular, on the form of religious activities. People who migrate bring in their tradition(s) and inevitably trigger tensions or revitalisations of the local practices.

4. Impact of modernity

The rather sudden and consistent expansion of the urban context of one's religious practice can be captured under the heading of 'modernity's impact'.

Contributions to the Volume

The volume presents a series of studies on the interface between urbanisation and religious or life stance traditions. The emphasis is on historical and ethnographic detail rather than grand models or theories. We are convinced that we need more in-depth studies like these in order to come to understand in a thorough way what the forms and shapes of religious and life stance traditions will become in a deeply and unalterably urbanised world. The Enlightenment proposal of the separation of church and state (or religion and politics) will only then be assessed in an informed way, in order to define viable formats for a world where many religious and life stance denominations will live together in urban, mixed contexts.

In Part I, Hirschon explicitly focuses on the nationality aspects and religion in the case of Greece. The Greek Orthodox Church had a strong impact on national politics, positioning itself as a fundamental factor of identity for the Greeks ever since the Ottoman Empire. The secularisation of systematically urbanising Europe thus was not followed up in Greece, and the latter's entering the EU (European Union) in 1981 launched the problem of 'national and Orthodox' identity, culminating in repeated controversy over the deletion of religious affiliation from the data on one's national identity card. This is followed by Drweski's intriguing overview of the developments in post-communist Poland. This new EU-member has a strong Catholic Church, which took a role of political and moral authority and leadership in the days of the decline of the communist regime. With the growth and the modernisation of the cities in Poland the Catholic Church (boosted under Pope John Paul II) is now struggling to reposition itself as either national-cum-rural or modern-cum-urban power. These two contributions looking at the impact of city transformations on churches shed a historical-anthropological light on matters.

Part II starts with Coleman raising the question why the Evangelical and the Pentacostal Protestants seem to have a huge success in the mega-cities, especially in the south of the world. His view is that mass communication and other political strategies and action forms, applied to large populations, makes them most effective. The role of building styles of the big cities (skyscrapers and large halls) has a supplementary impact on success. Coleman seems to suggest that what he calls 'urban religion' might exist and that it may well offer new perspectives for religious formats in the future. Next, Collins picks up the line of the impact of the 'urban ecology' defined as the built environment. He compares the architectural features of rural and urban contexts in an attempt to define the interrelationships between theology, the city contexts and politics in the new urbanised world as it emerges. His case is a typical one: the Quakers started out in the frame of mind of the rural believer and now position themselves more and more in an urban world of religious experience.

Part III consists of two contributions that highlight the role of immigration in the changing profile of Greek Orthodox religion. Vozikas focuses on the way the religious landscape is changing in one megapolis of Greece – Athens. Dikomitis then details the way Greek Cypriots, who have lived in the city of Nicosia for the past thirty years (following the division of Cyprus), imagine their village through religious representation. Although Athens and Nicosia cannot be compared on many dimensions, it is striking how the integration of former peasant groups in the city in both cases uses religious anchors and symbolic means to come to grips with the new predicament of the urbanite's life. Everyday rituals and religious imagination at the level of individual families and small groups shape the belonging and the practical integration in the city for the newcomers and these immaterial cultural markers sustain the identity formats and adaptation processes for generations.

Part IV comprises two studies on the developments of religious traditions and their institutions in two very different parts of the world. De Theije analyses the ways churches in Brazil's large cities influence the life and the appearance of the urban context through their political actions and organisational structures. Moreover, churches in that part of Latin America add considerably to the skyline and city structure through architectural projects. De Theije presents unique ethnographic material on these issues. A sinologist and ritual specialist on Chinese traditions Vercammen discusses how the Taijiquan tradition, which is best known for the Boxer Rebellion of the 1920s, evolves in the present era. In minute historical detail he describes how the age old tradition of 'ritual boxing' (an imprecise resume if there ever was one) changed over the past century. The nation-state China contained the tradition in a series of political moves, but the rapid and vast urbanisation of the past decades occasions deep adaptations of this ritual tradition. In a peculiar way the cultural identity processes of the Chinese empire have impacted the tradition. This impact is shaped by the exponential booming of the urban areas, hardly controlled by the Chinese nation and government. Within that new margin of semi-order the age old ritual tradition seems to find a new life.

References

Castells, M. 2002. *Conversations with Manuel Castells*. Oxford: Blackwell.
Davis, M. 2007. *Planet of Slums*. London: Verso.
Wyman, L. C. 1970. *Blessingway*. Tucson: University of Arizona Press.

PART ONE

NATION VERSUS CHURCH

RELIGION AND NATIONALITY: THE TANGLED GREEK CASE

Renée Hirschon

Greece stands out among European societies with regard to the way religion relates to social life. It has been one of the most homogeneous countries in Europe in terms of ethnic and cultural factors and it continues to present itself as such, despite widespread immigration over the past two decades from neighbouring Balkan and Eastern European countries and from the Third World. The continuing entanglement of religious and national identity is a particular feature of the country's modern history, and has had ramifications in all spheres of life. These features must be understood in the context of Greece's emergence as a nation-state in the nineteenth century, when it gained independence from the Ottoman state, which has left interesting residues (discussed below). Ultimately failing in its irredentist aspirations after a military defeat in 1922, Greece's vaunted homogeneity was largely accomplished through the terms of the 1923 Lausanne Convention – a unique international agreement specifying a compulsory population exchange between Greece and Turkey. This was effectively a programme of mutual 'ethnic cleansing', which removed the bulk of the Muslim population from Greece and the Orthodox Christians from Turkey, leaving only a small population in each country as a recognised minority (see Hirschon 2003). The assumption of a common religious and national identity is firmly rooted in public consciousness, and to be Greek it is commonly assumed that one is also an Orthodox Christian (discussed below). It is a distortion to conflate these features; nevertheless it is true to say that contemporary Greek identity is a complicated amalgam of national, cultural and religious features. Greece's continued homogeneity is reflected in current census returns, which indicate that over 90 per cent of the population is Orthodox Christian.

Other distinctive characteristics should also be noted. First, Greece is reckoned to be a nation with a high degree of religiosity. This is revealed in the observance of religious practices of various kinds and, even though church attendance may not have been high (though it has shown a marked increase from the early 1990s, with a decrease after 2005), it is the interweaving of the religious with so many aspects of daily life that strikes the outsider. Second, and related to the first characteristic, is the inapplicability of a sharp separation between 'sacred' and 'secular' or 'mundane'. The classic Durkheimian dichotomy is not appropriate for understanding Greek life, as many anthropological studies have indicated. I have analysed some unexpected aspects of this phenomenon in an urban quarter of the metropolis, as related to house furnishing (Hirschon 1993), seasonal activities, and in the philosophical outlook (Hirschon [1989] 1998, chs. 8, 9).

Similarly, the division between private and public, widely accepted in most Western European countries, assigning the religious to a private sphere, does not correspond to Greek ways of thinking or of practice. Church and state were, and continue to be, inextricably linked on all levels – institutional, official and informal, political, educational and personal. This feature proves to be a major obstacle for progressive reformers who wish to modernise old structures of civil administration (see Georgiadou 1996; Molokotos-Lieberman 2003; Prodromou 1998).

Transformations have nonetheless taken place through the various legislative and economic influences of the past twenty-five years, though their consequences are not always readily perceived (for the ramifications that affect notions of personal identity, see Hirschon, forthcoming). Changes have been provoked through the pressures of European integration (entry to the EU in 1981), and through the modernising programme of the PASOK (Panhellenic Socialist Movement) government, which was in power for almost twenty years. The ambiguous value of modernisation is hotly debated: far from being an uncontested area, political arguments about preserving Greece's national character continue in the face of a perceived threat to its consciously prized sovereignty and cultural integrity.

The questions underlying this chapter, therefore, ultimately relate to major issues such as globalisation, modernisation and westernisation, but my focus here is limited to showing how issues regarding religious identity and practice have certain unusual characteristics in Greece. One aspect of these larger processes, the question of secularisation, has a particular complexity in the context of contemporary Greek society. The analysis suggests that a more nuanced approach to the topic of secularisation is required in dealing with those societies that have not followed the western pattern (see Prodromou 1998). This chapter touches on wider issues regarding national identity as well as socio-personal levels of analysis. It is based on experience in the metropolis of Athens-Piraeus, where my activities were not limited to any specific locality but covered a wide range of urban settings and people of different social classes, from Kolonaki to Kokkinia.

Observations of Religious Practice/Religiosity

According to a recently published poll comparing the extent of religious devotion worldwide, Greece stands out among Western European countries in the proportion of its citizens who declare that they are 'religious' (86 per cent of those polled). It was among the top ten in the overall survey of sixty-eight countries on all continents.[1] During a two-month stay in Athens (October to December 2005) and again in the spring (March to April 2006), I had the opportunity to observe some aspects of religious practice on a daily basis. People who are used to living in a secular society, whether visitors to Greece, or even diaspora Greeks who have lived abroad, notice the frequency of outwards signs of religious practice while they are in Athens. This kind of 'diffuse religiosity' or what Prodromou (1998: 102) calls 'religious vitality' is not self-conscious; simply, it is common practice for people to make the sign of the cross when they pass a church, or enter inside to light a candle and venerate the icons, taking a break in the course of other activities to interact with the divine realm.

The city provides many places for such casual unplanned observances. Indeed, the Athenian landscape is marked by the presence of sacred spaces of all historical periods, predominantly around the ancient centre, the rock of the Acropolis and the old quarters of Plaka and Monastiraki. Here, the ruins and excavated expanses, evidence of temples, houses and graveyards from the founding of the city through the classical, Hellenistic and Roman periods are usually what attract the tourists' attention. But of more significance for contemporary city dwellers are the many churches, some dating from the late Byzantine period, others from the period following the establishment of the

Figure 1.1. An Eighteenth-Century Church Near the Main Square of Athens. Courtesy of the author.

Greek state. These little churches set on the main shopping streets, near markets, in small squares, provide points of reference, reminders of the divine realm, which transcends everyday concerns (see Figure 1.1). Small shrines (*proskinitaria*) also dot the urban landscape, erected to commemorate some event (accident or escape from it) are similar reference points.

Churches abound in all the residential areas of the city, many being of recent construction, often on sites of older churches. These buildings are not mere architectural features, they are set in a system of meaning and belief and they provide a locus for conventional religious practice beyond the home, a place of comfort and recourse for believers. Whereas some Athenians may bewail the decline in religious adherence while others mock what takes place as 'simple habit', it is clear that these spontaneous acts of worship constitute an expression of religious activity. It is worth noting that the practice of such religious devotion is public – it is conducted in the eyes of others, beyond the home, and in this way contrasts with the more private nature of much Protestant Christian practice.

Typically, as in other Christian societies, churches are used as geographical orientation points, for example, to designate neighbourhoods, or where stations and stops on public transport lines are named after saints or churches. This holds true for the train, bus, tram and trolley services, as well as for the new Metrolines, in operation since the 2004 Olympics (e.g. two major termini are named for St Dimitrios and St Antonios).

During Lent (*Megali Sarakosti*), I was struck by the numerous shops and restaurant signs that advertised 'fasting foods' (*nystisyma*), as well as radio and TV shows focussing on the preparation of such dishes. There was a marked public awareness of the Lenten fasting period, unlike the unobtrusive style of an earlier period when I lived in the city. My observation was reinforced by Greek colleagues who noted that this reaction could be interpreted as a kind of 'cultural resistance', both to the pressures of European integration and to a consciousness of the standardising process of globalisation. Indeed, we should note that religious practices constitute a major element in what is loosely characterised as 'Greek culture', in a society where religion is integral to worldview (see Hirschon [1989] 1998, ch. 10).

The point here is that the presence of the sacred in everyday activity is a feature of Athenian life which strikes the casual observer, but should not be subject to facile interpretations. Nonetheless some devout people who are observant of religious practices express anti-clerical sentiments and criticise the Church as a corrupt institution. This attitude was exacerbated after 2005, following scandalous revelations. Multiple accusations of financial mismanagement, homosexuality and links related to corruption in the judiciary rocked the Church of Greece and, at the time of this writing, were still under investigation. Certain bishops and some clergy close to the late Archbishop were implicated but the internal enquiry resulted in the prosecution of only one Bishop (Panteleimon of Attika), currently subject to an appeal (2008), with insufficient evidence said to have existed in the other seven cases. This was generally held to be a whitewash, produced many critical reports in the national press, and resulted in widespread disillusionment and disaffection in many circles.

Sceptics argue that the practice of going into church to light a candle or of signing oneself with a cross is merely a habit, an empty gesture without any real significance for the practitioner. This view was expressed to me by some educated Greeks who made it clear that they were not churchgoers; indeed, it is more common than in the past to hear urban educated people say that they are atheists. People in this group frequently noted their own contradictory conduct, saying that although they were non-believers they would go to the Easter church services because it was part of their cultural heritage and identity, and also that they enjoyed the experience for 'aesthetic reasons'. A clear illustration is provided by my historian colleague, a proclaimed atheist, who does not attend church but appears at major church festivals, saying, 'I'm not a believer, but I'm Greek, so I'm Orthodox' (cf. a similar example quoted in Ware 1983: 208). This is by no means a unique statement for I have heard such sentiments expressed by other leftwing, educated non-believers.

In dealing with this topic, therefore, it is important to distinguish among people's various degrees of involvement with the religious sphere, and to be precise about those whom we observe and with whom we engage.[2]

Religion and Identity

The interweaving of what in much of the western world would be seen as separate spheres, the religious and the civil, continues to be a salient feature of contemporary Greece, despite the legal reforms of the past twenty-five years. In 1983, the PASOK government's programme of modernisation introduced major reforms in the Civil Code, especially regarding family law. In particular, civil marriage and divorce were allowed for the first time as an alternative to religious marriage, constituting a radical change: until that time, marriages were contracted and dissolved only through the Church, or the equivalent religious authorities for Jews and Muslims. The new Civil Code also consolidated previous civil reforms, reinforcing the measures for registration of a child specified in Law 344 of 1976. That law had established the procedures whereby a child's name should be recorded in the civil registry office (*lyxiarcheio*). In doing so, it clarified the distinction between name giving (*onomatodosia*) and baptism (*baptisi*) (articles 22, 26) and the issues surrounding registration and naming are of particular interest in the context of this discussion.

In particular, the procedures required to register a child's birth demonstrate the resilience of cultural patterns ('habitus' in Bourdieu's terms). It is widely believed that a person's full membership in Greek society requires a record of their religious affiliation. This was essentially a baptismal certificate or its equivalent for the recognised religions, including Judaism and Islam but excluding Catholics who do not enjoy official legal status (K. Tsitselikis, personal communication, 2006; Frazee 2002; and for Orthodox Old

Calendarists see Ware 2002: 1–23).[3] People have long believed that without a baptismal name – or its equivalent for Jews and Muslims – a child could not be registered and therefore could not be enrolled in school. Public consciousness apparently continues to hold that a child's registration at school requires the registration of a baptismal name/production of a baptism certificate.

In fact, this is a misapprehension because it has long been legally possible to confer a child's name without baptism. It is interesting to note that the possibility of civil registration (without baptism) can be traced to the mid-nineteenth-century Greek Civil Code (*Astikos Ellinikos Nomos*, TZA' 1856), a measure that was reiterated in the statute books in 1976 and finally applied strictly after 1983 (see Alivizatos, email, December 2007; Lixouriotis 1986; Stathopoulos 2005). Nonetheless, it is a striking fact that even today the religious rites continue to be practised and only a tiny minority of people use the civil registration alone: the vast majority continue to employ baptism as the means of conferring names (Alivizatos, personal communication, 2006). The same is true with regard to marriage where only a small proportion of couples (5 per cent) prefer to legitimate their bond solely through a civil marriage while the overwhelming majority of couples continue to marry in church and, for a variety of reasons, many have both civil and religious ceremonies.

As already noted, it has long been possible to confer a child's name without a religious rite but in practise this was seldom done. The 1983 law requires the immediate registration of the child's birth in the civil registry office (*lyxiarcheion*), but a name need not be specified. A child can still be registered in the civil registry without a name until the parents decide on the name, which will be officially registered; after that it cannot be changed. A progressive measure in the 1983 Civil Code allows choice regarding the surname of a child, so that either the mother's or the father's can be conferred (Stathopoulos 2005). Once registered officially, however, the surname cannot be changed. Likewise, if a first name is registered at this time, it cannot be changed (*ametaklito*), even if baptism confers a different name later (e.g. if Leonidas is the name given at birth and Panayiotis is conferred at baptism, the only legal name is Leonidas). To facilitate the immediate registration of a birth, maternity hospitals in Athens provide registration forms that do not require a child's name to be specified, but only the its sex and parents' names.

The significance of the distinction between civil and religious naming practice is profound and should not be underestimated for it differentiates membership as a citizen in the state – that is, nationality – from that of religious affiliation. Though this might be a commonplace in Western Europe, from the Greek perspective it signals a radical break with the long-established equivalence of national and religious identity. The secularisation agenda is promoted, too, by the introduction of civil marriage and divorce as legal alternatives to the religious rites (divorce has always been permitted in the Orthodox Church), and both possibilities are provided for equally as options in the 1983 law. In 2005 the Hellenic League for Human and Citizen Rights, a legal pressure group, suggested a more radical initiative in a Draft bill aimed at the full separation of the Church from the state (see below), which proposed, among other measures, that all civil procedures of family law would be compulsory while the religious rites would be optional. The bill's proponents argue that they are following a common Western European model; in fact, it is actually based on the French case, and notably does not correspond with the situation in UK and Denmark which can still be called 'confessional states' where there is an established religion.

Historical Features

It is necessary to refer briefly again to Greece's special features in the context of contemporary European society. These can be traced to a specific historical trajectory and to cultural differences dating back to the early centuries of the Christian period when Rome and Constantinople became the two separate centres of the Roman Empire. The different developments of the 'Latin West' and the 'Greek East' (see Romanides 1975; Sherrard 1959) are crucial considerations in our understanding of contemporary processes of change in this region of Southern Europe and the Balkans, and can only be referred to briefly in this chapter.

Following the conquest of the Byzantine empire in the fifteenth century, the area that now constitutes the Greek state fell under Ottoman rule (for a general overview see Clogg 1979: 8ff). Under the Ottoman system of governance, the subject peoples of the imperial state were granted a considerable degree of communal autonomy if they constituted a group recognised as the People of the Covenant (*dhimmis*). As such they were organised into *millets* (literally 'nations'), the criterion of membership being that of religious affiliation. This was by no means a rigid system, but had varied considerably over time and in different regions of the empire (Augoustinos 1992: 33–38; Zürcher 1993: 2–13). The important point to recognise is that religion provided the basis for personal identity and for group membership. The Orthodox Christians of the Empire, the *Romioi/Rumlar,* were administered by the hierarchy within the *Rum millet,* which had jurisdiction over all family and inheritance matters, and even civil disputes (Braude and Lewis 1982). It was religion, not language or ethnicity, that determined a person's membership in the polity (see Kitromilides 1989).

It is an extraordinary irony of history, therefore, that national and religious identities are not separated in Greek consciousness, an approach that resonates with a central feature of the Ottoman past. In fact, to this day, these different criteria of identity can be seen as co-terminus for the vast majority of Greek citizens. What can be seen as a remnant of the Ottoman heritage is further illustrated by the legal status of the Muslims of Thrace. Following the provisions for minority rights entailed in the 1923 Treaty of Lausanne, these Greek citizens are adjudicated by a *mufti* under Islamic law for family and personal matters in an odd remnant of the *millet* system. Many complications arise, however, through the permitted application of two legal codes (see

Tsitselikis 2004). Again, it is an unusual fact that Greece alone among Western European countries allows the application of some aspects of sharia law.

The fact that it is religious identity that is seen to confer membership in the body politic is certainly resonant with the Ottoman system of administration (a point also noted en passant by Aarbakke 2003: 43 n.3; Kostopoulos 2003: 68–69). This is a remarkable irony, given the strong Enlightenment influence and Greece's engagement with Western ways of thinking through the Philhellenes and educated diaspora Greeks in the eighteenth and nineteenth centuries, the struggle for independence from the Ottoman empire (1821–29) and the development of nationalistic thinking over the nineteenth century (Clogg 1992: 6–14, 20ff; Kitromilides 1989; for variations in ways that Greek national identity was defined at different periods, see Hirschon 1999).

The fact that the religious rite of baptism was believed to be the main vehicle of personal identification for the vast majority of the citizens of the state and that the criterion for Greek nationality was based on an overall assumption of common religious identity as Orthodox Christians reflects the assumption of a homogeneous nation defined on religious criteria. The problems posed for minority groups who have other religious convictions have been a matter of increasing concern (see Aarbakke 2003; Alivizatos 1999; Christopoulos and Tsitselikis 2003; Pollis 1992; Stavros 1996; see also Clogg 2002).

Two points need to be reinforced: first, the fact that religion is so intricately bound up with national identity that these elements can barely be disentangled; second, that religion is not commonly seen to be an individual or a private matter. Instead, religious conviction and practice are open and not confined to the private sphere; they have a high public profile, for religious rituals accompany national celebrations and are openly celebrated (e.g. lighting candles, venerating icons).

The Identity Card Controversy

Given this context, the issue of a new form of identity card (*taftotita*, also known as *astynomiki taftotita*) revealed the singularity of some key features of Greek society and deserves attention. Interestingly, religion is a central aspect of the controversy around ID cards, a debate that has raged for at least two decades. As one involved commentator noted (Vlachos 2000: 27), the variable stance of successive governments, the changes in the law together with many related policy changes and their contradictions – some of which led to total reversals, and the persistent debate about the inclusion or omission of religious affiliation deserves a monograph in itself.[4]

Identification (ID) cards were introduced during the Second World War, when Greece was under Axis occupation. They are thus long established and do not provoke consternation, because people are used to being identified through a laminated card with a photo and thumbprint, and other basic data, including one's religious affiliation. In Greece, objections to the ID card are not to the innovation, as in the UK (where they are not yet used), but to the change in the form of the document (electronic) and to the data included (religion or not).

Over a period of at least fifteen years various governmental proposals for a new type of ID card were debated, laws and their amendments were passed, finally leading to a crystallisation of the tension between state and church in 2000. Among the PASOK government reforms was the 1986 Law 1599/86 on 'Church-State Relations, Adoption of New Type of Identity Card and Other Measures' (*Skeseis kratous-politia, kathierwsi neou typou deltiou tautothtas kai alles diataxeis*), proposing the adoption of a new type of identity card, among other reforms. The highly controversial change was that religious affiliation was to be omitted.

The Law 1599/86 also proposed a single identifying number for each citizen (EKAM, *eniaio kwdiko arithmo mhtrwou*, article 2), which would refer to the various numbers used in all other contexts ('*arithmo twn lhxiarchikwn praxewn, tou deltiou tawtothtas, tou eklogikou bibliariou kai tou diabatiriou, tou asphalistikou bibliariou, tou phorologikou mhtrwou, ths adeias ikanothtas odygou, tou mhtrwou arrenwn, tou proxenikou mhtrwou, tou dhmotologiou kai tou eklogikou katalogou*'). This single number would be used for all official records, including ID and passport numbers, driver's licence, local and national electoral rolls, health service and tax registration. Widespread objections centred on the assignment of a single identifying number for each individual and on the fact that a person would no longer be identified by name, thus dehumanising one. The similarity with concentration camps and political detention camps were pointed out while, on the extreme religious fringe, it was seen to be linked with the number '666', invoking the apocalyptic period heralding the last days and the end of the world. The use of a single number invoked great concern in wider circles in relation to the new technology: it would also involve an electronic chip, and would open up the possibility for storing secret data, and thus permit widespread surveillance.

The Law was passed despite widespread objections. Five years later in 1991, however, the government admitted that it had proved impossible to apply the law 'for practical reasons', but also 'because of the almost universal rejection by the people' of a single identifying number (Vlachos 2000: 31). Amendments proposed at this time eliminated the use of EKAM but the card would still be readable by electronic means (31–32).

In 1993 the debate about the inclusion of religious affiliation was reawakened when the Holy Synod (College of Bishops) released two statements (*egkyklia*) anticipating that the government was finally about to enforce the law. These asserted that the country was being subjected to external pressures and it called on the government not to proceed with the issue of this new type of ID, thereby 'bowing to foreign pressure' (Vlachos 2000: 34). It also made the strong statement that the Church would not allow 'the bond (*desmos*) between Orthodoxy and Hellenism [*sic*] to be broken' (32–34). But again no practical application of the law took place.

Early in 1997, however, under a European directive, the Data Protection Act (Law 2472/1997) was introduced regarding the 'protection of data of a personal kind' (*prostasia twn dedomenwn proswpikou characthra*). Finally, under this general rubric a break was made for religion could now be detached if it was given the status of a private matter. 'The Hellenic Data Authority raised the issue in May 2000, and the then Prime Minister Costas Simitis endorsed the Authority's decision and ordered the change of the relevant administrative act; the issue was not brought to Parliament' (Alivizatos, personal communication, email, February 2006; see Simitis 2005: 387–90).

In essence, this action reflects a clearly Western secular view, namely, that religion is a private matter, and thus religious affiliation should not be included on an identity document. Supporting this development is the view that 'religion is an element in the internal world of the individual (*'ws stoixeio tou eswterikou kosmou tou atomou'*) (Alivizatos 2001: 312), a notion not widely shared by the majority of Greeks. The antithetical view and central objection is expressed succinctly by Bishop Vlachos: 'For us Greeks, the identity card is not simply a public/formal document, but a document which declares our identity as a people/race' (*Yia mas tous ellenes i taftotita then einai aplws ena demosio eggrafo, alla eggrafo pou dhlwnei thn taftotita tou yenous mas*) (Alivizatos 2001: 38). This reveals another key issue, already noted, differentiating the Greek situation from most other Western countries, that of the public/private separation, a characteristic of the secular state, but which has a significantly different articulation in Greek social life (see Molokotos-Lieberman 2003). (In this respect, Greece and Israel provide interesting parallels.) The root of the conflict and controversy around the declaration of religious affiliation on an ID lies, in my opinion, in the entangled nature of personal identification where religious and political features are intricately linked.

From late 1999 through 2000 the issue finally reached a climax after the Greek government reintroduced proposals that the new identity card would not specify the religious affiliation of the holder. It reversed promises made earlier by government ministers to church leaders. The Holy Synod led by the late Archbishop Christodoulos, used the media and rallied support for their position. Negotiations with government ministers broke down and finally the clerics suggested that the people be consulted through a referendum. When the government did nothing to promote this proposal, the Church demonstrated its political clout with street demonstrations, public meetings and petitions. Over 3 million adults (in a total population of under 11 million) signed the petition for a referendum to decide whether information on religion might be offered voluntarily. The government did nothing in response to this pressure while everyone expected that public opinion would reject the new type of ID, widely seen as an infringement of national sovereignty through a European-driven initiative.

Certainly, one element in this reaction was purely political because the Greek government was seen to be succumbing to pressure from outside, reflecting a loss of autonomy – a situation Greeks do not easily tolerate. The resistance was noteworthy and shocked the liberal establishment. Flamboyantly exploited by some populist currents in the Church establishment, it brought into focus the problematic situation of church-state relations in the context of European integration. Paradoxically, many who supported the Church's petition were not observant believers (left wing and atheist protesters were objecting to the electronic card and the threat of surveillance) while, among the more religious, not all supported the petition as they felt that the Church was overstepping its role in a political arena.

What all this boils down to is a puzzle, and a challenge to any common sense or simplistic conclusions about modernity and secularisation in Greece. The short answer to why the vast majority rejected the government proposal to omit religious affiliation from the new ID cards is that religion in Greece is intimately bound up with national identity even today.[5] It is still widely held that to be a Greek is to be an Orthodox Christian. That this might pose a problem for the growing numbers of Muslims, Jews and other Christian denominations in the country has not been part of public consciousness until recently when increasing immigration, illegal and permitted, has affected marked demographic changes. Once a country of emigration, Greece in the past twenty years has become the receiving location for many nationalities, and is grappling with issues of immigration policy and immigrants' rights. Challenges to the notion of Greek national identity are at the forefront of many discussions in the media, and the situation is certainly one of ongoing debate.

Church and State – The Velvet Divorce

The degree of separation of church and state at the institutional level, and of religiosity at the popular level are two different but related criteria, which mark various expressions of democratisation and secularisation (see Prodromou 1998). Among the changes currently debated are those that challenge, both obliquely and directly, the long-accepted and deeply entrenched structures of church and state. Greece is still a country where the two institutions are not separated, a situation considered anachronistic by one section of the population, and as an unchallengeable and fundamental feature of the essential Greece by another. Heated debates take place about whether this is a negative or positive feature of the modern Greek nation-state.

The question then arises: What is entailed in the process of secularisation in a country where religion overlaps so closely with national identity? Certainly this differs from the process in those Western European states where private and public spheres have a sharper delineation. In the vanguard of the movement to create a secular polity, the Hellenic League for Human and Citizen Rights created a Draft Bill in December 2005 titled, 'Reorganization of the Relationship Between State and Church, Religious Societies and the Assurance of Religious Freedom'. The Bill's sponsors are motivated by a human rights agenda, and the proposals aim at ensuring complete religious freedom for all groups, regardless of the faith. It encapsulates radical measures in the Greek context for its proposals separate the spheres of religious authority from those of the secular authority in order to diminish the hegemonic power of the Church of Greece. Some of the articles proposed, for example, were to remove religious phrases from oaths taken in court and in parliament, to remove the ban on proselytisation, to permit cremation as an alternative to burial and various educational reforms. It was not, however, adopted as a package. Even those parties that favoured secularisation recognised that the 'political cost' would be too great. The Draft Bill gained support for only some of the twenty proposed articles, which were to be introduced piecemeal as parts of other laws (Nikos Alivizatos, personal communication, January 2006).

The important point to note here is the continuing struggle to define the areas of separation between the religious and the civil in Greece, a problem that has specific permutations given its different historical and political experience. The modernisation agenda of progressives and liberals is contested by strong resistance to disrupting the status quo. In trying to interpret the reaction in Greece to the proposal for a new form of ID, which conceals religious affiliation, it was clear that it touched a sore spot. The omission of religious identity from the ID card was apparently perceived as a threat to national and therefore personal identity. It provoked so great a public outcry that the government had to allow the issue to lapse until the solution was found under the cover of the Data Protection Act. In Greece secularisation is not following the 'expected' Western pattern for the essential difference remains: religious identity as Orthodox Christianity is part and parcel of national identity for the vast majority of its citizens, as a result of a long historical process. The challenge, then, for the reformers is how to secularise a society where this overlap remains a salient and fundamental feature.

Notes

In addition to being based on personal observations and long-term experience in Greece, the material for this study owes much to many friends and acquaintances for helping me see various perspectives on the situation. For guidance through the legal intricacies, I am deeply indebted to Nikos Alivizatos and to Ioannes Ktistakis, both of whom specialise in minority group rights. I am particularly grateful to Aigli Brouskou for the precision with which she pointed out the flaws in a previous draft and for her help in clarifying the issues. I am also grateful to Kostas Tsitselikis, who encouraged me to include information on the legal status of the Muslims of Thrace. Without their advice and responses to my many queries, I would not have been able to tackle this topic and I only hope that I have done justice to their explanations.

1. This survey conducted by Tnsicap and Gallup International Association was publicised on 16 November 2005 during a period when church-state relations were under scrutiny. It does not state the sample size or composition, but does indicate significant macroregional differences, the highest proportion of devout in African countries (overall average was 91 per cent). The lowest were Hong Kong (14 per cent) and Japan (17 per cent), while the overall average for Western European countries was 60 per cent (www.tns-global.com).
2. The varied aspects of Greek religious conduct before the 1980s are comprehensively dealt with by Ware 1983.
3. After writing this chapter, I obtained more precise information on the legal provisions for registration of a child. A striking finding is that the provision for naming without baptism, i.e. civil registration, has existed on the law books since the 1856 Greek Civil Code but it has been ignored in practice, was reinstated on the statute books in 1976 and finally applied strictly after 1983. It seems that public consciousness continued to emphasise baptism as the sole means of

identifying a child, while even legal professionals and civil servants reflected the mindset in which civil and religious identity were held to be coterminous, right up to the 1980s.
4. See the perceptive article by Molokotos-Lieberman (2003) and, from the Church's point of view, Vlachos (2000). Vlachos's detailed examination of this topic provided much of the information presented here, as did consultation with a constitutional lawyer, Nikos Alivizatos.
5. To Vima (4 August 2000) reported a sample street poll with the question 'Would you participate in the referendum about IDs (taftotites)?' to which five out of six replied positively. In an official poll (on 16 September 2000) reported in national newspapers, 77.4 per cent wanted religious affiliation to be recorded on the ID card, because they believe that this feature is an 'inextricable part of their self-awareness' ('anapospasto tmyma tis aftosyneidesias tous') (Iera Synodos tis Ellados 2000: 29).

References

Aarbakke, V. 2003. 'Adjusting to the New International Framework for Minority Protection – Challenges for the Greek State and Its Minorities', in *Jahrbücher für Geschichte und Kultur Südosteuropas/History and Culture of South Eastern Europe*, vol. 5. München: Slavica Verlag, pp. 43–54.

Alivizatos, N. 1999. 'A New Role for the Greek Church', *Journal of Modern Greek Studies* 17(1): 24–40.

———. 2001. *O Abebaios Eksyxronismos*. Athens: Polis.

Augoustinos, G. 1992. *The Greeks of Asia Minor*. London: Kent State University Press.

Braude, B. and B. Lewis (eds.). 1982. *Christians and Jews in the Ottoman Empire*. New York: Holmes and Meier.

Christopoulos, D. and K. Tsitselikis. 2003. 'Impasses in the Treatment of Minorities and *homogeneis* in Greece', in *Jahrbücher für Geschichte und Kultur Südosteuropas/ History and Culture of South Eastern Europe*, vol. 5. München: Slavica Verlag, pp. 81–93.

Clogg, R. 1979. *A Short History of Modern Greece*. Cambridge: Cambridge University Press.

———. 1992. *A Concise History of Greece*. Cambridge: Cambridge University Press.

Clogg, R. (ed.). 2002. *Minorities in Greece. Aspects of a Plural Society*. London: Hurst.

Frazee, C. 2002. 'Catholics', in R. Clogg (ed.), *Minorities in Greece. Aspects of a Plural Society*. London: Hurst, pp. 24–47.

Georgiadou, V. 1996. 'Kosmiko Kratos kai Orthodoxy Ekklisia: Skeseis thriskeias, koinonias kai politikis stin metapoliteufsi', in X. Lyrintzis, E. Nikolakopoulos, and D. Sotiropoulos (eds.), *Koinonia kai Politiki: opseis ths Ellhnikhs Dhmokratias 1974–1994*. Athens: Themelio, pp. 247–86.

Hirschon, R. 1993. 'Essential Objects and the Sacred', in S. Ardener (ed.), *Women and Space*, 2nd ed. Oxford: Berg.

———. [1989] 1998. *Heirs of the Greek Catastrophe: The Social Life of Asia Minor Refugees in Piraeus*, 2nd ed. Oxford: Berghahn Books.

———. 1999. 'Identity and the Greek State: Some Conceptual Issues and Paradoxes', in R. Clogg (ed.), *The Greek Diaspora in the Twentieth Century*. London: Macmillan, pp. 158–80.

———. (ed.). 2003. *Crossing the Aegean: An Appraisal of the 1923 Population Exchange Between Greece and Turkey*. Oxford: Berghahn Books.

———. forthcoming. 'Indigenous Persons and Imported Individuals: Changing Paradigms of Personal Identity in Contemporary Greece', in C. Hann and H. Golz (eds.), *Orthodoxy, Orthopraxy and Parádosis: Eastern Christians in Anthropological Perspective*. Berkeley: University of California Press.

Iera Synodos tis Ellados. 2000. *Ekklisia kai Taftotites*. Athens: Ekdosis Kladou Ekdosewn Epikoinwniakis kai Morphotikis Yphresias ths Ekklisias Ellados.

Kitromilides, P. 1989. 'Imagined Communities and the Origins of the National Question in the Balkans', in M. Blinkorn and T. Veremis (eds.), *Modern Greece: Nationalism and Nationality*. Athens: Sage, ELIAMEP, pp. 23–65.

Kostopoulos, T. 2003. 'Counting the "Other": Official Census and Classified Statistics in Greece (1830–2001)', in *Jahrbücher für Geschichte und Kultur Südosteuropas/History and Culture of South Eastern Europe*, vol. 5. München: Slavica Verlag, pp. 55–78.

Lixouriotis, I. 1986. *Koinonikes kai Nomikes Antilipseis gia to Paidi ton Proto Aiona tou Neoellinikou Kratous*. Giannena-Athens: Dodoni, pp. 329–30.

Molokotos-Lieberman, L. 2003. 'Identity Crisis: Greece, Orthodoxy, and the European Union', *Journal of Contemporary Religion* 18(3): 291–315.

Pollis A. 1992. 'Greek National Identity: Religious Minorities' Rights and European Norms', *Journal of Modern Greek Studies* 10(1): 171–95.

Prodromou, E. 1998. 'Democracy and Religious Transformation in Greece: An Underappreciated Theoretical and Empirical Primer', in P. Kitromilides and T. Veremis (eds.), *The Orthodox Church in a Changing World*. Athens: ELIAMEP, Centre of Asia Minor Studies, pp. 99–153.

Romanides, I. 1975. *Romiosyny*. Thessaloniki: Ekdoseis Pournara.

Sherrard, P. 1959. *The Greek East and the Latin West*. Oxford: Oxford University Press.

Simitis, K. 2005. *Politiki yia Mia Dhmiourgiki Ellada 1996–2004*. Athens: Ekdoseis Polis.

Stathopoulos, M. 2005. 'Prosopiki Katastasi kai Thriskeftikes Epiloges', unpublished manuscript. Athens: Hellenic League for Human Rights.

Stavros, S. 1996. 'Citizenship and the Protection of Minorities', in K. Featherstone and K. Ifantis (eds.), *Greece in a Changing Europe: Opportunities and Constraints*. Manchester: Manchester University Press.

Tsitselikis, K. 2004. 'Personal Status of Greece's Muslims: a Legal Anachronism or an Example of Applied Multiculturalism?', in B.-P.R. Aluffi and G. Zincone (eds.), *The Legal Treatment of Muslim Minorities in Europe*. Leuven: Peeters, pp. 109–32.

Vlachos, I. 2000. *Taftotita kai Taftotites*. Livadia: Monastery of the Birth of the Theotokos.

Ware, K. 1983. 'The Church: A Time of Transition', in R. Clogg (ed.), *Greece in the 1980s*. London: Macmillan, pp. 208–30.

———. 2002. 'Old Calendarists', in R. Clogg (ed.), *Minorities in Greece. Aspects of a Plural Society*. London: Hurst, pp. 1–23.

Zürcher, E.J. 1993. *Turkey, a Modern History*. London: I.B. Tauris.

A Church Lost in the Maze of a City without References

Bruno Drweski

The Catholic Church occupies a particular place in Poland. Its roots are certainly not as old or as deep as appears at first sight. Catholicism remained a relatively superficial phenomenon until the Counter Reformation when the majority of the population in rural areas distrusted the preachers, resulting in a wave of conversion that was decided by tribal chiefs. Notwithstanding the religious convictions of individual Poles, since the early twentieth century, the Church has constituted a visible element of continuity for people subjected to profound, painful and repeated upheavals. During the course of its history, the Church most certainly was not the patriotic institution the clergy pretended it to be. One need only refer to the example of the Protestants who created the basis for Polish literature, or think of the support the Catholic bishops lent to the Holy Alliance after 1815 when they asked Tsar Alexander I to reinstall censorship in Poland in 1819. Moreover, Catholic officials were very reticent vis-à-vis patriotic currents during the First World War; similarly one can point to the mass performed by Warsaw's Archbishop celebrating the victory of Russian armies. However, prior to 1918 the Catholic Church has often had the opportunity to fill the gap left by the absence of a legitimate and constructive state on Polish territory. Furthermore, during the socialist period of coercive modernisation it occupied a position of social counterforce, which was indispensable to counter authorities who refused to accept an independent political interlocutor altogether. Today the Church increasingly has to support the consequences of 'post-modern disenchantment' and the social effects that contrast with the system transformations of 1989. Finally, it has to deal with the ascension to the pontifical throne of a German pope, who cannot benefit in Poland of the same aura the son of a Polish peasant had. Indeed, the position of the Church in Polish society cannot be understood properly when its role, which John Paul II personified to perfection, for the recently urbanised and originally rural populations is not taken into account.

At the least two types of Polish Catholicism can be distinguished. One is Polish-centred and induces the withdrawal of a nation often menaced in the past. It seeks to reassure those who urge to find their place in a society which has become depersonalised, individualised and urbanised over the past half century. The other positions itself closer to universality, or at least to that of Western elites. Because contemporary Poles are divided between those who have profited from post-1989 opportunities and those who feel abandoned, these two components of Polish Catholicism find less and less room for convergence. Will the Church of the future be a structure of charity, refuge and comfort? Or will it participate in the changes underway, by either profiting from them or by offering innovating alternatives to them? Moreover, in what sense will the Church continue to be a socially useful force once urbanisation is fully deployed and individualisation of social ties is generalised?

Indeed, during the years of the 'construction of socialism' the Catholic clergy managed to become indispensable. It feared that industrialisation and urbanisation would entail the emergence of a working class and an intelligentsia who would be lay and indifferent to religion. But the cycle of social decomposition and restructuring by the communists has finally created a need for recognisable references. This entailed the re-implantation of the Church in new neighbourhoods of the cities and new industrial complexes. This evolution led to the phenomenon of 'Solidarnosc' (Independent Self-governing Trade Union 'Solidarity'). This happened in a climate where the old 'rural' distrust vis-à-vis a larger impact of priests on public life manifested itself inside the union. During the period of popular Poland the Church has thus acquired a position it never occupied in the course of a millennium of Polish history. Paradoxically, it was the 'socialist' modernisation, and most of all the fast urbanisation, that produced a Catholic following. Will this phenomenon soon reach its end? Or, will the post-1989 social changes give a new chance to the Church in a disenchanted Poland with joblessness, poverty, precariousness and lack of perspective and meaning in life?

During the Middle Ages the Church collided with the pagan heritage in the rural territories, and later on with the influence of Renaissance, Reformation and Enlightenment among the elites. These currents refused to accept that the Church would have an ideological monopoly and act as the spokesman of national identity. Many Poles regarded it as an egoistic and foreign force, which held back progress and national development. It was a rich power, attached to traditional hierarchies and in principle opposed to the democratisation of social relations. But at the same time the Church also enhanced the social promotion of children from a rural background. Its charitable activities combined making people dependent from the Church with acquiring an incomparable place in the social network. Since the 1989 transition to capitalism, the 'ideology of winners' once again gave the Church the monopoly over the discourse of welfare and well-being. Only the 'nostalgics' of socialism can approve the declaration of the conference of Polish bishops of 14–15 March 2001 that stressed the 'primacy of humans over things and of work over capital'. Few leftist political parties would dare to support such a position.

In the 1980s almost all dignitaries and intellectuals, Communist Party and Solidarnosc's sympathies shifted towards a hardboiled liberal ideology, sometimes a social liberalism. This left a quasi-monopoly position in the social discourse (even a paternalistic one) to the Catholics. This was not diminished by the fact that few upper class Catholics seem to strive for a social model, which is genuinely beneficial for the poor. But liberal individualism tends to downplay the traditional status of religion as a factor of social and national cohesion, while the Church has territorial structures in the 'deep country', which is not covered adequately by politicians and brokers. The 'deep country' is not necessarily the rural backwaters, but also the peripheral neighbourhoods of metropoles or the larger marginalised towns like the old mill town of Lodz. Apart from those there are the many small towns, which grew in the wake of 'real socialism': planning staffs of the 1950s and 1960s had the rule of thumb 'a small city – a large mono-industry'. When these industrial plants close down, the cities are often deteriorating. Hence, grave social menaces weigh on a majority of Polish society.

The Church has witnessed the dwindling of its position, which explains why part of the clergy has tried to consolidate its position institutionally. To that effect, they imposed the Catholic cult in public life, reaffirmed the ethno-Catholic version of Polish identity and refused to accept non-Catholic components of Polish and European origin. Many Poles, regardless of their religious convictions, have sympathy for freedom of thinking and social solidarity and refuse narrow nationalism. But their views are not accepted by the Church, and are appraised critically by liberal circles today. To give an idea of the potential power of critical Catholics one can estimate their group holds 95 per cent of officially baptised Catholics versus 46 per cent of churchgoers and 63 per cent of the believers who object against the church's zeal vis-à-vis the functioning of financial and political life (Zdaniewicz and Zembrzuski 2000, 2001).

However, dissatisfaction, the rise of criminality and delinquency in the suburbs and the 'satellite' cities with their disruption of social ties have yielded the urge in partisan groups of liberalism for a sufficiently legitimised force to stop and bar any organised expression of dissatisfaction. In that context the Church stands on a crossroad. The political, economic and media elites need it as a force of 'absorption' that controls deteriorating urban quarters, whereas lower classes did not abandon the idea that behind the comfort speech for the poor the religion holds a potential to reconstitute solidarity networks. Moreover, US imported sects, traditional Polish religions, Protestants and Islamic groups are all players in the conversion area. The Catholic clergy is obviously in an uneasy position, being solicited by the elites and lower classes and being attacked on their traditional status. The ethno-Catholic groups on their part appreciate the fact that, in the light of the right of dignity for those excluded by 'a real capitalism', they could reconstitute durable social networks. Interestingly, the success of the media system and its social network 'Famille

Radio Maryja' has yielded the resurrection of a 'national-Catholic' identity, especially in small cities.

Polish people tend to hesitate among harsh identity based on a fundamentalist Catholicism that is socially sterile, a small leftist alliance and liberal and social-liberal forces that support a weak and ill-bounded Europe. This evolution steers Poland to dangerous tensions. Indeed, while people and ideas do not freely circulate, financial fluxes do. In a recent past the Polish cities were marked by 'grey socialism' where workers, lower-level staff and professors were socially on an almost identical level of existence. Today, the new elites are locking themselves up in the 'gated cities of dreams' – the secure ghettoes of the elite with money and without roots. The price they pay for that is generalised fear for a growing insecurity on the one hand and distrust vis-à-vis the powerful and the foreign on the other. The impoverished middle class seeks to preserve the appearance of quietness in other neighbourhoods. Still, they left the concrete buildings of the past, where jobless people are crowding today. In this new cutting up of the urban landscape the Church cannot pretend to stand above the cleavages. Hence, the priests have to behave differently in different groups of following, which is hardly tenable.

An Element of Traceable Continuity in an Uprooted Society

As demonstrated earlier, the position of the Polish Church can be explained in terms of pre- and post-1989 identity forces, which are patriotic, social and political. By comparing the feeble implantation of the Church's networks in a few old workers neighbourhoods in 1945 with the mobilisation triggered in new workers quarters by the absence of established Catholic structures, one can explain why Catholicism was able to install itself in the 'new territories' after 1945. A typical example was the model socialist city of Nowa Huta at the fringes of Krakow, created in the 1950s. The planners of that time had 'forgotten' to build a church. After twenty years of intensive mobilisation the true followers were granted a church. The struggle of this urbanised population of peasant origin, without roots or promises, has stood as a symbol of the new Polish working class. In contrast to their 'red' predecessors of the pre-1939 era, they had no other parochial structures of socialisation which they claimed. To understand the challenge the Church had to face here one should examine how it was able to implant and reimplant after 1945.

One should recall the historical role the Church has played in the nineteenth century, especially in the countryside, in the formation and social promotion of the most talented persons from the lower classes. It is good to know that the institution of celibacy of priests, monks and nuns induced a complete overhaul of the institution after each generation, which contributed to securing a permanent authority for the Church in the eyes of the villagers. Their children were thus able to escape the meagre context they were raised in for generations. Indeed, migration towards the cities was considered risky before 1945. The wild and peripheral capitalism in Poland evoked ambivalent feelings of fear and fascination. In the cities workers structures of welcome were organised by unions, welfare banks, parties and workers universities. The Church implanted itself in the wealthier peasantry and in the small cities where workers culture was as good as absent. The larger cities stood symbol for 'dens of vice' in the minds of the Catholic practitioners. But in 1945 the role of the Church as a provider of secure social upward mobility was extended to the rural areas, over and against communist initiatives to the same effect. One reason was that Stalinist Poland never underwent a systematic anti-Catholic repression; being a priest in Poland was never dangerous, but rather represented an opportunity.

To this traditional role was added another one, due to the effects of generalised urbanisation, after the exterminations of 1939 and the reconstruction of the country in 1945. It is difficult to imagine the depth of psychological blows the Polish society underwent in 1939. The killings and deportation of people, the changes of borders and the 'exchange' of populations between 1939 and 1945, more than one out of four Poles changed residence places. Moreover, one should add the mobility inside regions (*voïévodie*). This phenomenon caused rural masses to move towards the cities. From 1950 on this trend was accelerated with massive industrialisation and bureaucratisation (the development of 'services' and of present-day middle classes). Within one generation half of the rural population has moved into cities. Today two-thirds of the Poles live in different environments from their parents.

This massive mobility, often accompanied by social promotion, is remembered fondly, which explains the nostalgic sentiments towards socialism found in present-day Poland. It is interesting that this phenomenon was analysed extensively in a publication by the Catholic Church, showing its interest in social questions. The research focussed on the question when Poles felt to be most happy and most unhappy. For 16.6 per cent of the interviewees the happiest period was identified as that between the two world wars, for 29.6 per cent that after 1989, but for 53.8 per cent that of socialist Poland. On the contrary, 41 per cent considered the socialist period as the unhappiest one, 21.7 per cent the era between the two world wars and 37.3 per cent the post-1989 period. Hence, the Church has to act in a society that is deeply divided over its aspirations (Zdaniewicz and Zembrzuski 2000: 351).

Even those who profited from accelerated mobility under the communists felt deeply uprooted. More so because the 'new urbanites' were often implanted in destroyed cities, which were left by their original inhabitants who moved towards so-called German territory. Indeed with 55 per cent of the Polish urban population killed in the war, either through genocide of the Jewish urbanites or the systematic destruction of Polish cities (especially Warsaw in 1944), the cities were emptied. Hence little or no core of initial urbanites was left to greet the rural migrants and help them integrate. Thus, for the mass of the migrants the importance of the psychological blows they underwent should not be underestimated, even if they had better conditions of lodging, work and so on in harsh times. In that context the bulk of new urbanites, with no link to the 'old intelligentsia' or to the 'traditional Polish values' of nobility or intelligentsia, and without contacts with the 'workers culture' (the working class perished by 1945) were ill prepared to confront this impersonal world and its 'civic' relationship in a city. The Church was often the only visible, sensible and structured element of continuity with the world they left. Hence many peasants who were distrustful of the bishop's institution before 1939 felt a new attraction to the Church after 1945, without refusing the opportunities offered by the communists.

> We should forget that the successes reached by the Vatican under the direction of the politician Karol Wojtyla were linked to the uprooted condition of the people of the countryside after communist industrialisation. These human beings, encaged in their concrete buildings, did no longer possess their own culture. It is then that the Vatican suggested to them the idea that it stood for their real "native" culture (Karbowska 2005).

Even if this judgment from a feminist historian appears a bit extreme, it nevertheless highlights the social role in a field without concurrence of the Polish Church in the midst of a population without social ties. The other player in this predicament was the small faction of the Communist Party, which concentrated on the reconstitution of the state, thus neglecting the necessary reconstruction of a workers culture. It is impossible to understand why the implantation or reimplantation of the Church in the new quarters of formerly German territories was a success within socialist Poland without taking this fundamental psychological need for known referents into account. This holds for all Poles, including communists, which explains their moderate position vis-à-vis the Church and its religious ceremonies.

In the centuries of serfdom, poverty and spatial and social immobility Catholic religion with its 'mystery' aura had promised the disbelieving peasant 'evasion' from the world they lived in. At the time when the consequences of modernity hit them straight on and showed them a concrete new world (first through the mass wars of modernity and then with the substantial displacements of people) Catholicism came to personify, in the eyes of many, the unique element of stability in the midst of massive changes. Religion constitutes the only known space of socialisation in a new cold and impersonal environment. The attempts of the communists to impose a 'socialist' ritual could not compete with the need for something known, intimate, 'archaic' or even childish. Poland of 1944 until 1989 was characterised by this 'hybrid' and for a long time accepted the marriage of socialism and Catholicism, of traditional and modernist appeals. This compromise was seen as viable and hence lasted for two generations, notwithstanding a variety of political opinions. This explains why the Poles have left in a massive way 'socialism' and looked backward rather than in front of them. Indeed, they were enthusiastic in 1918 and again during the 'great national communion' and the 'consensus' agreements of Gdansk in 1980, but scepticism has set in since 1989. But the new elites, which emerged from the bank compromise of church and state between 1944 and 1980 have slipped into postmodernism and individualism. The 'people' had difficulty in finding an identity. The Church clergy, who had become used to dealing with power at the least since 1956 (both with communists and with 'dissidents') has also shifted places in 1989. However, its social status is not anymore automatically assured in the cities, which became impersonal.

An Ambiguous Social Position

During the last decades of socialism the Church has mediated successfully with those in power so that censure would forbid critique of it and the abortion law would be up for discussion again in parliament. Today, it capitalises on the power it acquired as an intermediate institution before 1989 and moves towards a front position in a context where political elites are largely left aside. In this way, the presence of clergy is almost obligatory during official ceremonies. Both functionaries and military personnel are pushed to participate in pilgrimages. Abortion is penalised and the clergy does not hesitate to air voting advice, to intervene with political parties and to lend out its religious buildings for meetings to certain parties. Religious courses were introduced in the schools without consultation of the people. The arrogance it manifested in recuperating buildings which were nationalised under socialism or tsarism, the signature by the government to dispatch current affairs before the 1993 elections by a concordat with the Vatican, in the eyes of many Poles made plausible the thesis that the Church has totalitarian views and wants to create a quasi-theocratic state. Moreover, the parliament has passed a law in 1992, which forces the audiovisual media to 'respect the Christian values' within a definition given by the Catholic Church. All this in fact points to the new weakness of the institution of bishops who are losing the 'government of the souls' in an atomised, consumerised and disenchanted society.

Many among the clergy push back to the old nomenclature, or to the liberal circles emanating from Solidarnosc, the responsibility for social difficulties. However, they rarely react on these evolutions in any other way than through traditional charity activities. Indeed, the economic reforms have profited the Church as well, before the impoverishment of the followers who had their resources dwindle, that diminished their possibilities for charity. But the political forces which grew out of Solidarnosc have believed that the moral authority of the Church would suffice as a fender against social dissatisfaction. Even 'post-communist' leaders, who were often hurt by the hierarchy of the Church, hesitated when they came to power to push for the separation of church and state. When the clergy inserted itself in the decision processes at the national and local levels, the political elites often solicited the Church as well. In the contrasting light of capitalist transformation the disruption of society has favoured the fragmentation of political life as well as the emergence of small parties leaning on the Church. At first certain members of the clergy have resisted what they saw as an opportunity to cleanse the institution from the social effects of the 'shock therapy' and so constitute a durable social basis. These members at first went public with the little groups, who were subsequently marginalised in the elections of 1993. The Church clergy, who had regularly frequented the communist power circles since the 1970s, systematically ignored them afterwards in the opinion that they would disappear from public life. The bishops held to an exorbitant anticommunist discourse which contrasted with the ambivalent feeling of the majority of Poles on what popular Poland has stood for. All this could only undermine the position of the Church though, more so since the help for the needy was not within their power anymore, certainly not in the cities where access to food is becoming a problem for some.

The omnipresence of the Church in public life clashed with a passive resistance of very diverse sectors of society and facilitated the return to power of the official heirs of the communists in 1993. Since then a more important segment of the bishops has shown more reticence vis-à-vis politics. The Church continues to benefit from a position that differs clearly from what exists in most liberal democracies. It obtained fiscal advantages and exemptions for imported goods. Public powers, at the national and local levels, take into account the opinions of bishops before making any important decision. When the question of anti-Semitism has disclosed the divide in Polish society between partisans of an ethnocentric and those of an open and interdependent society, then the question of abortion has permitted to measure the impact of Catholic currents and triggered the emergence of feminist movements.

Many priests and bishops in socialist Poland were used to occupy a position that was both materially and morally comfortable, because they were courted by the governing powers and the opposition at the same time. With the end of censure for the first time since the destalinisation of 1956 one saw the reappearance of a press, which (like before 1939) took anticlerical stands. Religious indifference, which has deep roots in Poland, became visible again from the moment the visit of religious places stopped being a manifestation of independence vis-à-vis the party-State and the priests stopped 'producing social ties'. But through inertia they still constitute a force in the cities where sense and coherence dwindled.

Catholicism and Globalised Capitalism

The position of the Church has weakened through its interventions in political life, but also because of the growth in wealth of some of its dignitaries. The laws on reprivatisation, which recalled the decrees on nationalisation after 1945, have permitted the Church to recuperate goods in the countryside, but also in the cities. In many cases the users of places, hospitals, schools and rental buildings suffered from a lack of management, which has shocked onlookers. But the Church also directs charity activities, which earns it a definite political place in the eyes of others. When most political parties, unions and non-governmental organisations neglected to give a voice to the poor, the jobless and the excluded, the Catholic circles continued to stress social justice and did not focus all attention on the lack of initiative and responsibility of the poor for their difficulties. But even when the Church speaks of the poor and helps them occasionally, it remains defiant when needy groups seek to mobilise in an autonomous way. In 1993 cardinal Glemp denounced the strike of teachers by saying: 'being a teacher is not just a job, it is a national mission. . . . How can those teachers who close schools and leave their pupils alone teach the love of the country?' (Graczyk 1999: 74). On the contrary, in 2000 the archbishop of Lublin declared on the occasion of a strike by nurses: 'We should all live the drama of nurses in order for Poland not to become a land of contrasts, where some can think they were created uniquely to occupy functions of direction while others gain a meagre 440 zlotys a month, and this would not interest anybody' (*Tygodnik Powszechny* 2000).

The rather traditionalist declarations by John Paul II on moral issues and on public life were transmitted to the priests and their flock. But those statements that held a critique on the economic and social order have been cited rarely in extenso in the media or the sermons. In that context the 2001 funeral of the former first secretary of the Communist Party Edward Gierek, who had refused the participation of a priest in the ceremony, is telling in that it yielded massive attendance. Some compared the event with the mass drawn during papal voyages. Later on, Adam Gierek, son of the deceased, has triumphantly been elected first senator and then member of European Parliament. All this signals the decline of the power position of the traditionalist currents in Poland.

John Paul II underlined that 'Poles . . . either have the opportunity to enter in a consumer's society and occupy there the last place when successful, before the door would be slammed definitively for newcomers, or help to rediscover the great, profound and authentic European tradition by proposing an alliance of the free market with solidarity' (Graczyk 1999: 21). Even when the liberals could not openly attack the Polish pope, because they needed at least the tacit support of the Church to praise the renunciation of social struggles, they were hesitant for that part of his discourse where they saw an attempt to elaborate a middle road between socialism and capitalism. Many Poles experience sympathy for this approach, independent of their opinions of the Church. But the Church of Poland in a general way always has been chillier on social questions than John Paul II has been. Polish bishops nevertheless seem to question the pre-eminence of the market in domains of culture and information. In March 2001 they issued a declaration that supports 'the development of our culture and the way information circulates cannot . . . be subordinated to the laws of the free market'. One can see here a support of the international movement to promote cultural diversity at a time when the liberals claim it to be an appeal for censure. John Paul II appeared, willingly or not, as a 'caution given by God' to the Polish Church. His death, followed by the election of the German pope, already occasioned a growing cooling in Polish opinion towards the 'new' Vatican (Dominiczak 2005).

A Disorientated Church

The Church can only accept, although with reticence, pluralism. This is especially the case in Poland where the influence of paternalistic habits from the feudal centuries and of serfdom remains important, because modernisation and urbanisation of society only date back to the 1950s. Two poles manifest themselves in the heart of Polish episcopate. On the one hand, certain bishops wish that the Church would not intervene in political affairs. They fight religious and ethnic intolerance and rather favour a liberal economy. The old spokesman of the episcopate, Tadeusz Pieronek, approves of market economy on the condition that it integrates moral principles: 'the Church can not forget, by placing human beings first, that economic life functions according to its proper rules which should be respected, lest the Church will not develop in an efficient way' (Pieronek 2000). He was relegated to a minority, however, in the bishops' conference. This was due to his economic opinions, his reticence to see the Church engage itself in public life and the firmness he showed in condemning religious and ethnic intolerance. On the other hand, the refusal of 'moral relativism' and of a religion limited to the private sphere aligns all dignitaries of the Church, but not all followers. Some 76.3 per cent consider that the Church should not take a position on the politics of the government (Zdaniewicz and Zembrzuski 2000: 363). The question of abortion led to a split between the Church and lay liberal milieus. In order to construct a market society the liberals need credible rules and laws for all: they do not question the authority of the Church because, through education, it can contribute to calm the passions of those who do not find their place in a society based on mere competition. This is the main reason why parties of the centre-right tendency, but also those of the centre-left and of communist breeding, never confronted the Church directly. They did not even do that on questions like abortion or the place of religion in schools, even when opinion polls proved that a majority would have supported the position.

The milieus that feel menaced by 'capitalism without frontiers' often show a tendency to turn to the sectors in the Church that feel menaced in their traditional positions and hence develop a mentality of the victim, which is characteristic of being centred on Polishness. The 'national-Catholic' sensitivity is more perceived at the basis, particularly so in the small urban agglomerations. The 'liberal' current within the Church is weak in the lower clergy. The Catholic 'liberals' have succeeded in having the Church adopt the principle of the integration in the European Union, privatisations and the denouncement of anti-Semitism and intolerance. But the slowing down of economic growth, the budgetary crisis of the state, the economic and social failures of centre-left governments, the collapse of 'moderate' Catholic parties, the emergence of 'national-populist' currents and entry into parliament of the League of Polish Families (a party with nationalistic Catholic tendencies) all show the range of contradictions. One understands that no Catholic can really accept the liberal principles propagated by Polish media, which claim that 'freedom does not exist without a free market of ideas' and 'the pluralist order, within which values are in free competition with each other and in which the state renounces the task of educating citizens, leaves this task to the family, to religions and, finally to individuals' (Graczyk 1999: 47). One may understand that such discourse recalls in priests the experience they had under socialism, when their Church benefited from genuine autonomy but at the price of a press with limited editions, of marginalisation of Catholic practitioners in political life and restriction of their activities to religious ceremonies, charity and catechism. Nevertheless, this should not lead to what happens with many fundamentalist Catholics today – an amalgamism of Stalinism, Marxism, socialism, liberalism and some Enlightenment ideas.

At the same time one notices in certain Polish Catholic milieus the charismatic movement with sectarian expansion, which unites those who distrust capitalism. They entertain close relationships with Brazilian Catholic charismatic groups, who militate in the Brazilian workers party of radical left origin where they meet with liberation theologians and Marxists (Myslek 2001). After 1989 many Poles have witnessed, with some reticence, the emergence of a group of unscrupulous profiteers. During a pilgrimage from the monastery of Czestochowa organised for members of parliament from those parties that came out of Solidarnosc, priest Jan Pach warned against 'the pseudo-prophets who reached the summit on the back of the Polish workers' (Graczyk 1999: 24). This view corresponds all the better with the experience of many Poles now than during the socialist period where they came to know a power of workers origin that produced a nomenclature without scruples.

A Divided City

Today the Church reached a point where it can preserve its traditional place in society in such a way that currents better adapted to actual challenges really take shape. This distinguishes it from churches in the West. Because the left-right debate is still marked by the cold war climate of the end of the socialist era, it was logical after 1989 to see a radical anti-communist discourse triumph, which was solidly opposed to the ideas of Enlightenment and of social progress. The Church believed to be able to profit from this situation. However, after twelve years of 'shock therapy' the mass of jobless people, the impoverished peasants, the youth without a future and the urban neighbourhoods left to themselves all led to a small percentage of population that believes in a promising future when national sovereignty is diluted in the 'great Europe' the way it functions today.

In a climate where consistent political debate and innovating proposal are lacking the monopolisation of modernist discourses by liberal ideologues has triggered a return to tradition. In Poland, like elsewhere, tradition offers a comfort, of which part of the Church profits. Social discourse, however superficial and deserted by the official heirs of communism, has hence almost totally been monopolised by more or less fundamentalist Catholics. Nevertheless, one can see that they have not really succeeded to push through politically, notwithstanding the relative success of the League of Polish Families. Indeed, some Catholics remain faithful to another form of open society. Most importantly, the Church does not have the means to renew the charity operation to families in need that it organised in 1982 with the benefit of humanitarian aid from Western countries. On the one hand, the Church has the means to speculate in the centres of large cities, but on the other hand it lacks the means to keep up the parishes in the poor neighbourhoods of villages and small cities. Also, Poland is exporting its priests to the West. At the same time, the Polish cities start to link up with the interwar processes of decline of the Catholic presence, which was characteristic of the small cities. The priests are many and they hate to imagine that an autonomous organisation of 'lay' Catholics would emerge who would be able to promote new networks of solidarity and resocialisation.

After 1989 the Catholic Church has strived to conserve the territory acquired after 1944 and to take control over domains from which it was locked out. There is a contradiction that becomes more and more clear between two objectives. This explains the decline in moral authority. If its position was maintained until now, this is less due to what it offers in terms of religious dogmas than to the disarray, which became apparent after the 1989 elections vis-à-vis almost all political, social, media and economic elites. They have left the grassroots practices and the anchoring in large segments of society to concentrate exclusively on the administrative management in the context of a deregulated market. The workers became disorientated after they lost their role in legitimating policy, which was theirs under the communists and with Solidarnocs. The peasants see their private businesses disappear after they fought hard for their maintenance under socialism. The youth tries with diverging success to launch itself in the opportunities opened by capitalism. But the number of Poles who suffer is rising tremendously and the Church remains one of the few important institutions that can take this into account in a visibly recognisable way. The emergence of the homeless people simultaneously points to disruption of traditional family ties, in which Catholicism has its roots. This implies that the educational system of the Church has at the least been a partial failure. Moreover, the hierarchy of the episcopate distrusts the priests who have been concerning themselves with these layers of society after 1989, because they showed the tendency to push the population to the limits of legal action.

Notwithstanding a rather marked laicisation of Polish society (confirmed by sociological analyses) the Church was not met by massive anticlericalism, but rather by individual forms of rejection of some activities. Poles of today continue to live in an 'in between' society, looking out for any opportunities. However, the growing compartmentalisation of Polish cities in closed off neighbourhoods or the rich residential quarters for the precarious middle classes and neighbourhoods for the needy, has destroyed the social coherence that was still there at the start of socialism in Poland. It also demolished the form of 'interclass' social ties, which existed under socialism and which was the most powerful vector for the Church. The latter cannot pose as the neutral force today as it had been in a pacified society. The Church is as divided as the rest of the society today. But it is not used to accept and deal with internal differences and experiences more difficulties than others in granting that Poland has ceased to be a 'post-rural' urbanised society.

The Church has not genuinely been profiting from the respite it has enjoyed prior to 1989. Its future depends, on the one hand, on its capacity to adopt within Polish conditions the progressive social role played by a number of Catholics elsewhere in the world's poor neighbourhoods. On the other hand, there is the possibility of the emergence from current populist trends in Poland of a political and social force, which is better capable to canalise in a creative way the social discontentment. In 1989 one had promised America to the Poles, but one neglected to mention that it would be Latin America. And Polish Catholics today find themselves much more in a situation that is closer to that of Latin America than that of Western European countries. Finally, this occurs after having known under socialism a relatively 'modern' level of survival and a rather Western and lay way of life.

References

Dominiczak, A. 2005. 'Habemus Papem', *Bez dogmatu*, 64.
Graczyk, R. 1999. 'Przekleta Alternatywa', in Polski Kosciol-Polska Demokracja. Krakow: Universitas.
Karbowska, M. 2005. 'Jestem politycsna emigrantka', *Bez dogmatu*, 64.
Myslek, W. 2001. 'Kosciol jeszcze zroznicowany czy juz podzielony?', *Bulletin de l'Association des Marxistes Polonais*, 7.
Pieronek, T. 2000. 'Popyt na wolnosc', *Wprost*, 15 October.
Zdaniewicz, W. and T. Zembrzuski. 2000 and 2001. 'Kosciol I religijnosc Polakow 1945–1999', *Tygodnik Powszechny*, 25 June and 7 January.

PART TWO

Urban Transformations

THE PROTESTANT ETHIC AND THE SPIRIT OF URBANISM

Simon Coleman

The city has long been a site of both dangerous temptation and alluring opportunity for pious Protestants. For the Victorians, it offered threats to personal morality alongside landmarks of societal progress. Or, to reach further back into the history of the Protestant imaginary, we may remember that North American 'pilgrims' were faced with the task of creating a Christian civilisation – a new Israel – out of the apparent wilderness, while retaining the Puritan vision of a 'city on a hill' in their minds' eyes. The very origins of the evangelical[1] forms of Protestantism I explore in this chapter display powerful links with urban landscapes. Much of what we now think of as Conservative Protestantism was formed in the nineteenth and early twentieth centuries, in response not only to secularism but also to the challenges of urbanisation and immigration within expansive and dynamic urban conurbations. Pentecostalism even traces its origins to a specific, named, urban place – Azusa Street, Los Angeles – where the black preacher William Seymour orchestrated a revival of the Spirit in 1906. Seymour embodied the image of a rootless urban migrant, moving from town to town, away from his early life in rural Louisiana. Indeed, the story of 312 Azusa Street is itself one of a kind of urban regeneration: a tenement house that had previously been a Methodist church was converted into a powerful context for worship, demonstrating that the Spirit, as described in Acts, could fall into any place and at any time.

My claim is not, therefore, that contemporary developments in the relationship between conservative Protestantism and urbanism are without precedent. Instead, I argue for a resonance – even an affinity – between urbanism and revivalism. However, such an affinity should not be treated ahistorically, regarded as a transcendent principle of faith. I consider how a spiritualised morality of the urban might display both shifts and continuities, as industrial landscapes shade into their postindustrial counterparts. My more general point is that as contemporary urban social and material structures are changing with the impact of globalisation, we need to understand how specific sub-cultures react to – even construct – their own global processes.

Arguing for an affinity between revivalism and urbanism does not imply that tensions will be absent from the relationship. Quite apart from concerns over threats to personal piety, more evangelical forms of Protestantism have often tended to exhibit worries over the role of 'place' in religion. Attachment to locality can, it is argued, move into idolatry, a tendency to see more of God in one location than another, or at least an unwillingness to display the mobility required of a true servant of God, prepared to move where the Spirit listeth. Conflicts between the demands of community and those of mission can occur, and both are at a premium in urban surroundings. Yet, I would not go as far as Percy does (1998: 285) in declaring that there is no Protestant theology of place, or at least I would argue that that is not the whole story. As social scientists, we should not take at face value the Protestant assertion that place is irrelevant, that the move 'from temple to meeting-house' (Turner 1979) implies a simple denial of the role of the material in Protestant worship (see Coleman and Collins 2000). For the purposes of this chapter I focus on two dimensions of the urban, which map out the tensions as well as the resonances that I claim exist between urbanism and revivalism. First, I examine the physical, architectural forms of Protestant association, and how these have evolved at least since the nineteenth century. Second, I look at the much wider sense of a Protestant 'public', at how urban forms might interact with Protestant understandings of who their audiences might be. Although I appear to be juxtaposing two rather different manifestations of the urban – bounded spaces and unbounded publics – I also argue that the two are not quite as diametrically opposed as might initially seem to be the case.

This chapter draws broadly on both historical and contemporary material in its exploration of the Protestant spirit of urbanism. In the process, it is meant to challenge two common preconceptions of evangelical aesthetics and practice. First, as noted, that strict Protestantism and place have a necessarily antagonistic relationship. Second, that such conservative forms – not least in their historical manifestations – represent a purely 'redneck', rural and spatially peripheralised religious movement. Such a preconception comes in part from the ridicule heaped on southern fundamentalists after the famous Scopes trial in 1926, when a Tennessee school teacher was accused of teaching evolution in biology classes (see e.g. Wills 1990). Yet, my argument is that revivalism – taken as a whole, and in its various forms – not only needs 'the city' against which to position itself ideologically, it has also required urban social structures and spectacles to catalyse its constituencies and engage in some of the conversionist practices that form the basis of its religious commitment.

I focus largely on American and European manifestations of the faith, and in particular for my contemporary material on case studies drawn from a branch of conservative Protestantism, the Faith or Health and Wealth Movement. The roots of the Movement lie, in part, within North American revivals of the post-war period that emphasised themes of healing and material plenty (Coleman

2000, 2004). Currently, considerable followings for Faith teachings can be found in large urban areas with middle-class constituencies, such as South Africa, South Korea, Singapore, parts of South America and certain areas of Europe (Martin 2002), but the Prosperity message has also appealed to less advantaged groups who have maintained aspirations for personal (and sometimes wider) forms of transformation and empowerment. Both sets of interests are served by ideological contexts where the virtues and excitements of internationalism are stressed (Gifford 1998: 83), often bolstered by the use of electronic media. Before we delve further into the details of Protestant movements, however, we need very briefly to reconsider the character of the city, at least as it relates to the 'spirit' or urbanism we are examining here.

The City as Space and Place

Steve Pile (1996) asks a simple question: 'What is a City?' His answer includes the observation that cities intensify and focus interactions, while – certainly in contemporary Western contexts – building on the circulation and use of capital. In a sense there are two movements being described here: a centripetal attraction to a centre and also a potentially contrifugal, or at least network-based, extension of interconnections from the centre. Thus Massey (1999: 161), in a resonant phrase, talks of cities as embodying a kind of 'open intensity', speeding up links 'within an ever spatially-spreading web of external connections'. Massey also points to Simmel's observation that concentrated spatial proximity can – perhaps must, in some cases – co-exist with forms of social distancing.

The values embodied in the 'modernist' city just described can themselves be inscribed in styles of corporate architecture. Momosh (1992: 83) talks of how a self-consciously rational Modernism, imported into American architecture from Europe throughout the first decades of the twentieth century, spoke of a fit between design and function, encouraging displays of the technological underpinnings of the new city. Commerce might combine with art in the production of overtly flexible and expandable spatial arrangements, but also of places of display of identity in the context of the anonymising city.

More contemporary urban developments can be said to have taken some of the elements of the modernist city to their 'logical' conclusions. Hubbard and Hall (1998: 16), drawing on Harvey's (1989) influential work on capitalism and postmodernist spatialities, refer to the tensions resulting as time-space compression threatens people's self-identification with place (even if the mobility of capital can be exaggerated). Social relations themselves can become disembedded, 'distanciated'. In a post-Fordist environment, territorial politics may therefore become more salient as the establishment of locality comes at more of a premium. Furthermore, older models of urban spatiality may come to seem increasingly anachronistic (Hubbard and Hall 1998: 1) as spectacular new forms, such as out-of-town retail parks and heritage centres, emerge. These themes touch on the geographer Yi-Fu Tuan's much-quoted distinction (Tuan

1977; see also Jones 2000: 28) between the concept of neutral, undifferentiated space and that of meaningful place. His definition of neutral space in turn recalls the contrasts Marc Augé (1995) draws between *places*, marked by monuments, memory and dense forms of social life, and *non-places*, contexts, such as airports and motorways, to which people are connected in homogeneous ways and which involve forms of transit.

The argument so far is necessarily truncated and schematic. However, the basic point is twofold. First, the conservative Protestantism as I have described it has shared with modernist (and to some extent post-modernist) views of the city an uneasiness with – though not necessarily a blanket condemnation of – 'place'. Circulation, mobility and even technological development are ideally not to be compromised by inappropriate forms of stasis; technology can be used for divine purposes; and the message must be able to appeal to a loosely structured 'public'. Second, such resonance between revivalist and urban ideologies is not surprising if, in Weberian terms, we consider the partially common roots of evangelicalism and modernity. Yet, of course the Western, modernist city that I have described also appears to be a largely secular city, expressing the values of an ostensibly de-spiritualised capitalism. So how has conservative Protestantism attempted – both historically and in the present – to reappropriate the desacralised, urban forms from which it emerged, and which it even helped to create?

Taking Back the City

When we consider the emergence of evangelicalism as an urban force within nineteenth-century America, Jeanne Kilde's work (1999) is a key reference point. She argues for a close connection between religious revivals and the spaces in which they occur, and notes: 'From Billy Sunday's revival tents to Billy Graham's athletic stadiums to Robert Schuller's glistening Crystal Cathedral, twentieth century revivalism brings to mind the image of a multitudinous audience seated in an amphitheater-like auditorium – a large space housing a semicircle of ascending seats radiating from a center stage – and focused intently on a magnetic speaker' (Kilde 1999: 174). Within this passage we begin to gain a sense of historical continuities: the juxtaposition of audience with charismatic speaker, obviously, but more specifically the way effective spaces of revivalism not only facilitate the easy communication of the spoken word, but also the visual display of a mass audience, a body of fellow believers gathered around 'the Word' and, crucially, visible to each other. Note also how each of the architectural forms conveys a quasi-theological message: the tent as symbol of mobility; the athletic stadium as spiritual appropriation of secular space (as well as ideally containing the disciplined body); and the 'Cathedral' as reminiscent of the Gothic in its size and orientation towards the heavens, but startlingly transparent, as opposed to the opaqueness of cathedral stone, and internally much less differentiated and divided.[2]

Yet, as Kilde points out, however familiar the auditorium revival space is today, it was revolutionary in the nineteenth century. Its origins lay in the architectural iconoclasm of urban Protestant revivalists, who were eager to favour utilitarianism over convention. Theatre-style auditoria (and often former theatres themselves) demonstrated the ability of believers to adopt any spaces, while at the same time converting the urban secular to sacred use. While preachers might have demonstrated actorly skills in the past, earlier worship spaces cramped the rhetorical style of the speaker through being relatively modest in size, with columns obstructing views. Thus the transformation of traditional church plans commenced in the 1830s, in America at least, as evangelical Presbyterians attempted to broaden their appeal among urban working classes. Kilde quotes Lewis Tappan, writing to the famous preacher Charles Finney on 16 March 1832, when the latter had expressed doubt over the virtues of taking over popular dens of iniquity: 'The *sensation* that will be produced by converting the place, with slight alterations, into a church will be very great. . . . By taking this theatre appropriating it for a church the whole city will talk of it, wonder and inquire. . . . It will have the effect of storming a redoubt, or taking cannon & turning them upon the enemy, as in an army' (1999: 176). Tappan reveals the complex stance of affinity and repulsion between this form of conservative Protestantism and the urban entertainment to that it was supplanting. On the one hand there was the attempt to appeal to a mass and anonymous audience – made up not just of fellow believers (ideally if not always in practice being treated equally, despite social and other divisions) but also of potential converts – and open stages were designed precisely for sometimes histrionic displays of charismatic personality. On the other hand, the military metaphor expressed the self-consciously embattled sense of being surrounded by 'the enemy', who after all had previously occupied the theatre. Only urban contexts could provide mobile and mass publics to appeal to, combined with the sensation – increasingly crucial to some forms of evangelicalism – of defining the faith against a proximate and dangerous other.

In subsequent years (see Coleman and Collins, 2006) the auditorium style was to trade architectural blows in urban America with an alternative and very different genre, that of the neo-Gothic (Kilde, 1999: 182–83; White, 1964: 130). The tension between revivalism and romanticism revolved partially around the expression of clerical authority, with the Gothic constituted by overtly hierarchical and divided spaces that were anathema to many revivalists. It also invoked different attitudes to tradition; for instance, Finney's apparently rational and utilitarian 'new measures' for promoting conversion versus the neo-medievalism of the Gothic. In a broader sense, it reflected different attitudes to the nature of place itself. Revivalism, as noted, is constituted ideally by the sense that any space can be converted to God's purposes, that attachment to a specific place is liable to lead to stasis and the death of enthusiasm. Even while the Gothic was in the ascendant in the 1850s, amphitheatre designs were still adopted for periodic revivals and Finney himself had a large tent constructed in which to conduct camp-style meetings.

This is a story, then, of a faith that was adapting itself to cities made up of increasingly mobile, heterogeneous populations. New auditoria could use not only the charisma of the speaker, but also the self-referential 'charisma' implied by the spectacle of mass audiences to reinforce commitment – a technique exploited by Billy Graham and other leaders of city revivals in the post-Second World War period. This use of space complemented, and to some extent was also constituted by, a consciously rational attempt to adopt explicit and efficient principles of evangelisation and preaching, and the influence of the business world was never very far away from such an approach. The transcendence of denominational identities through (temporary) mini-revivals was always a possibility, and these methods were also complemented by other generic evangelical practices that were burgeoning in the new cities. Ladd and Mathison (1999) remark that D.L. Moody not only allied himself in the last decades of the nineteenth century with business people, but also with those interested in sports and the self-consciously disciplining approaches of the YMCA.

Furthermore, cities were key arenas for the ideological debates that were to help form the future developments of conservative Protestantism in the twentieth century. As Smith notes (1998: xi), it can be argued that evangelicalism has thrived precisely because of, and not in spite of, its confrontation with modern pluralism. The latter has constituted an apparently threatening ideological other against which to join forces. In the last quarter of the nineteenth century (1998: 5–6), as the battle lines between social and conservative versions of the gospel solidified, the northern cities of the United States were places where conservatives fought to expel liberalism in education and religion. Indeed, the movement that was to become the fundamentalist wing of conservative Protestantism, led by Dwight L. Moody, had its organisational bases in northern cities such as Chicago, Philadelphia and Boston.

From Suburbia to the Globe

A century later, the auditorium style is still in vogue among conservative congregations. However, many of the burgeoning mega-churches in America (and increasingly beyond) are located in areas where land is less expensive but mobility is not compromised, such as suburban housing developments and major freeway nodes (Kilde 1999: 185). The famous Willow Creek Community Church founded in 1975 outside Chicago can accommodate an audience of around 5,000 and continues, in modern form, the nineteenth-century attempt to enhance the perception of the preacher: sound amplification and video projection combined with spot- and laser-lights. Business marketing is again used, though now it is more explicitly orientated to forms of Christianity that are more comfortable with an expansion of leisure and consumer opportunities.

The architecture of Willow Creek has a deliberately corporate feel and the sense that a business aesthetic, incipiently present in the earlier period, has partially supplanted that of the theatre is also evident in the warehouse styles favoured by many believers, including those belonging to Prosperity-style ministries. Balmer and Winner (2002: 110ff.) describe the New Life Family Fellowship, which meets in a converted warehouse on Pacheco Road in Santa Fe, New Mexico. The ministry was founded in 1980 by a graduate of Rhema Bible Training Center, and Balmer and Winner characterise it as part of a new wave of American evangelicalism, combining an unwillingness to affiliate with any one denomination with openness to a heterogeneous congregation (in this case of Native Americans, Anglos and Hispanics). As such, it provides a good example of the Prosperity/Faith strategy of training pastors to establish their own ministries around the world, frequently in urban areas of high population density. As Stai (1993: 1) notes, such ministries worldwide are placing themselves in the parts of urban areas that exhibit the most growth, in keeping with an expansionist aesthetic that extends from body language to consumerist ideology.

Next, I consider this aesthetic and urban strategy in urban areas beyond the United States. While conducting fieldwork among Faith Christians in Sweden in 1987, I observed the construction of a new church by the Word of Life ministry in Uppsala. The group, created some four years earlier, had been renting premises in an industrial zone just outside the city and now wanted its own location. The new construction provided a form of architecture in which the revivalist mistrust of place was clearly evident (see Roelofs 1994: 220), but also a clear attempt to demarcate a particular kind of spiritualised territory within the urban realm.[3]

Thus, on one level the new Word of Life building clearly constituted a distinct and lasting context for the life of the church. The site, next door to the rented buildings, was determined partly by its availability and affordability, but also by a charismatic form of theophany. The head pastor of the group, Ulf Ekman, noted the following in a 1985 *World of Life Newsletter* article titled 'Now Is God's Time for Expansion':

> So one day, despite the fact that I had driven past this plot hundreds of times, I saw the plot. It gleamed. The Lord told me to ring the local authority immediately. When I rang the state planner said: 'It's strange that you're ringing just at the moment. I'm sitting with the plans for the plot and intend to build a road over it. We have a bit left, but you'd better hurry'.

If the initial vision was closely associated with the particular charismatic qualities of the head pastor, the plot was subsequently appropriated by congregation members as a whole who, after a Sunday service, spoke tongues into the ground upon which the new building would rise.

In other respects, however, the architecture and use of the building can be seen as a kind of denial of place and reassertion of Tuan's 'space' or Augé's 'non-place'. The building is vast and looks like a warehouse, blending into the industrial landscape by which it is surrounded. What marks the Word of Life sanctuary are the elements of audibility and visibility (Peacock and Tyson 1989: 118). The stage is visible from all parts of the high-ceilinged hall and congregants are visible to each other. No windows are placed at eye level, thus removing distractions from the outside. The visitor is subject to the panoptic gaze of the preacher, high up on the platform, as well as to the gaze of many fellow congregants throughout the hall.

The largely internally undifferentiated, rectangular sanctuary, marked by plain walls and rows of chairs leading to a stage, is surrounded by offices and smaller lecture halls, suggesting that the productive work of worship and of running the ministry's Bible school, media business and university are part of the same mission. At the time of its construction believers admired the size and technological efficiency of the building, but also expressed the hope that it, too, would one day be perceived as too small and in need of replacement by an ever-growing and progressing ministry. The building is thus seen as an architectural manifestation of the central charismatic (and broader evangelical) notion of outreach, the spreading of the Word to the unconverted.

Services held in the group's hall also contain the combination of promoting and denying place: size of congregation is always important, but services are also video- and audio-taped and thus made available in contexts that are widely dispersed in space and time. At the entrance to the building is a shop selling Faith products from around the world, indicating that the building is a context of extensive consumption as well as production. Group literature stresses the fact that the industrial zone outside Uppsala is a prime locus for the mobile: it is after all near an international airport. There are clear parallels here with the Toronto Airport Christian Fellowship, the catalyst for the globally diffused Toronto Blessing. We are also perhaps seeing a charismatic version of a modernist conception of the regenerative powers of travel (Featherstone 1997: 241), where the transcendent and the 'travelled' come together in a powerful ideology of movement. Most important, the ideal – and very often the practice – of bringing fellow charismatics from all around the world to the Word of Life building for conferences and preaching tours provides a contemporary counterpart, but also a transformation, of the gathering of nineteenth-century congregations in urban auditoria. The believer's gaze now takes in fellow worshippers not simply from around the city or the nation, but frequently from other parts of the globe, reinforcing a concrete sense of a fellow public that is massively expanded in scope.

Travel brings another important dimension into such contemporary, urban, Protestant experience: ironically enough, a form of temporality. As David Morgan pointed out, 'for many Protestants, the sacred is configured by a rhythm of events, encountered within the ritualised time of worship that culminates in prayer, song, ecstatic experience, the altar call, or the sermon. The "place" of the sacred is thus articulated within a temporal sequence, not a physical site. . . . In the case of many Protestants . . . the architecture of the sacred is one of time, in the activities of prayer, song or testimonial' (1998: 812). Although I agree that Morgan's characterisation fits the charismatic case well, I argue that the sense of mobility and flow provided by constant, temporary visitors to the group provides an equally important, if less obviously ritualistic, expression of the way sacralisation can occur by both denying place (mobility) and yet simultaneously exalting it (with the Word of Life's premises acting as a magnet for such mobility).

This church thus displays its own variations on a 'warehouse' style, involving the extensive annexation of space on the horizontal, and occasionally also the vertical, plane. Size is combined with the articulation and representation of movement so that it is not surprising to find the tent emerging as a potent architectural form among these Christians. On his website Reinhard Bonnke, a well-known preacher within and beyond Faith circles, tells the story of how his original 'Yellow Tent', which could seat a mere 10,000 souls, had to be replaced by the 'Big Tent', which had the capacity of seating 34,000 and, equally important, of going wherever Bonnke chose to conduct services. Predictably, even the Big Tent has at times proved far too small for Bonnke's congregations. Meanwhile, the Word of Life in Sweden has purchased its own tent, for use during conferences. In a sense the tent provides the ideal revivalist space, set off from the outside, yet inviting entry; internally undifferentiated and externally plain; capable of creating a temporary revivalist 'space' that need not be limited by the confines of 'place'.

When describing the Prosperity-influenced Universal Church of the Kingdom of God in Brazil, Lehmann (1996: 183) notes that in the early 1990s these Christians had numerous hangar-like, rented buildings in outlying areas. Ruuth (1995: 117) points to the Universal Church's tendency to choose buildings located in points of literal urban mobility – train stations, bus stops and so on. In his study of the same denomination, Kramer (2002) notes that the Universal Church's Temple of the Glory of New Israel is based in the working-class district of Del Castilho in Rio de Janeiro. The Temple complex – similar to many buildings I have described in this chapter – converts secular into spiritual space, as it occupies the site of an old tile factory. Furthermore, its location encourages and benefits from mobility, because it borders on train tracks that connect the outlying suburban periphery to the metropolitan terminus, Central do Brasil. One of the more extraordinary aspects of the construction activities of the congregation, however, consists of a concrete platform outside the building, stretching over approximately 11,000 square meters. The platform, at the time of Kramer's writing, was being prepared to house a 1 : 50 scale model of Jerusalem, made out of marble blocks quarried in Israel. The model would form part of a theme park, also including olive trees from Israeli seed and other items from the Holy Land. As Kramer notes, unlike circulating object media in the Church, the model would embody a place in which the believer could activate, or perhaps supercharge, the force of his or her faith in practice, while it seems likely that the Church's leadership intend the park to serve as a magnet for religious tourism.

Thus the model of Jerusalem described by Kramer goes somewhat further in its reconstruction of the urban than some of the other examples we have seen. It not only builds a material replica of the Jerusalem of the Bible, it incorporates some of the Holy Land into its very walls. Rather than simply building a church for the community of believers, it builds a whole city. As such, the model has the potential to prompt further mobility in the form of tourists, and Kramer argues that the model of Jerusalem and the complex of which it is part are part of a pattern of concentrating IURD (Igreja Universal do Reino de Deus or

Universal Church of the Kingdom of God) congregations in larger metropolitan and regional centres – both in Brazil and in urban centres elsewhere where large Latino populations exist, such as New York, New Jersey, California and Texas.

Concluding Remarks: An Urban Sublime

This chapter shows the ways in which urban contexts can provide key growing grounds for forms of Protestantism that valorise the abrupt conversion of the secular into the sacred and build mobility into material landscapes of action. It is also the case, however, that just as urban forms have changed over the past century, so evangelical spaces and places have undergone some changes in character. Massey's 'open intensity' has become ever more intense, and the contemporary evangelical auditorium has the potential to contain a far more cosmopolitan, or at least diverse, constituency. The distanciation of relations is far more evident now, with the often enthusiastic embrace of communications technologies on behalf of believers who are very willing to use contemporary methods to broadcast what they see as an unchanging and ancient message. And the evangelical counterpart to the out-of-town retail park is probably the Prosperity-style 'warehouse', accessing populations that no longer need to be at the centre of cities, which are likely in any case to be too expensive and densely occupied to facilitate the mass consumption of the product on offer.

My argument is not that the processes I have described are the only dimensions of evangelicalism, or that they are key to the practices of conversion for which this branch of Christianity is famous. One of the most significant developments in the broadly evangelical world in recent decades has been the so-called Alpha Course, a programme of lectures and socialising that has become a truly globalised phenomenon, which draws on smaller-scale (and not necessarily urban) forms of association. The process of becoming a believer is more likely to occur with the support of family or friends than it is through mass rallies. Furthermore, as I write in the summer of 2005, the evangelist Billy Graham is preaching – at the age of eighty-six – at what may well be his last great Crusade, in New York. Yet, we should not underestimate the significance of both the sight and the experience of the (physically or virtually) gathered community for these Christians. The evangelical gaze for much of the time is focused on a vision of the mass, the huge numbers of fellow believers and potential converts who have chosen to associate together. It is also a gaze that – in common with the exercise of glossolalia – is constituted by imagining the potentially infinite others who can be reached by forms of outreach (Coleman and Collins, 2006). Evangelicalism in the city may be bounded by the places its believers can occupy, but such places help cultivate a Protestant imagination that has no limit to its ambition.

Notes

1. Here, I use 'evangelical' as a catch-all term to encompass the many varieties of conservative Protestantism.
2. Perhaps there is an interesting parallel here with London's famous Crystal Palace Exhibition of the mid-nineteenth century, which deployed a giant transparent building to 'evangelise' for the idea of human progress (Stocking 1987).
3. Some of the description here is based on Coleman and Collins (2006).

References

Augé, M. 1995. *Non-Places: Introduction to an Anthropology of Supermodernity*. London: Verso.
Balmer, R. and L.F. Winner. 2002. *Protestantism in America*. New York: Columbia University Press.
Coleman, S. 2000. *The Globalisation of Charismatic Christianity: Spreading the Gospel of Prosperity*. Cambridge: Cambridge University Press.
———. 2004. 'The Charismatic Gift', *Journal of the Royal Anthropological Institute* 10(2): 421–42.
Coleman, S. and Collins, P. 2000. 'The "Plain" and the "Positive": Ritual, Experience and Aesthetics in Quakerism and Charismatic Christianity', *Journal of Contemporary Religion* 15(3): 317–29.
Coleman, S. and Collins, P. 2006. 'The Shape of Faith (Or, the Architectural Forms of the Religious Life)', in E. Arweck and W. Keenan (eds.), *Materialising Religion: Expression, Performance and Ritual*. Aldershot: Ashgate, pp. 32-44.
Featherstone, M. 1997. 'Travel, Migration, and Images of Social Life', in W. Gungwu (ed.), *Global History and Migrations*. Boulder: Westview Press, pp. 239–77.
Gifford, P. 1998. *African Christianity: Its Public Role*. London: Hurst.
Harvey, D. 1989. *The Condition of Postmodernity*. Oxford: Blackwell.
Hubbard, P. and T. Hall. 1998. 'The Entrepreneurial City and the "New Urban Politics"', in T. Hall and P. Hubbard (eds.), *The Entrepreneurial City: Geographies of Politics, Regime and Representation*. Chichester: John Wiley, pp. 1–23.
Jones, L. 2000. *The Hermeneutics of Sacred Architecture: Experience, Interpretation, Comparison. Volume Two: Hermeneutical Calisthenics: A Morphology of Ritual-Architectural Priorities*. Cambridge: Harvard University Press.
Kilde, J. 1999. 'Architecture and Urban Revivalism in Nineteenth-century America', in P.W. Williams (ed.), *Perspectives on American Religion and Culture*. Malden, MA and Oxford, UK: Blackwell, pp. 174–86.
Kramer, E. 2002. 'Making Global Faith Universal: Media and a Brazilian Prosperity Movement', *Culture and Religion* 3(1): 21–48.
Ladd, T. and Mathison, J. A. 1999. *Muscular Christianity: Evangelical Protestants and the Development of American Sport*. Grand Rapids, MI: Baker Books.
Lehmann, D. 1996. *Struggle for the Spirit: Religious Transformation and Popular Culture in Brazil and Latin America*. Cambridge: Polity.
Martin, D. 2002. *Pentecostalism: The World Their Parish*. Oxford: Blackwell.
Massey, D. 1999. 'On Space and the City', in D. Massey, J. Allen, and S. Pile (eds.), *City Worlds*. London: Routledge, pp. 157–71.

Momosh, M. 1992. 'Corporate Cultures and the Modern Landscape of New York City', in K. Anderson and F. Gale (eds.), *Inventing Places: Studies in Cultural Geography*. Melbourne: Longman Cheshire, pp.72–86.

Morgan, D. 1998. *Visual Piety: A History and Theory of Popular Religious Images*. Berkeley: University of California Press.

Peacock, J. and R. Tyson. 1989. *Pilgrims of Paradox: Calvinism and Experience Among the Primitive Baptists of the Blue Ridge*. Washington, DC: Smithsonian Institution Press.

Percy, M. 1998. 'The Morphology of Pilgrimage in the "Toronto Blessing"', *Religion* 28: 281–88.

Pile, S. 1996. 'What Is a City?', in D. Massey, J. Allen, and S. Pile (eds.), *City Worlds*. London: Routledge, pp. 3–52.

Roelofs, G. 1994. 'Charismatic Christian Thought: Experience, Metonymy, and Routinization', in K. Poewe (ed), *Charismatic Christianity as a Global Culture*. Columbia: University of South Carolina Press, pp.217-33.

Ruuth, A. 1995. *Igreja Universal Do Reino De Deus: Gudsrikets Universella Kyrka—En Brasiliansk Kyrkobildning*. Stockholm: Almqvist & Wiksell International.

Smith, C.1998. *American Evangelicalism: Embattled and Thriving*. Chicago: University of Chicago Press.

Stocking, G. 1987. *Victorian Anthropology*. New York: Macmillan.

Tuan, Yi-Fu. 1977. *Space and Place: The Perspective of Experience*. Minneapolis: University of Minnesota Press.

Turner, H. 1979. *From Temple to Meeting-House: The Phenomenology and Theology of Places of Worship*. The Hague: Mouton.

White, J. 1964. *Protestant Worship and Church Architecture: Theological and Historical Considerations*. New York: Oxford University Press.

Wills, G. 1990. *Under God: Religion and American Politics*. New York: Simon and Schuster.

The Ecology and Economy of Urban Religious Space: A Socio-Historical Account of Quakers in Town

Peter Collins

A sociological question often emerges along with the discernment of a pattern, or its absence. The starting point for this chapter is a simple, apparently naive, question: why are Quaker meeting houses in town larger than those in rural areas? Naturally, the question I have posed can be aired in a variety of ways. The most obvious response would be merely to present a series of population statistics indicating the sometimes astonishing increase in the urban population in Britain in the eighteenth and nineteenth centuries; however, this would be a crude and analytically uninteresting response. Although it is impossible to deny or ignore such statistics, I contend that the space constructed by Quakers in town bears a considerable symbolic load. I begin with a brief exploration of a trio of key terms: urbanisation, urbanism and 'urban ecology', drawing principally on work carried out by the Chicago School. I go on to consider the claim that religious space is meaningful and therefore open to interpretation. I then present a brief historical overview of the structure and (primary) functions of Quaker meeting houses. Finally, I narrow my focus and analyse the built environment, of Quakers in town.

Urbanisation, Urbanism and Urban Ecology

The path towards a greater understanding of 'the urban' can start from either of two places. First, we can consider the process that has come to be known as urbanisation, measured by the percentage of people who are urban in a society, a region or the world, and that statistically summarises the relationship between total population and its urban component. This has been a primarily demographic endeavour which can often lead to a dead end – though the practical implications of a town or city being defined as such can be very important indeed. A salient fact in this case is the extent of rapid urbanisation in Britain from around 1750 on.[1]

However, the pursuit of a single, objective definition of the urban (or of terms like hamlet, village, town, city) is inevitably fruitless. There may be reasonable heuristic reasons for calling any settlement of up to 100 people a 'hamlet' and those of over 250,000 a 'city' but the reasons for doing so had better be largely administrative because labouring over such classifications does little to advance theory. Weber recognised the theoretical futility of such definitions when he lamented: 'the many definitions of the city have only one element in common: namely that the city consists simply of a collection of one or more separate dwellings but is a relatively closed settlement' ([1905] 1958: 65). But like many others, Weber himself could not resist the temptation to define. The city, he avers, is a market settlement, a place: 'where the local inhabitants satisfy an economically substantial part of their daily wants in the local market' (66–67).

He adds that the city is a place which is too large for everybody to know everybody else. This last remark is very interesting. Weber is making an implicitly demographic claim about the city (that it is 'large') but qualifying it in a novel way by referring to the quality of social relations that characterise it. In so doing, he is moving from the quantitative to the qualitative, from talking about 'urbanisation' and towards 'urbanism'. Similarly, I am primarily concerned here with qualitative issues and specifically with developing an understanding of religious space.

Perhaps it was the Chicago sociologists under the tutelage of Robert Park who made the single greatest contribution to our understanding of urban ecologies. The result was a collection of often brilliant ethnographies.[2] These studies provided an early insight into the ways in which people might come to belong in cities. Given the large number of ethnographies undertaken, it is surprising that so little attention was paid to the religious life of Chicago. The Chicago school did not bequeath a particularly strong body of theory apart, perhaps, from Burgess's concentric zone model in which ecological niches form concentric circles from Zone I (the Central Business District, known in Chicago as 'the loop') out to Zone V (the commuter zone, on the outskirts of the city). Again, Burgess's work did not prompt those interested in religion to use his model as a means of religious belonging in the city. For instance, one might have begun by asking a simple question such as what did it mean for a congregation to be located in Zone I rather than Zone V?

Urbanism refers to a way of life experienced by city dwellers. We often feel strongly about cities and opinions are often represented as extreme visions. On the one hand, cities are the embodiment of culture/civilisation, exhilarating, exciting places full of vitality and creativity. On the other hand, they are typified as anomic and alienating concrete jungles, melting pots where the recipe has gone disastrously wrong. Louis Wirth in his seminal paper 'Urbanism as a Way of Life' (1938) developed Weber's ploy in arguing that the city has the following elements: permanent residence, high density and heterogeneity. Wirth's paper might be seen as the culmination of the Chicago School wherein the human ecology of urban areas received close and sustained scrutiny. Wirth's characterisation of the city has been extraordinarily influential and has a peculiar relevance to the issue at hand. Wirth supposed that these characteristics produced a particular kind of emotional and mental response – city dwellers become sophisticated, rational and relativistic. The lone individual counts for little in the modern city. In order to accomplish their goals individuals with similar interests join together to form (voluntary) organisations. Unlike rural folk, city dwellers do not owe their allegiance to any one group or community. How might this claim relate to the experience of religion in cities? Unfortunately, the Chicago scholars remained singularly uninterested in such questions.[3]

Wirth and the Chicago School largely and significantly ignored issues of power. An omission partially rectified by influential individuals writing from the perspective of political economy. For example, David Harvey (1985a, 1985b, 1989) suggests that cities are perhaps, above all, powerful places and despite the increased mobility of capital (Sassen 1991) remain principal sites of capital accumulation, as well as symbolic capital accumulation. In speaking thus of the urban one cannot but imply a particular view of the rural.

For much of written history, Raymond Williams (1973) argues the city, or urban ecology if you like, has been defined in terms of what the country is not: culture, civilisation, power and so on. As Lefebvre puts it, urban space 'gathers crowds, products in the markets, acts and symbols. It concentrates all these, and accumulates them. To say "urban space" is to say centre and centrality, and it does not matter whether these are actual or merely possible, saturated, broken up or under fire, for we are speaking here of a dialectical centrality' (1991: 101).

Bipolar definitions are prominent across various modes of representation – the media, novels, poetry, geography, sociology, anthropology. Some mid-twentieth-century writers, ethnographers for the most part, began to work out a slightly more nuanced classification, an urban spectrum. The most influential among them was Robert Redfield, who graded urban settlements on the Yucatan Peninsula in Mexico from less to more urbanised. In a sense it seems obvious that settlements vary from the very small to the very large – this is merely a matter of counting heads. Conversely it could be argued that thanks to the media and improved transport facilities, one can be 'urbanised' in the smallest village, that we live in an urban society regardless of our geographical location. Furthermore, according to Sassen (1991), Castells (1989) and others, we live in a global society, in a world in which there is one 'super' urban network. We now have access via the Internet, television and video to any number of cultures, and therefore any number of religions and also to those who worship with us, as it were, in faraway places; in this case it is easy to believe ourselves believers in a global church (Coleman 2001). This is not, however, always the case and British Quakerism has remained relatively parochial.

It is clear that the rate of urbanisation since around 1750 and its acceleration throughout the nineteenth century helped provoke an interest in the urban sphere among political economists (such as Marx and Engels) and those who were beginning to see themselves as sociologists (Durkheim, Simmel and Weber). However, the single most important point of this introduction is that we should not take for granted the meaning of the terms 'city' or 'urban ecology'. The consequences for religious faith and practice of urbanisation and urbanism vary depending on whether one concentrates on the legal, political, economic, demographic or symbolic. I am specifically interested here in the characteristics of the built environment, particularly on 'religious space', and the ways in which it varies between what we think of as the rural and the urban.

The Meaningfulness of Religious Space

Whereas the character of urban space has long been theorised, this is not the case with architectural space. For a long time architecture was assumed to be a practical matter, the primary function of a building was to shelter its occupants from the weather. There was considerable emphasis on external form over and above the space contained therein. Over time, increasing attention has been paid to the symbolic meaning of architecture (Zevi 1974). Recently, the built environment has come to be seen as more than simply a matter of design and engineering. For instance the Quaker meeting house, like almost any building, obviously serves to keep worshippers warm and dry as they worship and conduct their business. But meeting houses also have a symbolic valence. This is an area that I have explored in the past (Collins 1996a, 1996b, 2006; see also Coleman and Collins 1996, 2000) and I continue to develop these arguments here.

It is worth noting that comparatively little was published on the symbolic component of the built environment until the 1960s. Even in the late 1980s, Caroline Humphrey (1988) chides anthropologists for largely ignoring the built environment of their subjects. There has been some response to this clarion call, including Waterson's work on Toraja domestic architecture (1991). Important exceptions would be the structural analyses of Claude Levi-Strauss and Pierre Bourdieu. Significantly, despite the brilliance of Bourdieu's analysis of the Berber house and its relation to Berber cosmology (1973), few scholars took up the challenge to repeat such work. Since the 1970s Paul Oliver (e.g. 1977), an architect by training, has produced a number of comparative studies of domestic dwellings. Charles Jencks and George Baird edited an interesting collection of essays in 1969 (*Meaning in Architecture*) debating the usefulness of semiology in interpreting the meaning of buildings. Meanwhile architects have drawn on a range of sources (philosophy, sociology, anthropology, semiology) in an attempt to grasp the meaning of buildings. Drawing on the phenomenological approach of Heidegger, Merleau-Ponty and Bachelard, in 1979 Christian Norbert-Schulz wrote *Genius Loci: Towards a phenomenology of Architecture*, a wide-ranging and complex work that characteristically emphasises the elements or fundamentals of the built environment.

Cultural geographers Anne Buttimer and David Seamon edited an interesting collection of essays in 1980 including that of Amos Rapoport who had written other important essays on the meaning of the built environment before that (Rapoport 1969, 1977). More recently Tom Markus (1993) and Kim Dovey (1999) have written extensively on the ways in which buildings signify power, and in 1994 Parker and Richards edited an excellent collection on the same subject. In 2001 architect Bryan Lawson published an introductory textbook titled *The Language of Space* (with a bias towards psychology), indicating the establishment of a sub-discipline. Lawson argues strongly and compellingly for the importance of buildings in forming and sustaining our identities.

In terms of religious space in particular Peter Hammond's book *Liturgy and Architecture* (1960) assesses the impact of the latter on the former. Turner's *From Temple to Meeting House* was something of a landmark when published in 1979 but mostly ignores analysis of buildings' meanings. Drawing on the work of semiotician A.J. Greimas, Lukken and Searle (1993) carried out a pioneering semiotic study of the Church of SS Peter and Paul (Tilburg), though the growth of structuralist and semiotic studies seem to have slowed down considerably during the past decade. We should also remember Belden Lane's stimulating though idiosyncratic book *Landscapes of the Sacred* (1988) in which he describes the spatial production of various American spiritualities.

Many of these accounts draw either directly or indirectly on Lynch's *The Image of the City* (1960) to the extent that they focus on the elements or fundamentals of the built environment, rather than on styles or genres. Lynch suggests that urban areas consist of relatively few elements that connect in various ways: paths, edges, districts, nodes and landmarks, forming the basis of a system of classification. He therefore introduces a level of abstraction equal to that of Lukken and Searle (1993), but relatively rare in analyses of the built environment. This approach, both taxonomic and comparative, has been adopted by Thomas Barrie in *Spiritual Path, Sacred Place* (1996), and more impressively by Lindsay Jones in *The Hermeneutics of Sacred Architecture* (2000). Jones has provided perhaps the most complete taxonomy of the meanings of religious buildings, identifying three primary 'ritual-architectural priorities' (fundamentals of religious space if you like), which he subdivides to form a basic taxonomy, or system of classification: 'I. architecture as orientation (that is, the *instigation* of ritual-architectural events); II. architecture as commemoration (or, the *content* of ritual-architectural events); and III. architecture as ritual context (or, the *presentation* of ritual-architectural events)' (Jones 2000: vol. 2, appendix).

This careful study undoubtedly provides us with a useful taxonomy and the fact is that this suggests that the space in which the religious life is lived is still relatively little understood. We can each run down the list, ticking off those features that best characterise the religious group in which we are particularly interested. In Jones's terms, Quaker meeting houses for instance, include IA (homology: sacred architecture that presents a miniaturised replica of the universe and/or conforms to a celestial archetype), IB (convention: sacred architecture that conforms to standardised rules and/or prestigious mythico-historical precedents) and IC (astronomy: sacred architecture that is aligned or referenced with respect to celestial bodies or phenomenon); IIC (politics: sacred architecture that commemorates, legitimates or challenges socioeconomic hierarchy and/or temporal authority); and IIIA (theatre: sacred architecture that provides a stage setting or backdrop for ritual performance), IIIB (contemplation: sacred architecture that serves as a prop or focus for meditation or devotion) and maybe IIID (sanctuary: sacred architecture that provides a refuge of purity, sacrality, or perfection). These 'ritual-architectural priorities' may be more or less apparent, depending on design, some more obviously apparent in some meeting houses than others as we are dealing with spectra here rather than black and white distinctions. We can see, then, that the function of the Quaker meeting house, purely in terms of the religious, is a complex phenomenon just as much so as an Anglican cathedral, a Sikh temple, or a mosque.

Despite the usefulness of Jones's scrupulously careful classificatory schema it does have a major flaw, inherited from many if not all previous accounts: it focuses entirely on the explicitly religious character of 'religious architecture'. Jones assumes that 'the religious' is a hermetically sealed environment, purified and wholly separated from the rest of social life. I argue that although this is a necessary focus, it is a mistake to ignore the profane, secular or non-religious facets of the built religious environment. The point here is that the meaning of religious space is generally assumed to be 'religious' and I believe that this is to take too much for granted. In order to explain myself I focus on the case of the Quaker meeting house.

The Quaker Meeting House

Quakers have written voluminously and on a wide variety of subjects since the 1650s. In the seventeenth and eighteenth centuries, in particular, they spilt a great deal of ink on what members should and should not do: proscriptions and prescriptions issued thick and fast and covered virtually every aspect of life from the shape of gravestones to the use of umbrellas. Given its role in the creation and maintenance of identity, it is somewhat surprising therefore that there is so little advice on the construction of the meeting house. We might assume that Quakers simply knew from experience what a meeting house should look like, that such an understanding was a part of their habitus (Bourdieu 1977: 78–87). However, the shape of Quaker space was originally defined by an unusually basic liturgy (which involves worshippers sitting quietly, the silence occasionally broken by a worshipper standing to minister) and their broader testimony to plainness meant that in the case of the Quaker meeting house form follows function. There should be a room large enough for Quakers to meet for worship and hold regular meetings for transacting church business.

In the 1650s and 1660s Quakers spoke to crowds wherever they could, in market places, in churches (often during services) on the fell-side, especially in the north and west of England, that is in the predominantly rural counties of Cumberland, Westmoreland, Lancashire and Yorkshire. These 'threshing meetings' generated interest in some who later gathered in smaller groups in houses and barns (Braithwaite 1955). The first meeting houses were built towards the end of the seventeenth century and were simple, vernacular buildings: generally low stone buildings, forming a single space (sometimes partitioned) with a bench set aside for the elders and ministers. Spatial pragmatism was furthered by the addition of a second, smaller room (or an area that could be temporarily partitioned off) in order that women could hold their meetings for business within the same building and simultaneously with the men. Meeting houses were built in this manner for the next century (Butler 1999; Lidbetter 1979). See Figures 4.1 and 4.2 for two typical examples of early, rural, Quaker meeting houses.

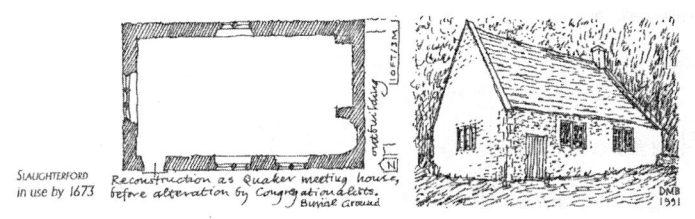

Figure 4.1 Slaughterford (West Country, before 1673). From Butler, David. *Quaker Meeting Houses of Britain*. Friends Historical Society, 1999. Reprinted with permission.

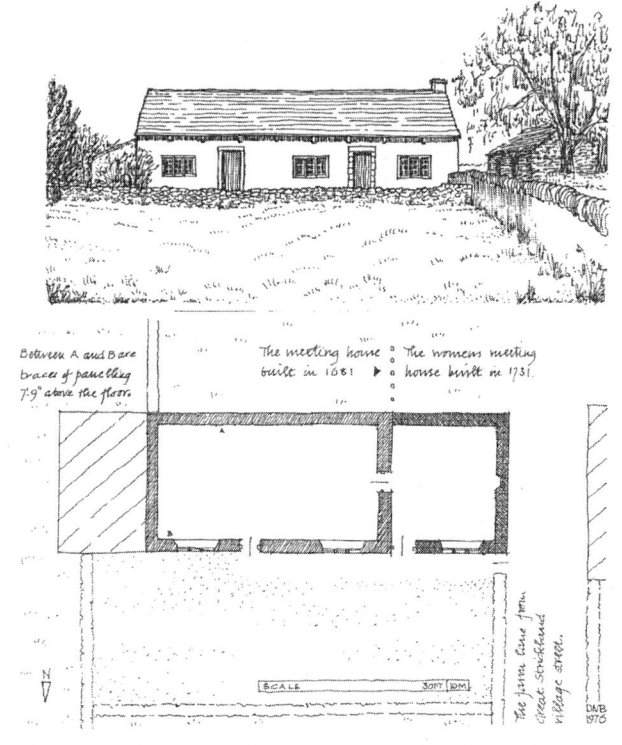

Figure 4.2 Strickland (Lake District, 1668). From Butler, David. *Quaker Meeting Houses of Britain*. Friends Historical Society, 1999. Reprinted with permission.

By 1800 meeting houses were being constructed not only in rural, but also in urban, areas. The buildings tended to have a different structure in each type of location (see Figures 4.3 and 4.4).

Figure 4.3 Coalbrookedale (1808, country meeting house). From Butler, David. *Quaker Meeting Houses of Britain*. Friends Historical Society, 1999. Reprinted with permission.

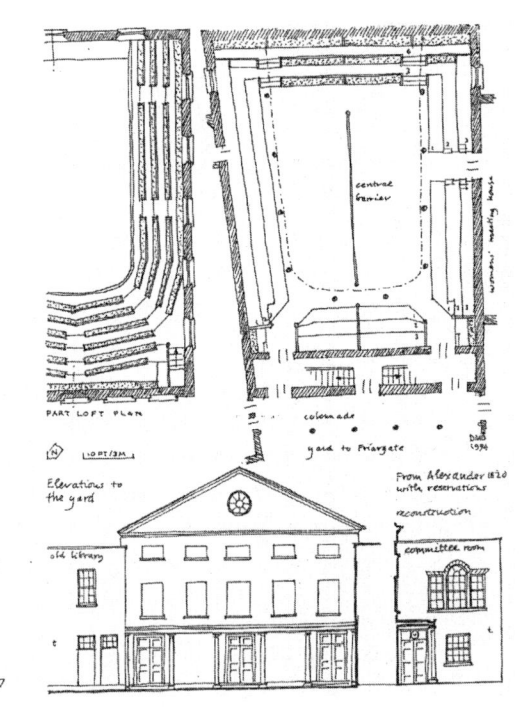

Figure 4.4 York (1817, town meeting house). From Butler, David. *Quaker Meeting Houses of Britain*. Friends Historical Society, 1999. Reprinted with permission.

The design parameters were set by the testimony to simplicity or the plain. Meeting houses, however large or complex were very seldom adorned, either within or without. It remains true, however, that meeting houses were being built on a larger scale, and with a more complex structure, in towns.

The Development of Urban Quaker Space

This chapter opened with a claim, or rather assumption, that urban Quaker meeting houses are larger than those in rural areas. This section considers three representative English cases, each of which confirms my argument that the nonreligious cannot be discounted in interpreting the meaning of religious space: Bolton in the industrial North West; Darlington in the northeast; and Cheltenham in the south.

The Quaker meeting house in Bolton, Lancashire provides a more or less typical historical trajectory. In the seventeenth century Bolton Friends met in houses or barns; in the eighteenth century, in rented accommodation in the town that was growing rapidly; in the nineteenth century, in a larger meeting house, built in dressed stone and including warden's accommodation; finally, in the twentieth century this meeting house was demolished to make room for a by-pass and was replaced by a striking and relatively complex building.

In general, by the start of the nineteenth century urban meeting houses tended to be larger, more complex in plan and more obviously stylised, broadly following first Georgian and then Victorian design. Tipping Street meeting house in Bolton, built in 1820 is clearly not a vernacular building. It extends the single or double cell arrangement of earlier meeting houses. The new building, clearly Georgian in appearance, included large and smaller meeting rooms, toilets, cloakrooms, a library, schoolroom and warden's cottage; a relatively imposing building for its time.

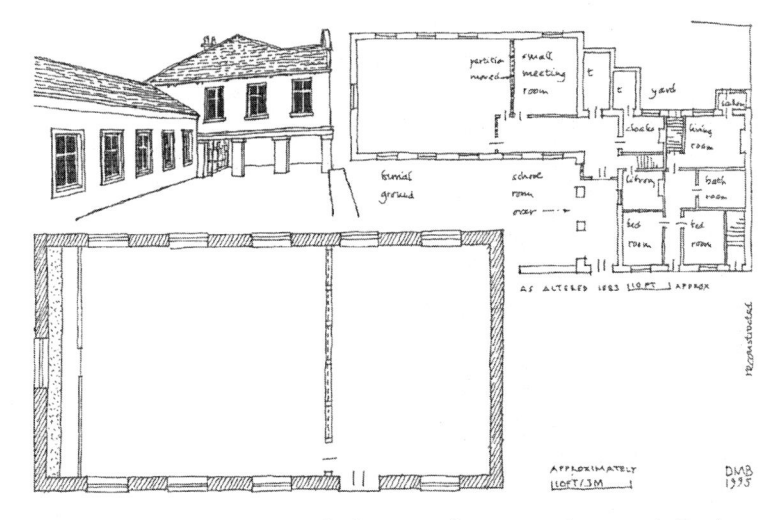

Figure 4.5 Tipping Street Meeting House (Bolton, 1825). From Butler, David. *Quaker Meeting Houses of Britain*. Friends Historical Society, 1999. Reprinted with permission.

In each case, and together they represent a clear trend, meeting houses in these three places were small, simple (few cells) and vernacular in style, over time becoming larger, more complex (a proliferation of cells) and adopt a national/international style. Nineteenth-century meeting houses were often Georgian in style, though somehow muted. They were generally built of brick, for example, Darlington (Butler 1999: 208–10) or dressed stone, for example, Cheltenham (Butler 1999: 157–60); front elevations were generally symmetrical, with steps up to a portico-columned entrance, opening onto a high and airy wood-panelled hall. The large Cheltenham meeting room seated over 200, wooden benches were likely to be banked, windows were sash-corded with regular multiple lights and there were subtle quotations of the classic orders, such as bold crowning cornices. Architectural historian Banister Fletcher describes such buildings as 'dignified' and Quaker architect Hubert Lidbetter notes that even when they manifest some outer embellishment, they mostly 'escaped the Victorian Gothic influence' (1969: 8). The Quaker version was, of course, subdued; for example, chimney stacks were relatively unobtrusive. Manchester is a particularly good example of the nineteenth-century urban meeting house (see Figure 4.6).

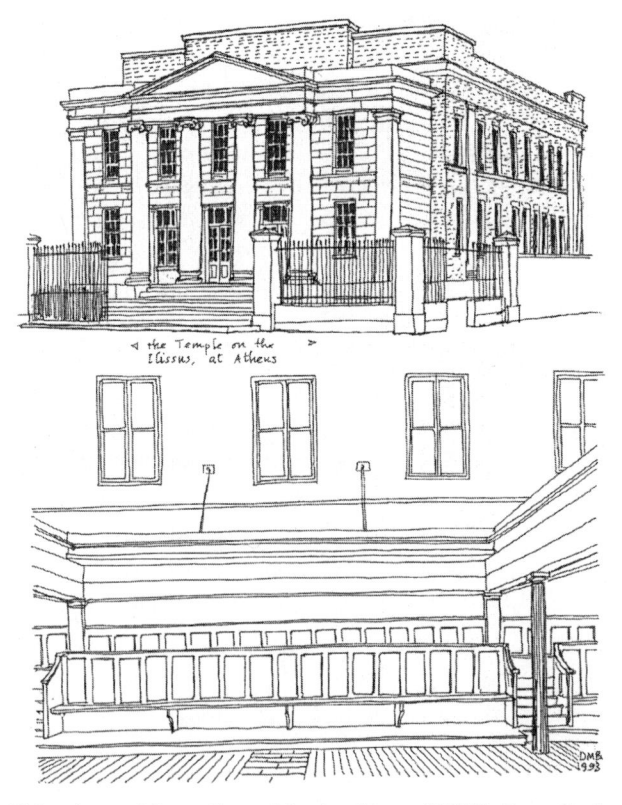

Figure 4.6 Manchester Mount Street Meeting House (1830). From Butler, David. *Quaker Meeting Houses of Britain*. Friends Historical Society, 1999. Reprinted with permission.

Such buildings clearly reflect an orderly and relatively prosperous community – the Mount Street meeting room could seat upward of a thousand people. Here, in microcosm, are the twin processes of urbanisation and urbanism, from the period just before the Industrial Revolution to the present. In these buildings, and there must be many other examples (both religious and overtly secular), we observe those features that represent the modern city: increasing sophistication, complexity and the accumulation of wealth. First, meeting houses were built primarily in rural areas. This process had more or less come to a halt by 1750, by which time the exodus from country to town had developed tremendous momentum. Britain, remember, was the first country to urbanise. Second, Quakerism was itself changing. For most of the eighteenth century the Society of Friends had been going through a Quietist period, shunning the world and progressing in splendid isolation. By 1760 it was already becoming evident that the precious remnant was becoming threadbare as the growth of national population accelerated rapidly, the number of Quakers declined not quite as dramatically, but very significantly (from around 20,000 in 1800 to 14,000 in 1850). The Methodists, in particular, were stealing the Quakers' thunder across the country, and Quakers were well aware of this. Quietism gave way to a more outward-going, open outlook.

Nineteenth-century meeting houses were larger and still more complex. This was partly due to the turn to an evangelical mode and the construction of rooms given over to the Adult School – sometimes constructed on a separate site, but often an integral part of new meeting houses built after 1830. The Adult School Movement was warmly nurtured in many Meetings and those coming into meeting houses formed an increasingly heterogeneous group, and certainly included those who could not easily be slotted into that category sometimes called 'the middling sort' from which stock Quakerism had, since the 1650s, drawn its membership. During the mid-nineteenth century, Quaker marriage laws were suspended and the Quaker meeting became an increasingly differentiated community.

The larger meeting houses served ever growing Quaker congregations, as mentioned earlier, numbers declined nationally until the 1850s and even then the up-turn was lethargic. We have to look for more subtle reasons for the building of what might be called 'grand' meeting houses. Quakers were of course excluded from a number of middle-class employment opportunities: the Church, the army, higher education, and were pushed or pulled into industry and commerce. I propose therefore (and this is a rather contentious claim) that wealthy Quakers living an urban life (and there were plenty of them) could and would not stretch their interpretation of the testimony to the simple life to include a place of worship that was a crudely built hut, situated in the middle of nowhere. Meeting houses became – to use Wirth's term – more sophisticated.

Indeed, many of the urban meetings included Friends who were of considerable influence, not only locally but also nationally, and in several cases internationally. Urban-based Quaker businessmen in industry and commerce include household names such as Barclay, Lloyd, Fry, Rowntree (York),

Cadbury (Birmingham), Coleman (Norwich), Clark (Street), Huntley and Palmer (Reading), Allen and Hanbury (London) (Raistrick 1950; Walvin 1997). It is hardly surprising that such men should ensure that their places of worship might stand beside the best. The Ashworths were cotton factors and for much of the nineteenth century formed a considerable and influential presence in Bolton. They were Friends of Cobden and Bright (famous for their part in repealing the Corn Laws) and hobnobbed with members of both Houses of Parliament and captains of industry throughout Europe. They numbered influential Anglicans and notable Methodists among their acquaintances. They lived outside Bolton in considerable affluence, enjoyed hunting, shooting and fishing, travelled extensively, acquired precious artefacts on their sojourns abroad and established a considerable collection of fine wines. Several family members held positions of authority in the town (Boyson 1970). In brief, and to draw on Bourdieu, they actively cultivated their stock of symbolic capital. Why not devote a little of their wealth on their meeting house? The Pease family of Darlington was probably more influential and certainly wealthier. Their business acumen led them into banking, the new railways and real estate; they built the town of Middlesbrough from scratch. Henry Pease was the first Quaker MP. Edward Pease made several entries in his diary regarding the building of the new meeting house and the family clearly took more than a passing interest in its development (Orde 2001). The Darlington meeting house retains an excellent library and many of its books have the family name 'Pease' stamped within.

The new large/complex meeting house is a result of changes in other aspects of Quakerism (theology, demography, organisation, etc.) but also concretises and presses those changes. However, the driving force behind their construction was the growing presence of sophisticated, influential, cosmopolitan and wealthy men (or, rather, dynastic families) whose tastes were both urban and urbane.

The twentieth century saw further changes to the urban meeting house. One could argue that modern meeting houses are just that: 'modernist' and therefore representative of recent trends in architecture. However, it is difficult to generalise and the style of recently constructed meeting houses range from anonymous and domestic to striking and public. To return briefly to Bolton, the Tipping Street meeting house was demolished in 1968 to make way for a by-pass and the borough council provided funds for a replacement which was eventually built nearer the centre of town, adjacent to the parish church (see Figure 4.7).

The new Bolton meeting house is a relatively complex building with a large meeting room, spacious concourse, children's room, toilets and cloakrooms, and on the second floor a library and committee room, again, a warden's house is attached. Hardly a vernacular building, not obviously a religious building, but strikingly modern. See Figure 4.8 for the 'anonymous and domestic' style and Figure 4.9 for the 'modernistic (based on the steel frame and concrete) and public' style.

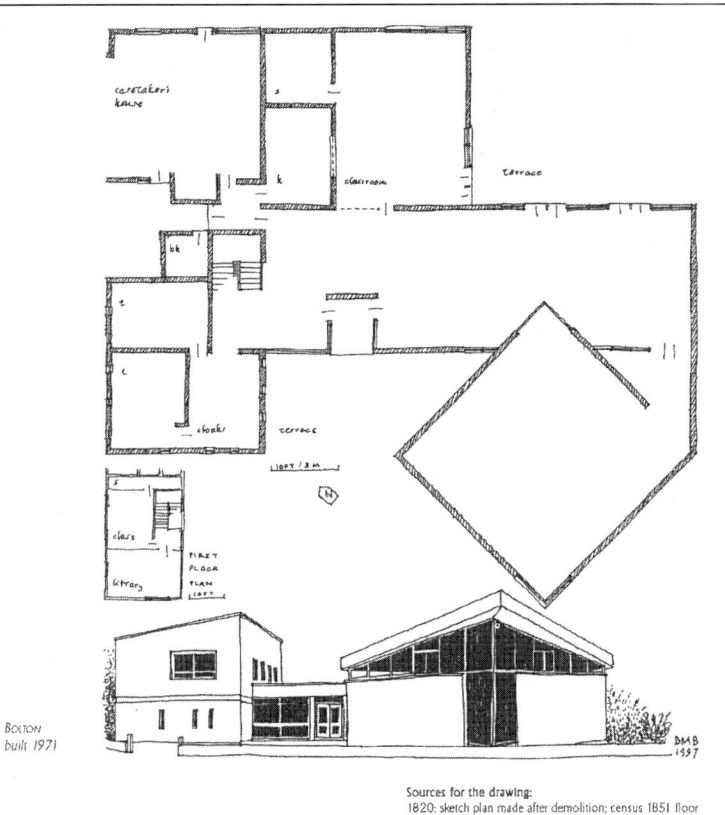

Figure 4.7 Silverwell Street Meeting House (Bolton, 1970). From Butler, David. *Quaker Meeting Houses of Britain.* Friends Historical Society, 1999. Reprinted with permission.

Since 1850, almost without exception, meeting houses have been built in town. In terms of internal design they have become increasingly rationalistic – *machines for living* – to use Le Corbusier's well known term. In the seventeenth and eighteenth centuries a Quaker came to worship once or twice a week and perhaps attended a business meeting once or twice a month. The Quietist decades of the eighteenth century gave way to a more committed, public engagement with social and political issues (Kennedy 2001). The second half of the nineteenth century saw a sharp growth in the Adult School Movement, in which congregations opened their doors to those seeking the educational opportunities denied them elsewhere. Meeting houses were also used increasingly for public meetings in which social concerns (alcohol abuse, betting and gambling, militarism) were aired and debated. Those attending business meetings have always been in the minority. But since 1900, Quaker organisation – at least at the local level – has grown increasingly complex. In addition to formal business meetings there are meetings for elders and overseers, children's committee, retreat committee, library committee, wardenship committee, finance and premises committee, outreach committee, peace committee and ad hoc meetings for clearance, creative listening, learning

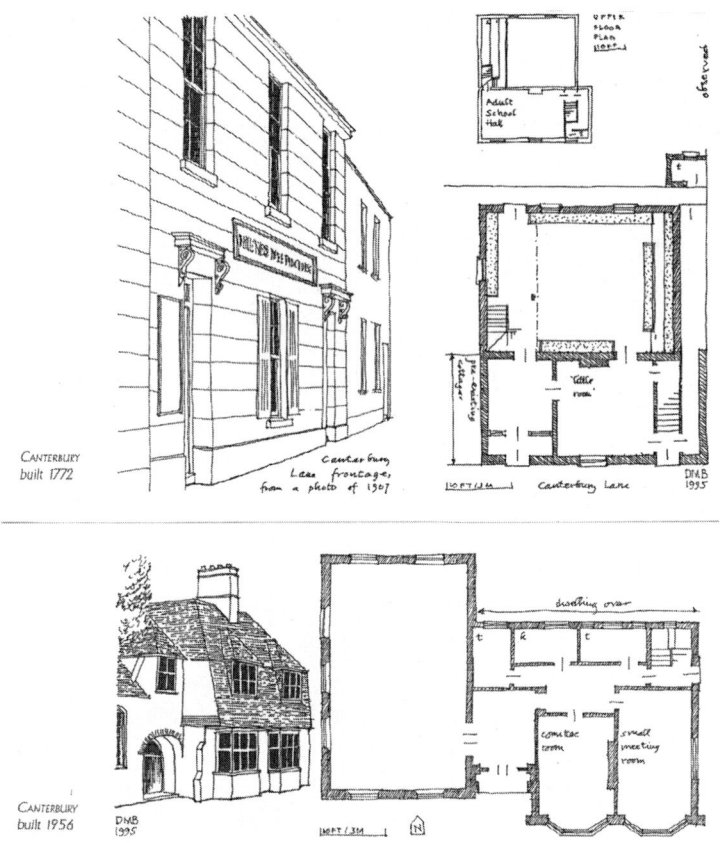

Figure 4.8 Canterbury (1772 and 1956). From Butler, David. *Quaker Meeting Houses of Britain.* Friends Historical Society, 1999. Reprinted with permission.

about Quakerism, visits from outside speakers and so forth. Active members find themselves attending numerous meetings both at the meeting house and elsewhere. We must not forget the importance of the religious organisation as a voluntary association. And so the modern meeting house is designed to cater to such meetings: often five or more rooms of various shapes and sizes (large and small meeting rooms, committee rooms, classrooms, library, etc.), a kitchen, toilets and cloakrooms, often with a warden's house attached. Devices such as folding partitions reflect a further shift towards the secular.

Quakerism has continued to develop along liberal lines: joint membership is now accepted and attenders play an increasingly important role. Now that Quakers live fully in the world, meetings encourage others to use their premises and given the paucity of cheap meeting space in the centre of many towns, meeting houses can become very busy places. The cost of upkeep of a meeting house in some cases has been the primary driving force behind the way it was planned. Letting rooms brings in a useful and perhaps necessary income. This has become increasingly true with the disappearance from the society of wealthy benefactors. In a few cases, the Quaker meeting house has become a part of a fully fledged community centre of community-based facility – for

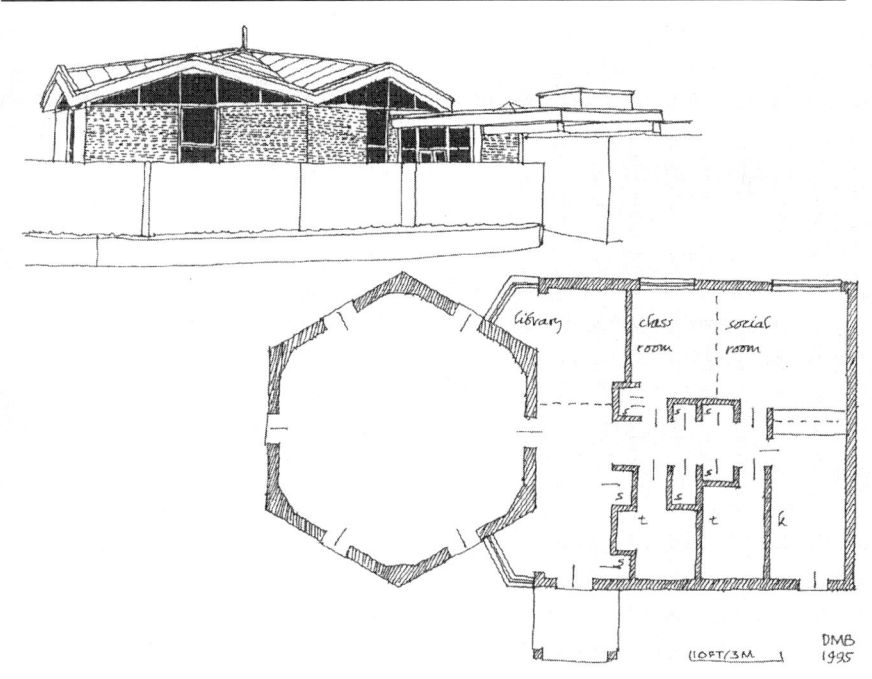

Figure 4.9 Maidstone (1956). From Butler, David. *Quaker Meeting Houses of Britain*. Friends Historical Society, 1999. Reprinted with permission.

example, the Rochester meeting house is partly inhabited and owned by Age Concern; other meeting houses (such as Wisbech) are a part of sheltered housing schemes.

There are at least two reasons that pressure Quaker meetings to maximise the use of their premises. First, meeting houses are increasingly expensive to maintain, especially given the dwindling numbers of members. Second, the growing need felt by religious groups (at least in the mainstream) to appear 'useful', in a secular sense. In town, space is at a premium and should be put to optimal use. The meeting house that was once used only on a Sunday is now likely to be used every day of the week for various purposes: the Bolton meeting house, for example, provides rooms for the local coroner's court, held in a number of meeting houses because they are perceived to provide 'a neutral venue'; Royal School of Music examinations are held there and rooms are let to many charitable organisations. A local Buddhist group meets regularly in the library and Hindu weddings have occasionally colonised the entire building.

Conclusion

The meeting house in town is a religious building in so far as it is used by a voluntary, avowedly religious, association: the Religious Society of Friends. But to see such space entirely in religious terms is a mistake. Friends' meeting houses built in towns are larger and more complex than those built in earlier times in rural areas: they are texts that can be read in a number of ways (Geertz 1973). There are a number of reasons for this. First, they reflect the national urbanising trend of the eighteenth and nineteenth centuries. Second, they form a stock of symbolic capital in those locations occupied by dynastic Quaker families. Third, internal complexity represents a shift from the inward looking Quietist eighteenth century to the more outward looking evangelistic tendencies of the Victorian era and the development in particular of the Adult School movement. Internal complexity continues to characterise modern meeting houses, which have come increasingly to function as community centres, appearing quite often as wholly secular buildings. These developments are not unique to Quakerism, and similar developments are evident in Methodism, Anglicanism and Roman Catholicism. To conclude, I want to re-emphasise my earlier point that in interpreting religious space we impose on ourselves an unnecessary limitation if we fail to look beyond the religious. Our physical environment is as much a social phenomenon as it is a physical one,p and the social extends well beyond the religious. Even a partial account of urban meeting houses suggests that the category of 'the religious' cannot entirely contain the meaning of 'religious' architecture.

Notes

I thank David Butler for permitting me to reproduce his excellent plans and elevations and the participants in the 2002 British Sociological Association (religion study group) annual conference held in Birmingham for useful comments on the content of an earlier draft of this chapter.

1. In 1750 the population of Britain was around 6 million (15 per cent urban); in 1901, just over 38 million (85 per cent urban).
2. Perhaps the most famous among them being Anderson (1923), Thrasher (1927), Zorbaugh (1929) and Cressey (1932).
3. Interestingly, a research team led by Lowell Livesey (2000) has been asking these questions of present-day Chicago.

References

Anderson, N. 1923. *The Hobo*. Chicago: Chicago University Press.
Barrie, T. 1996. *Spiritual Path, Sacred Place*. Boston and London: Shambhala.
Bourdieu, P. 1973. 'The Berber House', in M. Douglas (ed.), *Rules and Meanings*. Harmondsworth: Penguin, pp. 98–110.
———. 1977. *Outline of a Theory of Practice*. Cambridge: Cambridge University Press.
Boyson, R. 1970. *The Ashworth Cotton Enterprise: The Rise and Fall of a Family Firm, 1818–1880*. Oxford: Clarendon.
Braithwaite, W.C. 1955. *The Beginnings of Quakerism*. Cambridge: Cambridge University Press.
Butler, D.M. 1999. *The Quaker Meeting Houses of Great Britain*, 2 vols. London: Friends Historical Society.

Buttimer, A. and D. Seamon (eds.). 1980. *The Human Experience of Place and Space*. London: Croom Helm.
Castells, M. 1989. *The Informational City: Information Technology, Economic Restructuring, and the Urban-Regional Process*. Oxford: Basil Blackwell.
Coleman, S. 2001. *The Globalization of Charismatic Christianity*. Cambridge: Cambridge University Press.
Coleman, S. and P. Collins. 1996. 'Constructing the Sacred: The Anthropology of Architecture in the World Religions', *Architectural Design* 124: 14–18.
———. 2000. 'The "Plain" and the "Positive": Ritual, Experience and Aesthetics in Quakerism and Charismatic Christianity', *Journal of Contemporary Religion* 15(3): 317–29.
Collins, P. 1996a. '"Plaining": The Social and Cognitive Practice of Symbolisation in the Religious Society of Friends (Quakers)', *Journal of Contemporary Religion* 11(3): 277–88.
———. 1996b. 'Auto/biography, Narrative and the Quaker Meeting', *Auto/Biography* 4(2/3): 27–38.
———. 2006. 'Reading Religious Architecture', in E. Arweck and P. Collins (eds.), *Reading Religion in Text and Context: Reflections of Faith and Practice in Religious Materials*. Aldershot: Ashgate, pp. 137–56.
Cressey, P.G. 1932. *The Taxi-Dance Hall*. Chicago: University of Chicago Press.
Dovey, K. 1999. *Framing Places: Mediating Power in Built Form*. London: Routledge.
Geertz, C. 1973. *The Interpretation of Cultures*. New York: Basic Books.
Hammond, P. 1960. *Liturgy and Architecture*. London: Barrie and Rockliff.
Harvey, D. 1985a. *Consciousness and the Urban Experience*. Baltimore: Johns Hopkins University Press.
———. 1985b *The Urbanization of Capital*. Baltimore: Johns Hopkins University Press.
———. 1989. *The Urban Experience*. Oxford: Blackwell.
Humphrey, C. 1988. 'No Place Like Home in Anthropology: The Neglect of Architecture', *Anthropology Today* 4(1):16–18.
Jencks, C.A. and G. Baird. 1969. *Meaning in Architecture*. New York: George Braziller.
Jones, L. 2000. *The Hermeneutics of Sacred Architecture. Vol. 1: Monumental Occasions* and *Vol. 2: A Morphology of Ritual Architectural Priorities*. Cambridge: Harvard University Press.
Kennedy, T.C. 2001. *British Quakerism, 1860-1920. The Transformation of a Religious Community*. Oxford: Oxford University Press.
Lane, B.C. 1988. *Landscapes of the Sacred: Geography and Narrative in American Spirituality*. New York: Paulist.
Lawson, B. 200. *The Language of Space*. Oxford: Architectural Press.
Lefebvre, H. 1991. *The Production of Space*, trans. D. Nicholson-Smith. Oxford: Blackwell.
Lidbetter, H. 1979. *The Friends Meeting House*. York: William Sessions.
Livesey, L.W. (ed.). 2000. *Public Religion and Urban Transformation: Faith in the City*. New York: New York University Press.
Lukken, G. and M. Searle. 1993. *Semiotic and Church Architecture: Applying the Semiotics of A.J. Greimas and the Paris School to the Analysis of Church Buildings*. Kampen: Pharos.
Lynch, . 1960. *The Image of the City*. Cambridge, MA: MIT Press.
Markus, T. 1993. *Buildings & Power: Freedom and Control in the Origin of Modern Building Types*. London: Routledge.
Oliver, P. (ed.). 1977. *Shelter, Sign and Symbol*. Woodstock, NY: Overlook Press.

Orde, A. 2001. *Religion, Business and Society in North-east England: The Pease Family of Darlington in the Nineteenth Century* (Studies in Northeastern History). Donington: Shaun Tyas.
Parker, M. and C. Richards (eds.). 1994. *Architecture and Order: Approaches to Social Science*. London: Routledge.
Raistrick, A. 1950. *Quakers in Science and Industry*. London: Bannisdale Press.
Rapoport, A. 1969. *House Form and Culture*. Englewood Cliffs, NJ: Prentice-Hall.
———. 1977. *Human Aspects of Urban Form*. Oxford: Pergamon.
Sassen, S. 1991. *The Global City: New York, London, Tokyo*. Princeton NJ: Princeton University Press.
Thrasher, F.M. 1927. *The Gang*. Chicago: Chicago University Press.
Turner, H.W. 1979. *From Temple to Meeting House: The Phenomenology and Theory of Place in Worship*. The Hague: Mouton.
Walvin, J. 1997. *The Quakers: Money and Morals*. London: John Murray.
Waterson, R. 1991. *The Living House*. Oxford: Oxford University Press.
Weber, M. [1905] 1958. *The City*. Translated and edited by D. Martindale and G. Neuwirth. New York: Free Press.
Williams, R. 1973. *The Country and the City*. London: Chatto and Windus.
Wirth, L. 1938. 'Urbanism as a Way of Life', *American Journal of Sociology* 44(1): 1–24.
Zevi, Bruno. 1974. *Architecture as Space: How to Look at Architecture*. New York: Horizon Press.
Zorbaugh, H.W. 1929 *The Gold Coast and the Slum*. Chicago: Chicago University Press.

PART THREE

Urban Migration

Rural Immigrants and Official Religion in an Urban Religious Festival in Greece

Giorgos Vozikas

※

This chapter deals with religious experience in the particular form it takes in the Greek Orthodox religion and as the worship is carried out in an urban context. With reference to the migration and conditions that have shaped economic and social development of Greece, I examine the role of the rural background of the inhabitants in the conceptualisation and application of official religion by a local community in urban space.

The area on which my interest centres is the locality of St Marina (*Aghia Marina*), in the Athenian municipality of Ilioupoli. The area owes its existence to the *astyphilia*, phenomenon of internal migration in Greece to urban centres. St Marina today has 35,000 inhabitants, who have migrated there from various provincial areas of Greece. As my ethnographic example, I choose a particular ritual context, religious festival (*panegyri*),[1] held by the local church.

In my study of the religious festival, I employ the concept of 'rural background' as analytical tool, in the sense of a socially and culturally defined past, which is expressed in the collective memory of the inhabitants of the locality. This category I tie up to a second analytical category 'official religion', thereby implying the existence of a link between literate and popular culture to be found in the same religion. On the one hand, we have religion as expressed by the Church Fathers, such as Gregorios o Theologos, by the theoreticians of Christianity and the priests of the local church. On the other hand, we have religion, as it is experienced by the inhabitants of the locality via their convictions and patterns of religious behaviour (Dubisch 1990).

I suggest that, thanks to the late development and incomplete urbanisation of Greece, the inhabitants of the locality retain basic structural elements from their rural cultural capital. It is in these terms that they approach and interpret the religious festival, while at the same time, undermining the hegemonic role of the official version of religion, thereby endowing the festival with a popular dimension.

The Development and Urbanisation of Greece: The Birth of an Athenian Locality

The locality of St Marina is situated on the slopes of Mt. Imittos, one of the mountains that encircle Athens and the Piraeus. Founded in the 1930s, the locality of St Marina acquired its present form much later. With the appearance of the *astyphilia* phenomenon, the area underwent particular development in the 1950s and 1960s.[2] The inhabitants who decided to settle there were former members of the agricultural population who had migrated relatively recently to Athens. They were of a low educational level and correspondingly limited economic power. The educational and social features of the inhabitants, in combination with the uneven terrain of the area and the equally poor street planning of the locality, made for a local entity that was substandard compared with the other areas in the Ilioupoli municipality. Thus St Marina has a reputation of a working-class area of Ilioupoli.

Although the inhabitants of the area may have uprooted themselves from their place of descent, they nevertheless have not severed the umbilical cord. Many have not transferred their voting rights from their birthplace to Athens, even after many years of residence there. Each year some of them use the opportunity afforded by various short public holidays or by larger festivals, such as Christmas, to visit their villages. Even during the summer, many families spend the holidays in their place of descent and considerable numbers still maintain property in their village of origin.

Finally, a feature that reveals the desire to maintain a link with one's place of descent and its culture is the existence of various local associations. These local associations are groupings of the residents formed on the basis of their place of origin. Their aim is to maintain their members' bond with their place of origin and to reinforce their cultural identity (Kakamboura-Tíly 1999; Kenna 1983; Meraklis 1989).

The inhabitants of St Marina and, in particular, the migrants of the first generation retain vivid memories of their rural past. They express these memories through the medium of stories. At times, such stories take the form of an oral narrative. At other times they take the form of a ritual (Connerton 1989; Hirschon-Philippaki 1993). I regard these narratives as a means of forming concepts that shape reality, rather than simply reflecting it. I therefore lay particular stress on the metaphors (Sapir 1977) employed in the interpretation of St Marina's martyrdom and of her personality and of the religious festival in general. I attempt to find common points that allow communication between official and popular religion, as well as locating the differences between the two.

Saints and Places

In traditional Greek culture, the church is the symbol of the sacred. It is employed to order space, set boundaries, endow the space with meaning and to offer protection. In the Greek countryside, churches and shrines dominate the space of the community, encircling it in a protective ring. The church constitutes the foundation symbol of the community. The saint to whom the church is dedicated is the protector of the community (Du Boulay 1995: 153–54; Kenna 1977). It is to the saint that the community turns at times of danger. It is at the church that the community gathers to celebrate the great festival of the village on the day in the Orthodox religious calendar on which the memory of the saint is honoured. Saints are to be met with in the city, as 'saints who hold the city' (*poliouchi aghii*), to whom the cathedral of the city is dedicated.

The forming of the locality of St Marina and its conversion from a space to an area incorporating cultural features that distinguish it from other inhabited places is a process closely tied up with the sacred and the sanctification of the space. It is also tied up with the assigning of a name, as a means of giving identity to a place. The accounts that are offered regarding the foundation of the church and its dedication to St Marina offer parallels to the practices customary in traditional culture to which people resort in personal matters and at times of crisis. The practice in question here is the vow (*tama*).

In Greek traditional culture, the word *tama* means both the object dedicated to a church and the process of dedication itself. The *tama* as process is usually a type of prayer, which includes a promise to reciprocate and constitutes a means of gaining the good offices of the divine for the faithful. It is usually a promise to God, to the Virgin, or the saints, to acquire an object or to secure some kind of help or service, on the condition that the divine beings will aid in the solution of the problem in question (Papadakis 1971).

When the first internal migrants settled in the locality and began to assemble a local identity distinct from those of other communities, they attempted to define the place and render it familiar. Their first act was to found a church for the carrying out of their religious duties (see Chryssanthopoulou 1993: 115–18). The church, founded in the same year that the community was officially recognised, was built with the active participation of the community, which took the form of the offer of labour or of money. The church was built, initially without permission, on one of the many bare building plots, which happened to belong to a large landowner in the area. Following a long ordeal, the church was eventually granted planning permission. Oral tradition states that 'on the day they set up the shed (*paraga*), a lady placed an icon [of St Marina] in the middle of the church and at that moment, they said, *Aghia Marina*, help us, so that this church stands and they don't pull it down, and we will call it '*Aghia Marina*'.

The happy outcome as pertains to the church and, metaphorically to the whole district, which over time has come to be identified with the church and the saint, is to be understood as the result of the protective intervention on the part of St Marina. The local community kept its promise and dedicated the church to the saint, whereafter the locality embarked on a particular relationship with the saint. She became part of the process of the localisation, having become the patron saint of the locality and her mediating role with God on behalf of the local community having been recognised. The result of the process was the identification of the locality with St Marina as a collective entity and the giving of her name to the whole locale.

The relationship of St Marina with the local community is not restricted to the collective level, to the level of the settlement or the inhabitants *en masse*. Instead, it acquires more personal features, as many of the inhabitants of the area enjoy a special relationship with St Marina. Most of them keep her icon on their domestic 'icon stand' (*ikonostasi*) (Hirschon 1997: 81), turning to her for help at times of worry and when all hope seems to have vanished.

The special features of the saint, her sex and the age at which she was martyred, have contributed to her being seen by the inhabitants as the protector of children, in particular of girls. It is for this reason that the inhabitants of the locality turn to her when their children are facing problems. They perform *tama* to the saint and reciprocate the help given them by the saint. This personal relationship between saint and inhabitants assumes an extreme and dramatic shape, when an individual is given the name of the saint and is thereby symbolically dedicated to the saint. There is a long tradition in Greek folk culture of parents dedicating a child endangered by some serious illness to a saint in order to save the child. One method of symbolically dedicating a child is to give him or her a saint's name (Alexakis 2004; Hirschon 1998: 204–6; Meraklis 1999: 37–46; Vernier 2001). The child takes the name of the saint and is thus identified with the saint, who then dwells within the child through the name and assumes the role of the personal protector of the child. This tradition continues to hold in the locality of St Marina, as there is a fair number of inhabitants who have symbolically dedicated their children to the saint during periods of danger. Subsequent professional and social successes enjoyed by the child are attributed to the protection afforded by the saint whose name the child bears.

The Sacred Places of the Locality: The Church

In the locality of St Marina, there are numerous systems for organising the experience of space. Some of these systems enjoy the support of official institutions of the state, whereas others are shaped unofficially by the inhabitants of the locality themselves. There are two dominant systems, which coexist and complement each other. The first system concerns the organisation of space as dictated by the provision technical services, whose guiding principle is the satisfaction of the practical needs of the inhabitants. The second system concerns spiritual and cultural dimensions. Here we are dealing with the organisation of space based on the church as a sacred place of worship and as a landmark (Kyriakidou-Nestoros 1979: 15–40).

The Church of St Marina, the main church of the locality, occupies a central position in the locality and in the system of symbolism of the inhabitants. The manner in which the local church deals with the physical church building (*naos*) sheds light on its concerns and interests in connection with the sacred. Thus the local church stresses the metaphysical nature of the church building and does its utmost to maintain the sanctity of both the church and the surrounding area.

However, the role of the church and of the saint whose name the church bears is not restricted in the locality to the spiritual dimension alone. Instead, it involves complementary social parameters. The need to support the construction work on the church contributed to the development in the local community of a type of collective effort on behalf of the church. To build the church, a considerable number of local builders offered their services for its construction. Others contributed financially to various appeals organised by the church.

The material link between the church building and the locality has made the church building emblematic of the area and its identity. The church was originally a wooden shed. Later, thanks to the contributions made by the inhabitants of the locality, it was rebuilt in more substantial materials and increased in size. The church acquired its monumental character because all the inhabitants wanted a church consonant with the sanctity of the building, to express faithfully the brilliance and glory of the sacred and to represent the locality in worthy fashion, decorating it with its presence (*ena stolidi tis sinikias*, 'an ornament to the area').

Thus it is apparent that the role of the church and of the saint to whom it is dedicated is not restricted to the spiritual. Instead, it had complementary social parameters. It is closely connected with the existence of the community as a local entity and the cultivation of the feeling of belonging to the area.

Time, Festivals and St Marina

Time is marked in the locality by large religious festivals, such as Easter (*Pascha*), Christmas (*Christougenna*) and Epiphany (*Theophaneia*). However, apart from major religious festivals that break the linear flow of time and enrich it with elements taken from circular time, there are also the feasts of the saints of the Church. These multiply and spread over the religious festival time and qualitatively change the daily life of the locality.

In Greece, the feast days of the saints are extremely important. As has already been noted, in Orthodox religious tradition the saints enjoy a particular and personal relationship with mankind, who regard the saints as protectors and whose names they give their children (Ware 1964). This personal relationship of saint to man becomes even more intense when, as the result of some *tama*, the individual is symbolically dedicated to the saint and so takes the name of the saint, thereby becoming identified with him or her. For example, Eleni who lives in the locality, baptised her child after making a *tama*, in the name of the saint. She believes that the saint played a major role in the successful progress of her child. 'Thanks to the saint's blessings, my girl has done well. She made a good marriage and has a good husband. She has a very good time and I think that's because of Aghia Marina. She's looked after my child'. The involvement of the saint in the life of an individual who bears the name of the saint endows the festival with a personal importance for such a person.

Thus the feasts of the saints are linked to one's name. In the locality of St Marina, as is the case through all of Greece, names are celebrated and a nameday festival is a day of honour for the saint in the yearly cycle. In the locality of St Marina, the name day of the saint is established as a widespread social event of great importance and value to the community, unlike birthday celebrations, which continue to be relatively unimportant and restricted to children. The factor that contributes decisively to the recognition in Greece of the importance of the name day part from the religious parameters, is the name itself, 'the baptismal name' (*vaptistiko*) and the consequent symbolic power that the name wields in the identification and the placing of the individual in society as a result of bearing the saint's name (Oikonomidis 1962). The name borne by an individual, apart from indicating a relationship with a saint, also defines the relationship of the individual with his or her ancestors, with his or her relations and with society in general (see Hirschon 2009).

Although in the St Marina locality the name day is not celebrated as intensely as it was in the past, it nevertheless continues to be an important day for those who are named after the saint and for their families. Relatives and friends pay visits, if the celebrant desires it, in order to offer their good wishes. Indeed, it is regarded as a social obligation to offer one's good wishes and failure to do so may upset social relations. Some attend a church service on the name day and take *prosforo*, although their numbers have dwindled.[3] Some, even fewer in number, actually fast in preparation for taking Communion.

For the inhabitants of the locality of St Marina, one of the most important moments in the cycle of time is the festival of the saint herself. Besides the individuals actually named after her, the locality as a collective entity bearing her name celebrates its own name day and honours its protector. The residents of St Marina wish each other 'many years' (*chronia polla*), that is 'many years of life', and 'our help' (*voithia mas*), that is, 'may the grace of the saint help us'. In addition to the feast of the saint protector of the locality and all the obligatory religious celebrations, there is a number of economic and recreational activities. During the whole duration of the festival, the daily life of the locality is disrupted, albeit only temporarily, as it follows the pace of the saint's festival.

The Festival of the Protecting Saint

The church festival is a special day for the neighbourhood. The church and the main roads of the area are decorated with Greek flags. In cafes and in various shops, the programme of the religious festival is displayed for the benefit of the local inhabitants. During the afternoon and evening of the eve of the festival, the insistent tolling of the church bells announces the start of Vespers and the beginning of the whole ritual of the religious festival.

Arriving from the various neighbourhoods of the area, the local inhabitants begin to gather in the area where the festival is being held. In the courtyard of the church, portable icons of St Marina have been set up at various points, together with Greek flags, flags of the archbishopric and various other small flags displaying religious symbols and Christian sayings. In the same area, a small distance beyond these objects, beggars importune the worshippers for help. Beyond these, monks, who may or may not be genuine, have set up stalls and are selling objects intended for the religious observances of the faithful, such as icons of saints, rosaries or incense. Still further away are the gypsies who have also set up stalls selling *keria* (candles) and *lampadhes* (large candles) for the faithful to perform their ritual obligations to the saint.

Inside the church, a large crowd of worshippers waits patiently in line, to venerate the icon of St Marina located there. It is a large icon, decorated with flowers and is used in the procession. In accordance with the rules of the Orthodox Church regarding the religious decoration of the church, another icon is located on the icon screen. This icon is decorated as a bride with flowers and a long white veil. In front of the icon stand two white wedding *lampadhes*, also decorated with flowers and long white ribbons. Various votive offerings hanging from the icon complete its decoration, recalling the holiness and curative powers of the saint depicted on the icon.

The major event of the religious festival is the processing of the icon of St Marina along the roads of the neighbourhood. The icon emerges from the church, accompanied by priests and the chanters of the church. The bells ring insistently and festively, indicating that the icon has left the church and the procession is starting. The inhabitants of the area then come out onto their balconies and hold lit candles. The procession is strictly hierarchical and is notable for its pomp and seriousness.

The procession opens worldly and religious symbols of the Church, such as the flag of the local religious association – the Greek flag, with St Marina superimposed on it, and the banners of the church. The girls from the catechism class follow in groups, with each group commenting in its own fashion on the martyrdom of St Marina and thereby doing her honour. They are followed by the municipal band and the church chanters, who sing the hymn in honour of St Marina. The kernel of the procession is the icon of St Marina, which is carried by the oldest girls of the catechism class, the so-called brides (*nifes*), who are dressed in white, with white gloves and white ribbons in their hair. In front of the icon process other girls, also dressed in white and holding large wedding *lampadhes* – the votive offerings made by the inhabitants of the area – in their hands. The icon is decorated with flowers and with long white veils, the ends of which are held by other girls from the catechism class. The icon is accompanied by the army. Behind the icon come the priests of the Church of St Marina. Behind these, accompanied by deacons, follows the bishop who blesses the multitude. The sacred part of the procession is followed by the secular notables of the area, including the mayor, leaders of political parties on the local council, politicians and others. This group is followed by the rest of the celebrants. The procession finishes on its return to the area outside the church, where the national anthem is performed after the ritual.

Near the church a street market is set up for the duration of the *panegyri*. Enjoyment is an important part of the festival. For the *panegyri*, local cafés are turned into restaurants serving roast meat and become places of entertainment, fashioned after the Greek rural festivals. During the festival, folk music groups perform in cafés for the entertainment of festival visitors. Dance forms an inseparable element of the enjoyment of a *panegyri*. People dance in the cafés all night long to traditional Greek music performed on the clarinet, an instrument that represents mainland Greek folk music.

Between the Sacred and the Profane

A *panegyri* is one of the most long-lived cultural institutions of Greece (Loukatos 1963: 81–89; Vryonis 1981). The religious *panegyri* is an important event for the community to which the church belongs, the reason being that in traditional culture, Greek rural communities are identified with their church and the protecting saint of the village to whom the church is dedicated (Megas 1949: 107–9).

In general terms, the Greek religious festival, as it is celebrated in rural communities as well in the locality of St Marina, is notable for its extravagant character and for the religious celebratory element, which is rather rich in comparison with other religious feasts. The festival lasts two days and culminates in the processing of the icon along the streets of the community.

The festival of St Marina, in the way that it is celebrated in the locality, is a privileged field on which the local community and the cultural system of Greek society may rally round its central values. The religious element serves as an occasion for the family to pray together in the church, and to enjoy itself together in the market place and during the other accompanying activities at the festival. The festival, whose central feature is the feast of the patron saint, fuses a locality to shape its identity, in social and symbolic terms (Cohen 1989), as part of the wider national identity. It is this concentration at the festival of many important social and cultural parameters that accounts for the fact that religious festivals are generally regarded as an epitome of the cultural heritage.

The Church, as it expresses itself through the words of the Church Fathers, does not subscribe to this manner of celebrating the festival. For the Church the day, despite its celebratory character, is not self-evidently intended as an opportunity for entertainment with dancing and singing. Rather, the Church regards the festival as an opportunity for a turning of the spirit towards something better. In the view of official religion, the religious festival expresses a metaphysical orientation towards God and its purpose is to honour the memory of the saint who was martyred on the day of the festival. Although the day is connected with death by martyrdom, this fact is regarded as an occasion for a festival (Kotsonis 1952). The day is regarded in terms of a rite of passage celebration (van Gennep 1977) and the church regards it as a birthday for true life, rather than a day of death, whereby the saint is united with God (Fitrakis 1955: 64).

This is the view of the festival that the Church wishes to communicate to the world. It wishes thereby to maintain its hegemony over the assignment of meaning to the feast, employing the rights that it enjoys in the organisation of the festival. The stance of the Orthodox Church towards the people is ambivalent. On the one hand, it recognises the fact that it is the people who maintain Orthodoxy. On the other hand, for the Church, the piety of these lower levels of society recalls superstitions and idolatrous or secularising behaviour. Nevertheless, to win over the people the Church occasionally puts up with such practices, although it endows them with a different, metaphysical character.

The metaphysical perspective that the local church attempts to impose on the feast is removed by the participation of the people themselves and by the cultural prototypes relating to the *panegyri* as type of feast. Far from regarding the *panegyri* as a strictly religious event the inhabitants of St Marina conceive it as a composite whole, consisting of elements set around a religious core, which cannot be separated from each other.

The Icon

The icon is the nucleus of the festival and the reason for visiting it (cf. Dubisch 1995: 162). It is also a celebratory object and a symbol, whose meaning is difficult to trace, because 'celebratory objects stand for many things and thoughts at once' (Turner 1982: 16). Because of their nature, they are more easily experienced than explained.

In daily life, the presence of the icon of St Marina is highly noticeable in both public and private space. One may see it on the icon stand in the kitchen or in the bedroom of a house. It is even to be seen as depicted on a wall calendar in hair salons, cafés, bakeries and in other area establishments. At the festival the icon of St Marina dominates all. Its presence is manifold within and without the church, set on various objects, such as calendars, books, printed icons, icons produced for the domestic icon stand, on portable icon stands and on the small bell tower. The icon even circulates among worshippers in the form of a self-adhesive badge, which the local church offers to promote the collection of funds and places on the worshippers' lapels. This highly noticeable presence of the icon of St Marina, both in daily life and at the festival indicates that her icon, as well as religious icons in general, have a particular significance for the inhabitants.

During the festival, the icon becomes the object of a series of pious and devout gestures involving, above all, the *proskynisi*.[4] For the inhabitants of the area, however, the *proskynisi* at an icon is both a gesture of respect towards the saint and a means of transmitting the joy that the saint holds, which is to be conveyed to the worshipper who makes obeisance via the icon. Thus the *proskynisi* derives from an understanding of how closeness functions. The nearer one is to something, the less easily the boundaries between oneself and the object are to be distinguished and the more easily the qualities of one are to be transmitted to the other. In some areas of Greece, the faithful regard it as an honour to carry the icon around the village in their arms or on their shoulders. Similar behaviour is exhibited by the inhabitants towards the icon of St Marina during the procession. Because the icon is flanked by girls from the catechism class, who hold the icon during the procession, a considerable number of inhabitants who wish to obtain the blessing of the saint urge that their daughters be the ones holding the icon. By means of this process, the icon is converted into an insoluble whole, consisting of metaphysical and material parameters, wherein the sacred acquires material dimensions and the material is sanctified. Through the gestures directed during the course of the festival towards the icons it becomes obvious that the distinction between the material that constitutes the icon and the saint depicted in the icon is not always clear. This is particularly obvious in the respect paid to the icon, when some worshippers supplement the ritual of the respect by resting their aching or broken body parts on the icon, while others caress the icon piously and so on.

'Like a Glorious Bride . . .'

In the *synaxari*, a genre that describes the life and martyrdom of the saints, St Marina is presented as a beautiful young girl, born in AD 230, under Diocletian, at Antioch in Pisidia. She became a Christian at a young age and at fifteen underwent martyrdom. The cause of her martyrdom was her meeting an officer of the area, who, struck by her beauty, wished to make her his own. After St Marina refused him and made a proud declaration of her faith in Christ, the officer gave orders for her to face torture, in the hope that she would renounce her faith in Christ, before finally executing her. Her memory is commemorated on 17 July (Doukakis 1893: 226–35).

The features that St Marina presents in the verbal narratives retold by the inhabitants of the locality and the relationships among these features reveal a multidimensional personality (Hart 1992: 193–223). Sometimes she is presented as a saint with no local restrictions, while at other times she is presented as the protector saint and emblem of the locality. On some occasions, she personally intervenes with God on behalf of the inhabitants of the region and on others she is a woman who reveals in concentrated form cultural prototypes relating to womanhood that relate to the moral code of pre-capitalistic agricultural communities. Sometimes she is presented as the protector of small children, particularly of girls. All these aspects of the saint are concentrated, made public and commented on during the procession of the icon. The processing, in the particular form it takes during the festival of St Marina, constitutes a dramatised, symbolic presentation of the values that are negotiated in the *synaxari* of the saint. The ritual manner in which they are presented provokes intense feelings in the participants and spectators, as it charges with feeling the ideological content projected onto the ceremony (Smith 1972: 170; Turner and Turner 1978: 246–49).

In the view of the *synaxari*, St Marina's martyrdom is also to be understood as marriage to Christ. It is on this metaphor that the hymn 'like a glorious bride' (*os nimfi peridoxos*) rests. This hymn is sung during the procession. The metaphor of marriage that is employed during the festival contributes to the process whereby symbols employed during procession of the icon are capable of being interpreted on two levels, the earthly and the metaphysical, which in turn correspond to the sacred and the womanly nature of St Marina. The symbolisms tied to this metaphor consist of the decoration of the icon, the clothes worn by the brides and the wedding *lampadhes*. The womanly nature of the saint, her youth and purity are represented by the sex and age of the children who take part in the procession of the icon.

The theatricality of the *synaxari* in the procession of the icon is a recent innovation and is the creation of an energetic member of the local catechism class. The local church was happy to accept this theatrical approach to the martyrdom of the saint in the procession of the icon, because it agrees with the *synaxari* of the saint. It was therefore in accord, at least in the view of the church, with the educational aspect of the feast as a commemorative event and with pastoral work of the church.

The inhabitants are happy to accept this approach to the martyrdom of St Marina, although they may read it differently according to circumstance and individual preference. What makes it possible for the local community to communicate with both the martyrdom of the saint and the saint herself is the cultural basis common to both the *synaxari* and the rural background of the inhabitants. The metaphors employed in the *synaxari* also exist in rural culture. The result is that the symbolisms employed are familiar and are accepted because they agree with the cultural prototypes of the inhabitants.

In particular, the linking of death to marriage and vice versa is very common in rural tradition. The separation of the bride from her family environment has, in rural tradition, been invested with a large number of emotionally charged social practices. These customs express the emotional state of the participants and at the same time form a rite of passage, which marks the passing of the bride to her next social condition. Amid the joy of the circumstances, there are also tears, sad songs, the ritual silence (*kamaroma*) of the bride (Meraklis 1989: 33–58; Politis 1931: 276–82), all of which highlight the close relationship between separation from the paternal house and the separation that death brings. Yet, death is very often correspondingly likened to marriage, especially if the deceased is young and unmarried. Indeed, in the past it was the custom for a dead unmarried girl to be buried in a bridal dress, while a young dead man was buried dressed as a bride groom (Antzoulatou-Retsila 2004: 100). In such cases, death is viewed as marriage, sometimes to Christ, 'because then she marries Christ' (*pantrevete to Christo*) and sometimes to *Charos* 'she marries *Charos* [the personification of death in Greek folklore]' (*pantrevete to Charo*) (Antzoulatou-Retsila 2004: 102–4). The interpretation offered by the inhabitants of the symbols surrounding the procession depends on the level of education, the nature of their relationship with the Church and the cultural background.

Conclusions

In this chapter I trace the features that religious experience employs in an urban context, using as an example the locality of St Marina and the religious festival of its church. As is evident, the saint in Orthodox religion plays a defining role, In this case, she constitutes a basic element in the founding myth of the locality and through endowing the locality with her name endows it with an identity rich in cultural content.

In this context, the religious festival of St Marina ceases to be merely a narrowly religious festival of a general character. On the contrary, the saint becomes localised, which allows the festival to acquire local and social references. Along with the patron saint, the whole area and its local community are celebrated. Falassi states that 'both the social function and the symbolic meaning of the festival are closely related to a series of overt values that the community recognizes as essential to its ideology and worldview, to its social identity, its historical continuity, and to its physical survival' (1987: 2). In similar terms, Turner states, 'when a social group, whether it be a family clan, village, nation, congregation, or church, celebrates a particular event or occasion, such as birth, harvest, or national independence, it also "celebrates itself". In other words, it attempts to manifest, in symbolic form, what it conceives to be its essential life, at once the distillation and typification of its corporate experience' (1982: 16).

At the festival, St Marina is publicly displayed and celebrated as an element in the identity of the inhabitants. She is celebrated as a sacred personality and as an icon. She symbolises the local community (Nitsiakos 2003: 160–69; cf. Hirschon 1998: 225).[5] The local church attempts to impose its own interpretation on the festival, showing a preference for a metaphysical interpretation. Nevertheless, the inhabitants themselves, who take part in the festival, to the degree that they accept or reject the official interpretation offered by the church, alter the quality of the festival by their spontaneous religious behaviour and their own interpretation of the meaning of the festival. As has been described in the introduction to this chapter, they adapt it to the terms of reference and the anxieties of the local community.

Notes

1. The word *panegyri* derives from the ancient Greek word *panegyris*, which derives from 'pan' + 'agyris', meaning 'gathering of a multitude' (Andriotis 1983: 261).
2. The National Statistical Service reported the following population figures for Ilioupoli: 529 inhabitants (1928), 3,911 (1940), 8,052 (1951) and 27,638 (1961) (cited in Leontidou 1989: 331).
3. *Prosforo* is sacred bread that is distributed at the end of the communion service.

4. *Proskynisi* is a gesture of respect towards the icon, employed in the Orthodox Church, consisting usually of kissing the icon or kneeling before it.
5. On the desire to experience the feeling of 'communitas' as a basic motive behind participation in such activities, see Turner (1969: 82–83).

References

Alexakis, E.P. 2004. 'Onomatothesia ke stratigikes metavivasis tis periusias stin Kea Kykladon', in *I Ellada ton nision apo tin Fragokratia os simera*, vol. 2: *Praktika B' Evropaiku Synedriu Neoellinikon Spudon*. Athens: Ellinika Grammata, pp. 365–84.
Andriotis, N.P. 1983. *Etymologikon lexiko tis kinis neoellinikis*, 3rd ed. Thessaloniki: Aristoteleion Panepistimion Thessalonikis.
Antzoulatou-Retsila, E. 2004. *Mnimis tekmiria*. Athens: Papazisis.
Chryssanthopoulou, V. 1993. *The Construction of Ethnic Identity Among the Castellorizian Greeks of Perth, Australia*, Ph.D. dissertation. Oxford: Wolfson College.
Cohen, A.P. 1989. *The Symbolic Construction of Community*, 2nd ed. London: Routledge.
Connerton, P. 1989. *How Societies Remember*. Cambridge: Cambridge University Press.
Doukakis, K.C. 1893. *Megas synaxaristis panton ton Agion ton kath' apanta ton mina Iulion eortazomenon*. Athens.
Dubisch, J. 1990. 'Pilgrimage and Popular Religion at a Greek Holy Shrine', in E. Badone (ed.), *Religious Orthodoxy and Popular Faith in European Society*. Princeton: Princeton University Press, pp. 113–39.
———. 1995. *In a Different Place: Pilgrimage, Gender and Politics at a Greek Island Shrine*. Princeton: Princeton University Press.
Du Boulay, J. 1995. 'Time and Society in Rural Greece', in S. Damianakos et al. (eds.), *Les Amis et les Autres. Mélanges en L'Honneur de John Peristiany/Brothers and Others. Essays in Honour of John Peristiany*. Athens: Centre National de Recherches Sociales (E.K.K.E.), pp. 147–62.
Durkheim, E. 1995. *The Elementary Forms of the Religious Life*, trans. K.E. Fields, New York: Free Press.
Falassi, A. 1987. 'Festival: Definition and Morphology', in A. Falassi (ed.), *Time Out of Time. Essays on the Festival*. Albuquerque: University of New Mexico Press, pp. 1–10.
Fitrakis, A.I. 1955. *Lipsana ke tafi martyron kata tus tris protus eonas*. Athens.
Hart, L.K. 1992. *Time, Religion, and Social Experience in Rural Greece*. Lanham, MD: Rowman and Littlefield.
Hirschon, R. 1997. 'Essential Objects and the Sacred: Interior and Exterior Space in an Urban Greek Locality', in S. Ardener (ed.), *Women and Space. Ground Rules and Social Maps*. Oxford: Berg, pp. 70–86.
———. 1998. *Heirs of the Greek Catastrophe. The Social Life of the Asia Minor Refugees in Piraeus*. Oxford: Berghahn Books.
———. 2009. 'Imported Individuals and Indigenous Persons: Changing Archetypes of Personal Identity in Contemporary Greece' in C. Hann and H. Goltz (eds.), *Orthodoxy, Othopraxy, Parádosis: Eastern Christians in Anthropological Perspective*. Berkeley, CA: University of California Press.

Hirschon-Philippaki, R. 1993. 'Mnimi ke taftotita. I Mikrasiates prosfiges tis Kokkinias', in E. Papataxiarchis and T. Paradellis (eds.), *Anthropologia ke parelthon. Symvoles stin kinoniki istoria tis neoteris Elladas*. Athens: Alexandreia, pp. 327–56.

Kakamboura-Tily, R. 1999. *Anamesa sto astiko kentro ke tis topikes kinonies: I syllogi tis eparchias Konitsas stin Athina*. Konitsa: Pnevmatiko Kentro Dimou Konitsas.

Kenna, M.E. 1977. 'Greek Urban Migrants and Their Rural Patron Saint', *Ethnic Studies* 1: 14–23.

———. 1983. 'Institutional and Transformational Migration and the Politics of Community. Greek Internal Migrants and Their Migrants' Association in Athens', *Archives Europeennes de Sociologie* 24: 263–87.

Kotsonis, I.I. 1952. *To enthusiastikon stichion is tin Ekklisian ton martyron*, Athens: Damaskos.

Kyriakidou-Nestoros, A. 1979. *Laografika Meletimata*, 2nd ed. Athens: Nea Synora–A. Livanis.

Leontidou, L. 1989. *Polis tis siopis. Ergatikos epikismos tis Athinas ke tu Peirea, 1909–1940*. Athens: Politistiko Technologiko Idrima ETVA.

Loukatos, D.S. 1963. *Synchrona Laografika (Folklorica Contemporanea)*. Athens.

Megas, G. 1949. 'Zitimata Ellinikis Laografias', *Epetiris tu Laografiku Archiu* 5–6: 86–144.

Meraklis, M.G. 1989. *Laografika Zitimata*. Athens: H. Bouras.

———. 1999. *Therata Laografias*. Athens: Kastaniotis.

Nitsiakos, V. 2003. *Chtizontas to choro ke to chrono*, Athens: Odysseas.

Oikonomidis, D.V. 1962. 'Onoma ke onomatothesia is tas doxasias ke synithias tu Elliniku lau', *Laografia* 20: 446–542.

Papadakis, N. 1971. *Ellinika laika argyromata*. Athens: Morfologiko Kentro Athinon.

Politis, N.G. 1931. *Laografika Symmikta*, vol. 3. Athens: Akadimia Athinon.

Sapir, D.J. 1977. 'The Anatomy of Metaphor', in D.J. Sapir and C.J. Crocker (eds.), *The Social Use of Metaphor. Essays on the Anthropology of Rhetoric*. Philadelphia: University of Pennsylvania Press, pp. 3–32.

Smith, R.J. 1972. 'Festivals and Celebrations', in R.M. Dorson (ed.), *Folklore and Folklife: An Introduction*. Chicago: University of Chicago Press, pp. 159–72.

Turner, V.W. 1969. *The Ritual Process. Structure and Anti-Structure*. Middlesex: Penguin.

———. 1982. 'Introduction', in V. Turner (ed.), *Celebration. Studies in Festivity and Ritual*. Washington, DC: Smithsonian Institution Press, pp. 11–30.

Turner, V. and Turner, E. 1978. *Image and Pilgrimage in Christian Culture*. New York: Columbia University Press.

van Gennep, A. 1977. *The Rites of Passage*, trans. M.B. Vizedom and G.L. Caffee, 3rd ed. London: Routledge and Kegan Paul.

Vernier, B. 2001. *I kinoniki genesi ton esthimaton. Prototoki ke ysterotoki stin Karpatho*. Athens: Alexandreia.

Vryonis, S. 1981. 'The Panegyris of the Byzantine Saint: A Study in the Nature of a Medieval Institution, Its Origins and Fate', in S. Hackel (ed.), *The Byzantine Saint*, (14th Spring Symposium of Byzantine Studies, University of Birmingham), London: Fellowship of St Alban and St Sergius, pp. 196–226.

Ware, T. 1964. *The Orthodox Church*. Middlesex: Penguin.

From the City to the Village and Back: Greek Cypriot Refugees Engaging in 'Pilgrimages' across the Border

Lisa Dikomitis

❖

There were so many questions Kyriacos (forty-nine) wanted to ask when he first returned to his village. After he became a refugee he had travelled all around the world and lived in cities for almost three decades. Now he was back in his own house, which at the same time, was not his house. The air was the same, filled with the smell of jasmine, the old trees in the courtyard were packed with fruits, the pigeonholes he had built with his father remained intact, but everything carried a sense of unfamiliarity. Kyriacos was sitting opposite the present inhabitant of his house, a Turkish Cypriot Mehmet, who answered many of his questions. He offered Mehmet a cigarette and lit one for himself, although he never smoked. He looked like a nervous teenager, trying a cigarette, warily looking around with a knot in his stomach, not knowing how to behave. He only asked, with a voice heavy with emotions: 'Do the swallows still come? (*Erkountai ta selidonia akoma?*)' Before he returned to the city, Kyriacos filled a jerrycan with water from the village well and picked some fruits from the trees in his fields.

During the twenty minute ride from the city to her village Fanoulla (seventy-six) muttered repeatedly under her breath '*o theos einai megalos* (God is great)', while she commented on the landscape that had changed over the past thirty years. When we passed the *trouli*, a dome-shaped hill marking the entrance to her village, Fanoulla's eyes watered. She quickly recovered her voice and decided the places we would go. We visited her house with the small kitchen garden, her fields on the other side of the road, the small neglected cemetery outside the village, the monastery, the main village church, two little chapels and the village fountain. In some places Fanoulla picked up something to serve as a reminder of her visit, including a brick stone from her house and a bunch of wild flowers from the monastery's garden.

Since the checkpoints opened Georgia (fifty-five) frequents her and her husband's villages on a regular basis. In the two localities she visits the religious sites: the local church, the monastery and little chapels. In all these places Georgia always carries out the same ritual: fresh flowers are arranged near the makeshift *ikonostasis* (altar screen of icons), the icons are dusted, the oil lamp is refilled and new candles are lit. Georgia blesses the place and says some prayers. She kisses the foot of the icons one last time and leaves the site, by now thickly scented with incense. Then Georgia drives to the next place of worship and carries out the same rituals.

Kyriacos, Fanoulla and Georgia are only three of the thousands of Greek Cypriot refugees who visited their villages since the opening of the border in April 2003, but their stories reflect practices that are common among refugees. This chapter explores rituals regularly performed by Greek Cypriot refugees, who now live in the capital city of Nicosia, and the ways in which these rituals allow them to recreate the sense of belonging to a community that has been lost.

A Period of Transition

Cyprus has been divided since Turkish troops invaded the north of the island in 1974, following a brief Greek Cypriot coup orchestrated by the then Greek military regime. Greek Cypriots living in the north were forced to move to the south and became refugees in their own country (Loizos 1981). The Green Line established in 1964 following the first round of hostilities between Greek and Turkish Cypriots became a rigid partition line running across the middle of the island and cutting right through the heart of Nicosia. Since 1975 there have been several diplomatic attempts to resolve the so-called Cyprus Problem both in and outside Cyprus, but no solution has been found and the island remains divided. In recent years, as Cyprus was preparing to join the European Union, the pressure was on to resolve the long-standing partition of the island. This climate triggered the unexpected opening of the checkpoints on the Green Line in April 2003. One year later a referendum was held on the proposed United Nations solution for the reunification of the island (the Annan plan). Sixty-five per cent of the Turkish Cypriots voted in favour of the plan and 76 per cent of the Greek Cypriots voted against it. As a result, the Cyprus Problem remains unresolved and only the Greek Cypriots entered the European Union (May 2004).

In this period of transition the dividing line in Cyprus was transformed from an impenetrable border to a border that can be crossed. Greek Cypriots deal in various ways with this new opportunity to cross the Green Line. Some refuse to cross the border, others cross the border frequently to engage in everyday things and some cross the border to visit their former villages and houses. Although Greek Cypriots do not recognise the border as legitimate, this refusal is expressed in different and often paradoxical ways (Dikomitis 2005).

In this chapter I investigate urban Greek Cypriot refugees' attempts to recreate their shattered identities and communities. In order to arrive at some understanding of why these city dwellers engage in a range of activities in their former rural localities I consider their return visits as a form of 'pilgrimage'. For this purpose, certain aspects of the conventional concept of pilgrimage are revisited (cf. Delaney 1990). An analysis of these pilgrimages offers an avenue for exploring the symbolic nature of their activities across the border. In using 'pilgrimage' as an analytical tool I break down the heterogeneous urban refugee body and explore how similar actions can be conceptualised in different ways.

The main contention of this chapter is that although Greek Cypriot refugees may have varied attitudes towards religion and religious practice, they all engage in ritual routine when they visit their former villages in the north of Cyprus. The choice of ritual, the frequency and the intensity of their performances reflect the different ways in which they exercise agency and recreate community, albeit in a partial and provisional manner.

An Urban Refugee Community

It is important to understand the context of the Greek Cypriot refugee experience. Therefore I briefly sketch how the former inhabitants of villages in the north of Cyprus maintain a sense of community with their fellow villagers after three decades of displacement. I focus on one urban refugee group, the Larnatsjiotes, among whom I am conducting fieldwork.[1] Their experiences illustrate well how communities have been shattered after 1974 and the ways in which Greek Cypriots are dealing with a refugee identity in their everyday lives (see Dikomitis 2003; Hadjiyanni 2002; Loizos 1981, 2003; Papadakis 2005).

Currently the Larnatsjiotes are scattered in the south of Cyprus. Some live in mountainous and coastal villages or in provincial towns such as Paphos and Limassol, but the largest part lives in the biggest urban centre of the island, the capital city of Nicosia. These urban refugees form no homogenous body; the community is made up of people from different social strata and age groups. Although some Larnatsjiotes live in the same neighbourhoods, most of the villagers are dispersed throughout Nicosia and its suburbs.[2] Several refugee families were able to build their own houses in the south of Cyprus, but there are still many families who live in Turkish Cypriot houses or in a *synoikismos*. *Synoikismos* are refugee estates, apartment blocks and neighbourhoods with identical houses that were erected in the south of Cyprus shortly after the 1974 invasion to provide housing for the large number of refugees.[3]

This physical break-up of the village community is an important factor of the Greek Cypriot refugee experience. During one of our morning talks, Nitsa (fifty-four) sighed and said, 'I was a queen in my house [in the village] (*imouna vassilisa sto spiti mou*)'. What Nitsa was implying – and her sentiment is shared by other refuges, even those who own houses – is that she does not feel 'as a queen' in her everyday life in the city, that the status she had enjoyed in the village is now lost. Social life in Larnakas was primarily organised around the neighbourhood (*yeitonia*) (cf. Hirschon 1989: 166–91). The intensity of neighbourhood life has largely disappeared in the sociability patterns of the city. Day-to-day encounters are now centred on the nuclear family, whereas in the village social relations were centred around much larger networks. The refugees' nostalgic discourses repeatedly revolve around the sharp contrast between their former lives in a small rural village and their present lives in an urban milieu. Christos (fifty-five) told me that 'real life does not allow us [the Larnatsjiotes] to be a close community'. He explained that because of the loss of physical proximity, the hectic city lifestyle and the development of new social relations the Larnatsjiotes 'have lost touch with each other' (*khathikan*). Christos readily added that strong bonds between co-villagers remained; if one needed a job to be done certainly a co-villager would be asked first.

Despite the fact that Larnatsjiotes live 'far' from each other now and are entangled in the web of contemporary urban life, there are still many occasions where members of the former community meet. Particularly older, male Larnatsjiotes meet each other on a frequent basis in the coffee shop of their *syllogos* (association) to play games such as backgammon, cards, or bingo, or simply to have a drink. One Larnatsjiotis told me he frequents the *syllogos* because there he can talk about the old days (*na miliso gia ta palia*). The refugee associations organise events (such as day trips, dinners, dancing nights and talks), which are widely attended by whole families. The most frequent encounters among Larnatsjiotes involve Orthodox rituals. As Dora (nineteen) said to me, 'I know the Larnatsjiotes from church things. We attend each other's baptisms, weddings, funerals and *mnimosina* (memorials)'. Especially for a wedding celebration, the most important social event on the island (Argyrou 1996), all Larnatsjiotes are invited and attendance is required. It is no coincidence that co-villagers invite each other for these religious rituals – they are events that all villagers would have attended had they still been living in their former villages – the social world in villages was organised around the religious calendar and participation was largely inevitable (Hirschon 1989).

Larnatsjiotes frequently tell stories about the religious dimension of their lives in the village. They describe at length how they celebrated their patron saint's feast day (*paniyiri*) and they vividly recall details about the religious sites in their village. As in Greece (Dubisch 1995), Greek Cypriot communities are tied around the holy personages to whom the local churches are dedicated. In Larnakas tis Lapithou the local monastery was build in honour of the *Panagia ton Katharon* (Virgin Mary of the Pure). Many Larnatsjiotes have personal experiences with the miracle-working power of the main icon of the monastery. Kostas (fifty-seven), for example, told me with considerable emotion how he suddenly became paralysed as a young child. When the Panagia appeared in his mother's dream, she took her son to the monastery and fulfiled a vow. After a while, Kostas's seemingly untreatable condition was miraculously cured and he could walk again. Even those refugees who are sceptical towards religion and the Greek Orthodox Church take a great interest in particular churches or icons. One evening I was invited to dinner at a Larnatsjiotis's house because the village's former teacher (*o daskalos*) had come over from England. A group of Larnatsjiotes had gathered around the dinner table and when the conversation turned to the village one Larnatsjiotissa told us about a video she had seen showing Turks or Turkish Cypriots who were selling icons in the harbour of Kyrenia (one of the occupied coastal towns). Information was exchanged about the state of Orthodox sites in the north of the island.[4] When our host showed us a replica picture of the icon of 'their' Panagia everybody, including those who are known to be sceptical about religion showed great interest.

Refugees, whose daily life is still inextricably entwined with religion, feel at a loss in the urban environment where their saints are not worshipped and where they cannot practice their local traditions. For example, Loring Danforth (1989: 168–213) suggests that for the refugee community of the Kostilides in Greek Macedonia, the Anastenaria ritual of firewalking and spirit possession is a symbol of their shared identity and serves as a celebration of their past. Greek Cypriot refugees have no specific religious ritual that can help them deal with their loss and suffering (Loizos 1981). However, they engage in a number of 'acts of memory' (Bardenstein 1999: 148) through which they preserve important symbols of their village identity in different aspects of their everyday life. To list only a few examples: businesses (such as stores and restaurants) are named after their villages, the icons of the local saints on the household shrines are maintained with special care, photographs of meaningful localities in the north are exhibited in central places of their houses and trees and plants that grew in their village are now cultivated in their gardens in the south (Jepson 2006).

The most ordinary, but perhaps also most powerful, 'act of memory' of Greek Cypriot refugees is the repetitive storytelling about their way of life in the village, with emphasis on the material culture (buildings, flourishing trees, fertile fields and places of exceptional natural beauty). The Larnatsjiotes passionately recall the perfect harmony in the village ('it was a paradise') and celebrate the uniqueness of their place of origin ('nothing compares to our village'). The recounting of these stories, reiterated and reproduced by the media and the educational system, has led to a collective nostalgia, which has been transmitted to second generation refugees and to non-refugee Greek Cypriots. Accordingly, an overwhelming yearning to return to their villages is expressed by refugees: '[Our] passion is to go to our house [home] (*O pothos mas einai na pame sto spiti mas*)'.[5]

When in April 2003 the checkpoints opened, Greek Cypriot refugees had the possibility to visit their former villages and other meaningful localities in the north of Cyprus.

From the City to the Village and Back

Although numerous Greek Cypriots rushed to the checkpoint to visit the north, which had been inaccessible for almost three decades, there were many who were hesitant to cross the border. Some, who initially refused, did cross after hearing enticing stories of co-villagers. Others crossed once and decided not to go again because the visit had been too emotionally draining or had proved a disappointing experience. There remains a group of Greek Cypriots, refugees and non-refugees, who refuse to cross at all (Dikomitis 2005). At the time of writing, almost three years after the opening of the border, the crossings have found their way into everyday Cypriot life and are not discussed as frequently and intensively as in those first weeks.

I joined many refugees on their first visit to their villages and accompanied the same persons several times in subsequent visits. These first border crossings were remarkably different from the frequent return visits discussed in this chapter.[6] As one refugee, Petros (sixty), told me in retrospect: 'The first time I only went to see (*epiga mono gia na do*). I did not know if my house would still be standing, if it was inhabited and if so, who the occupiers are: Turkish Cypriots, mainland Turks or foreigners. I wondered for so many years whether my fields and trees had been looked after'. These first visits were characterised by profound sentiments in the search for answers to basic questions. Most refugees responded with strong emotions to the first encounter with their village and its present inhabitants: they were crying, trembling, or cursing, depending in what state they found their houses and properties. I witnessed one woman collapse as we drew closer to her house. Refugees reacted in different ways to the generally cordial hospitality from the present occupiers of their houses. People who are usually quiet were chatting non-stop to hide their unease. Others who are usually talkative almost did not speak when offered a coffee and shown around in their own house. Take Kyriacos for example: when he was received as a guest in his house, he only asked whether 'the swallows were still coming'.

Even before we left the village, some refugees already decided not to return. For example Charalambia (fifty-seven) who told me: 'The trees are not there anymore, there is a man inside my house who talks Turkish. My house is dilapidated. I do not want to return'. Or Aleksandra (thirty-five) who complained about the present state of the village: 'Dirty Turks. The village is not clean. *Tourkika*. They turned the village into a Turkish village. They built extra fences around our house. In yellow and grey! And they painted the walls green. It is their culture. Do you understand? (*Katalaves*)'. Other refugees, equally emotional, decided that they wanted to go back to the village. Georgia, for example, who is still engaging in frequent return visits, told us after her first visit: 'I saw the many acres of my fields, all the trees are cut (*ekopsan ta*). I noticed the condition of the houses and the village. The army is everywhere. It is the reality (*i pragmatikotita*). Every time I go I will cry and it will hurt me, but people should go (*o kosmos prepi na pigeni*)'.

During the months following the border openings everyone was discussing their negative or positive experiences and the talk of the day was whether one should pay a return visit or not. Often the opinions I heard echoed the official political debate. Refugees such as Spiroulla (fifty-four), who discovered that her house had been turned into a cowshed, recited time and again: '*Dhen mboro*. I can't [go there anymore]. My house became a stable (*stavlos*). I was ready to commit suicide (*eimouna etimi na aftoktoniso*)'. Others agreed with Georgia: however painful the return journeys might be, refugees have to visit their villages. Petros explained why he still returns to his village more than two years after those initial visits:

> The second time and all the other times I went back to my village it was because it is mine (*einai diko mou*). It is our heritage (*i klironomia mas*), our history (*i istoria mas*). Not only the churches and the buildings in the village, but also our holy grounds (*ta agia mas chomata*). It is my place (*o topos mou*). I go and I venerate the land of my village (*proskino to choma tou choriou mou*). And my fields are my heritage as well as

the things [which grow] on my field (*ta pramata tou chorafiou mou*). You want it (*to theleis*), you ask for it (*to zitas*). From a very young age I was working on those fields. I perceive my soil as holy (*ta theoro agia ta chomata mou*). I will never forget these things (*den prokeitai pote na ta ksexaso*). Not even now, after so many years. It is mine. It was my father's [land and village], my grandfather's (*itan tou patera mou, tou papou mou*).

Other refugees who regularly cross the border in order to visit their former villages provided me with related accounts about why they often return.

Similar to Delaney (1990), who compared the journeys of Belgian Turks to their natal village in Turkey to the *hajj*, I analyse refugees' return visits as a 'pilgrimage': a ritual process during which these city dwellers undertake repetitive, symbolic performances in their former rural localities (Turner and Turner 1978). Place is a prominent characteristic of all pilgrimages (Dubisch 1995; Turner 1974). Greek Cypriot refugees do not visit an established pilgrimage site, but a rural locality, which has been described to me on many occasions as a paradise-like place. As Dubisch (1995: 35) pointed out, a pilgrimage focuses on a place that is 'different from other places'. It is indeed the case, as I have shown, that these urban refugees perceive their village as an 'extraordinary' place. Petros's choice of words, notably *agia* (holy) and *proskino* (to venerate), indicates the spiritual and powerful qualities he attributes to his village. Also in poetry about their village, written by two Larnatsjiotes, I came across a similar vocabulary which is normally used in a religious context. Refugees who took up the opportunity to visit their villages repeatedly 'create' a pilgrimage site through these very visits (Dubisch 1995: 36).

'The House of God Feels Like My House'

The religious practices I outline in this section entail rituals that are familiar in Orthodox Christianity. These activities, performed by urbanites in their former rural localities, involve the care taking of religious sites, venerating the icons, lighting candles, crossing themselves, blessing the place and praying. These performances follow the same pattern repeated by a variety of refugees in different places: middle-aged men and women who attempt to purify profaned religious sites, elderly refugee women who carry out their religious duties at the cemetery and individuals who regularly go to worship a specific holy personage. A close examination of these rituals reveals that almost identical practices carry different meanings.

One of the most shocking experiences during the earliest visits, frequently discussed by the refugees, was the confrontation with the neglected and sometimes vandalised religious sites. Several refugees decided to restore the sacred character of these sites: the village church, the local monasteries and the many small chapels in the villages and around the countryside. I came across many such endeavours, some undertaken in a subtle manner and others in a more visible way.

The first case I encountered took place in the chapel dedicated to *Agios Fanourios* (Saint Fanourios), located in a cave on a seaside cliff in the Agios Georgios village near Kyrenia. This cave had been turned into a toilet; all the icons and religious paraphernalia had disappeared. One could not imagine that this terrible, reeking, empty cave was once a sacred site. In the summer of 2003, some months after the borders opened, a few refugees decided to reclaim the site. They took cleaning materials and tools on one of their return visits and restored this cave, to the best of their abilities, to its original state. They brought icons of *Agios Fanourios*, fresh flowers, water, oil, candles, matches and *livani* (incense used during Orthodox ceremonies). Most of the cleaning and restoring (removing the dirt from the cave, arranging the icons and flowers, lighting the candles and blessing the cave) was done by the women. The two men present were standing outside, talking and admiring the landscape and only occasionally interfering when one of the women asked for their help. It is no coincidence that women took on the major part of this work. Anthropologists working in the Mediterranean have provided detailed analyses of the involvement of women in religious activities (see Dubisch 1983, 1995; Hart 1992; Hirschon 1983, 1989; Rushton 1983).

I observed another telling example of reclaiming a sacred space in my field site, the village of Larnakas tis Lapithou. The monastery Panagia ton Katharon was in a very bad condition. On my initial visit in April 2003 I saw goats in and around the building. All the paint and icons were gone and the walls had been vandalised with graffiti. The original church floor was destroyed and broken tiles were scattered among animal excrement. In the summer of 2003, Georgia (fifty-five) and her husband Antonis (fifty-eight) decided to clean the monastery so that the place would be ready for the saints' days, in this case the festival of the Assumption on 15 August and 8 September when the Larnatsjiotes celebrate the *Panagia ton Katharon*. Georgia and Antonis brought all the necessary tools from the city. They removed the dirt with a shovel and a spade and then cleaned the church of the monastery with a dust broom. Antonis made a little tower with the original tiles (*toufla*) and, as he explained, put those on the place where the altar (*agia trapeza*) once stood. They whitewashed one corner wall in order to have a provisional *iconostasis*. Antonis did not paint over one slogan well known to Greek Cypriots, probably written by a Larnatsjiotis: 'I don't forget and I fight (*Den ksechno kai agonizomai*)'. The *iconostasis* is the most prominent feature of an Orthodox church, typically consisting of one or more rows of icons and a set of royal doors in the centre. Because there is no *iconostasis* left in the monastery, Georgia arranged the icons on the wall after the paint had dried. She then prepared to bless the place, using oil, water, candles, matches, incense, olive leaves and small pieces of charcoal (*karvounakia*). Antonis and Georgia lit the candles and the oil lamp, venerated the icons and said prayers. They left the village and returned to the city, where Georgia told her relatives what they had done: 'I could not [see the church in this state] (*dhen mborousa*). We had to clean it (*eprepe na tin katharisoume*). We painted [the church of the monastery] so it would be clean and ready (*tin vapsame na einai kathari tsje etimi*)'.

Throughout the north of Cyprus one can find many illustrations of ongoing attempts to restore neglected Orthodox sites, especially in local village churches, which have not been converted into mosques, cultural centres or cafés. During the past three years (2003–2006), urban refugees continued to rejuvenate the religious sites in their former villages. For example, I noticed that new icons and a wooden candelabrum had been taken to the monastery of Panagia ton Katharon. Icons regularly disappear, are smashed or burned. When icons were replaced for the second time in the Agios Fanourios chapel, refugees paid a local Turkish Cypriot carpenter to make a door so that the cave can be closed. In the monastery of Panagia ton Katharon Georgia recently put some icons high on the wall in order to prevent them from being stolen. She asked me if I knew the Turkish Cypriot *muhktaris* (village president) to ask his permission to remove the fig tree because its roots are destroying one wall of the monastery. The silent presence of icons, candles and flowers in the churches in the north point to the regular visits of Greek Cypriots. Chapels and small roadside shrines are less visible in the religious cartography, but are equally important to refugees as the more prominent churches. Many of these chapels were privately erected and maintained, hence in these places 'the sacred is localized and individualized' (Dubisch 1995: 64). These small churches (*eklisakia*) can be particularly meaningful to refugees because they commemorate specific past events in their lives. Chapels located in the villages' surroundings may also have been built in a 'continuous attempt to domesticate the wilderness' (Stewart 1991: 165). Stewart further notes that in Greece villagers perceive their locality as 'a divinely protected enclosure or circle' (1991: 166). Greek Cypriots hold the same belief. I saw a refugee family restoring a small chapel in Larnakas, dedicated to *Agia Marina* (Saint Marina). This chapel is merely a hole in the soil, a tiny space in the shoulder of a street, hidden under some trees a bit lower than street level. A Larnatsjiotis removed the wooden board that was obstructing the chapel. His sister cleaned the interior and arranged an icon, oil lamp and some candles. The others crossed themselves three times and lit a candle.

The practice of purifying religious sites can be interpreted in two ways. First, it can be understood as an effort to restore the spiritual unity of their village. When the possibility arose, urban refugees attempted to reclaim their community, through purifying the spaces that symbolise the protection of God. Second, it may be interpreted as an attempt, in a symbolic way, to reclaim their houses. In Cyprus, as in Greece, the house is the 'central nucleus' of village life (Du Boulay 1974: 140). Refugees wondered what happened with their household shrine, expressing the hope that the present occupiers might have saved the icons. Du Boulay (1974: 54) portrays the importance of the material culture of Orthodoxy in the privacy of homes: 'What is a house without icons? A shelter for animals'. In this case, most houses are devoid of Orthodox religious features and some are now actual animal sheds. Refugee cannot change their houses because they are inhabited by others. They can, however, alter the next closest thing, namely the sacred spaces in the village. Hart analysed the strong link between the house and the church: 'If the separation between home and church is emphasized in some respects (for the church is exalted as a hallowed place and as a public realm) it is diminished in others. If holy paraphernalia are incorporated into the house, domestic rituals are also extended to the church' (1992: 148). This argument is confirmed by how Georgia explained her actions to me: 'The church is the house of God and it feels like my house (*i eklisia einai to spiti tou theou kai tin niotho san to spiti mou*)'.

In the same vein the local cemetery can be perceived as an extension of the house (Hirschon 1983, 1989; Sarris 1995). The small cemetery of Larnakas is located at the top of the village. The marked headstones are broken and scattered around. The low wall that encloses the cemetery is falling apart and thick tangles of weeds are covering most of the graves. The names on the stone crosses are barely visible. One scene I observed at the cemetery was particularly moving. I sat crosslegged on a part of the wall that was intact and was watching the women I had accompanied. Irinou (seventy), wearing spectacles with thick lenses, is nearly blind. She descended into the graveyard and was searching for the headstone of her parents and her brother. The others were preoccupied with the blessing of the crosses. Irinou found the cross of her brother, touched the letters carved in the stone for a while, and silently cried. Then she carried out her rituals: putting an oil-lamp at the foot of the cross, blessed the grave with incense and praying. The cemetery in Larnakas is frequently visited by refugees, mainly elderly women. Several of them have told me they are grateful that they can finally perform the graveside rites in their village.

Next to the actual restoring of these sacred places and carrying out religious duties at the cemetery, many urban refugees visit various religious sites in their village where they engage in religious rituals. They venerate the icons, light the candles, bless the place and place flowers next to the icons. I agree, however, with Hirschon's (1983: 121) point that when Greek city dwellers visit shrines in the countryside there is no strict division between the religious and recreational aim of the visit (see Bowman 2000 for Orthodox pilgrimage in Jerusalem). In Cyprus refugees go, especially on weekends, for a 'walk' (*mia volta*) in their former villages, and while they are there also perform rituals in the churches and chapels.

Others undertake pilgrimages asking for the help of a specific saint and bringing an offering. In that case, the pilgrimage is undertaken because they have made a vow. Many refugees go to a well-known pilgrimage site in Karpassia, the monastery of Apostle Andreas. Refugees of my acquaintance also go on pilgrimages to the sites described above. In the weeks preceding the referendum on the Annan plan I observed refugees at the Agios Fanourios cave praying for a positive outcome. They left a banner, which they draped under the icons. On the green-white banner it said *Nai stin Kipro* (Yes to Cyprus). This banner can be seen as a *tama* (object exemplifying the vow). In this chapel I saw from time to time leftovers of a *Fanouropita* – a cake baked with seven specific ingredients and taken to the saint as an offering.

Figure 6.1. A Political Banner as a *Tama*. Courtesy of the author.

Four Larnatsjiotes went as pilgrims to the local monastery to pray for their son-in-law who lost his hand in a work accident with a concrete mixer. Their devotions were intensely emotional; they were crying and asking the Panagia to grant their prayers for a quick recovery of their son-in-law. Their pilgrimage coincided with Georgia's weekly visit. She told me that these Larnatsjiotes later called her to ask if she had been chanting hymns or if there was clergy around, because the four of them heard hymns (*psalmous*) as they were leaving the monastery. Georgia told them that she had not been praying aloud and that no one else was around that moment. For Georgia, this was an indication of a miraculous occurrence.

In concluding this section, I want to emphasise that although all of these routines (maintaining sacred sites, carrying out religious duties at the cemetery, worshipping at a specific shrine and engaging in traditional pilgrimages) are common rituals, they have to be adjusted and reinvented according to the present circumstances. There are, for instance, no priests or church employees around and the prayer services (e.g. on a saint's name day) are conducted by the refugees themselves.

Figure 6.2. Refugees Conducting a Service. Courtesy of the author.

'This Is a Place of Miracles'

Another set of rituals performed by refugees on their 'pilgrimages' is related to the material culture and natural elements of their villages. Even though these rituals are also performed by devout refugees who regularly visit the religious sites, they are more passionately enacted by refugees, like Petros, who explained he frequents his village because it is 'his place' (*o topos mou*). These city dwellers follow an unwritten fixed route along the places that are meaningful to them. Consequently, the whole journey is turned into a ritual and this sequence of practices is repeated when they go back to their village.[7]

One essential stop is at the village fountain (*vrises*). The Larnatsjiotes collect water for themselves and for co-villagers who could not come. They bring jerrycans, small containers and plastic bottles to fill up with 'their water'. They usually spend some time at the fountain, washing their faces with the water, drinking and collecting it. On one visit Kyriaki (sixty-six) exclaimed, 'I would give all my money to have this water in Nicosia! *Panagia mou* (my Mother of God). You should drink it. It is the purest water. Drink some more'. For them, this is not just ordinary water; it is assigned a spiritual meaning. Back in the city, they would offer guests 'water from our village (*nero tou choriou mas)*'.

Besides water they also collect fruits, herbs and flowers from their former gardens and fields. Refugees, whom I visited in their houses in Nicosia, showed me other things they took back from Larnakas: a brick from their house (*petra apo to spiti mou*), a piece of wood and an old picture they were given by the Turkish Cypriot inhabitants who found it when they settled in. When I joined Danae (forty-six) on a visit to Larnakas she showed me around the places she had strong memories of: the fields she used to play on, a picnic spot in the mountains, her old school, the houses that used to be coffee shops and so on. When we arrived at her paternal house, she was very disappointed that the old carob tree (*teratsia*) had been cut. Danae collected some soil in a jar from the spot where the *teratsia* once grew (the roots were still visible). She kept part of the soil in her refugee house and brought the remainder to her mother's grave in the cemetery in Nicosia. Danae explained, 'It is a part of me, a part of my past life'. I encountered a similar practice, one afternoon, when I accompanied Kyriacos to his village. He took me to the local cemetery and showed me his father's grave. Kyriacos did not engage in any religious action, but picked up a handful of dirt from the graveyard and poured it into a plastic bag. Like pilgrims who bring a keepsake from their journey, refugees take things from their village as a reminder of their visit (Coleman and Elsner 1995). That afternoon Kyriacos's eyes gleamed when he guided me through Larnakas. He told me stories about specific places, referring to them with their old names: *farangas, lacharopetra, kaminatzia* and so forth. We often stopped to inspect a tree. He told me whose tree it was and how, as children, they stole *karidia* (walnuts) and other fruits. For a while we watched the village's shepherd and his flock. Kyriacos told me how much he missed the jingling of the goat's bells. He constantly complained about the city: the fruits are not sweet enough there and the water has no taste; there are not enough open fields and the trees are worthless compared to the village trees. Kyriacos snapped dozens of pictures, declaring that 'this is a place of miracles'. He even taped, with his digital camera, the sound of the running water and the birds' songs. I have seen loads of videos and pictures taken by refugees, which are now displayed in their houses, next to the few old photographs they were able to take with them when they left. Nikos (sixty) has a picture of the grim pile of stones where once his house stood. Danae collected a pile of pictures of trees, rocks, fields and she regularly shows them to her friends. I also got many requests from refugees to take 'a good picture' of their house.

Urban refugees do the ordinary things they used to do when they were living in the village (e.g. collecting water, picking fruits and walking through the fields). The only difference is that now these things are no longer ordinary. These rituals can be conceptualised as 'acts of memory', even if performed in the actual locale they want to remember.

Conclusion

In this chapter I show how Greek Cypriot refugees now living in the city deal with the possibility of returning for day-trips to their villages of origin. I considered these visits as 'pilgrimages' through which they attempt to recreate the religious and cultural cartography of the village. The sense of continuity and the village community, which is less apparent in the city where they live, is to a certain extent re-established in the rural locality where refugees coincidently meet. The movement between city and village, engaging in 'pilgrimages', allows them to exercise agency and recreate community. However, this can only be done in a fragmentary mode, because they have to return to the city. Depending on their attitudes towards religion and religious practice the rituals vary from familiar religious routines to ad hoc rites, such as collecting material elements from particular sites in the village.

Notes

I thank Peter Loizos, Rik Pinxten and Marios Sarris for their encouragement and many helpful comments. I also thank Ireni and Niki Dicomitou for their constant support during my fieldwork.

1. The Larnatsjiotes come from the village Larnakas tis Lapithou, located on the southern foot of the Pendadaktylos mountain range. Most of the ethnographic data I use in this article was collected during several fieldwork rounds among the Larnatsjiotes between April 2003 and March 2006. I also include some events I have observed during visits to the north when joining refugees other than Larnatsjiotes on their return visits.
2. According to the last official census (at the end of 2001) the total population of the Republic of Cyprus numbered 689,565 of which 68.8 per cent reside in an urban area. The district of Nicosia has a population of 273,642 (http://www.mof.gov.cy/cystat).
3. Approximately one out of every four Greek Cypriots is a refugee. The 2001 census states that 5.6 per cent of the population live in refugee estates and 1.8 per cent occupy Turkish Cypriot houses. For more details about the rehousing policy of refugees in Cyprus, see Zetter (1982, 1987).

4. Through different sources (media coverage, tourists' accounts of their visits to the north and the stories of the few Greek Cypriots who had been allowed to visit the north) Greek Cypriots had some knowledge, before the opening of the border, of which religious sites had been neglected and even vandalised and which were well preserved.
5. Zetter (1994) investigated the dilemma of a possible return. See also Loizos (2008).
6. For detailed impressions on the first border crossings see Dikomitis (2004), Loizos (2006) and Papadakis (2005: 239–51).
7. See the pictorial narrative in Dikomitis (2004) for illustrations of these secular rituals.

References

Argyrou, V. 1996. *Tradition and Modernity in the Mediterranean: The Wedding as Symbolic Struggle*. Cambridge: Cambridge University Press.

Bardenstein, C. 1999. 'Trees, Forests, and the Shaping of Palestinian and Israeli Collective Memory', in B. Mieke, J. Crewe and L. Spitzer (eds.), *Acts of Memory: Cultural Recall in the Present*. Hanover, NH: University Press of New England.

Bowman, G. 2000. 'Christian Ideology and the Image of a Holy Land: The Place of Jerusalem Pilgrimage in the Various Christianities', M. Sallnow and J. Eade (eds.), *Contesting the Sacred: The Anthropology of Christian Pilgrimage*. Urbana: University of Illinois Press, pp. 98–121.

Coleman, S. and J. Elsner. 1995. *Pilgrimage Past and Present: Sacred Travel and Sacred Space in the World Religions*. London: British Museum Press.

Danforth, L.M. 1989. *Firewalking and Religious Healing: The Anastenaria of Greece and the American Firewalking Movement*. Princeton: Princeton University Press.

Delaney, C. 1990. 'The Hajj: Sacred and Secular', *American Ethnologist* 17(3): 513–30.

Dikomitis, L. 2003. 'Nothing Compares to Our Village: Gendered Memories of Greek Cypriot Refugees', MA thesis. Ghent: University of Ghent.

———. 2004. 'A Moving Field: Greek Cypriot Refugees Returning "Home"', *Durham Anthropology Journal* 12(4): 7–20.

———. 2005. 'Three Readings of a Border: Greek Cypriots Crossing the Green Line in Cyprus', *Anthropology Today* 21(5): 7–12.

Dubisch, J. 1983. 'Greek Women: Sacred or Profane?' *Journal of Modern Greek Studies* 1(1): 185–202.

———. 1995. *In a Different Place. Pilgrimage, Gender, and Politics of a Greek Island Shrine*. Princeton: Princeton University Press.

Du Boulay, J. 1974. *Portrait of a Greek Mountain Village*. Oxford: Oxford University Press.

Hadjiyanni, T. 2002. *The Making of a Refugee: Children Adopting Refugee Identity in Cyprus*. London: Praeger.

Hart, L. 1992. *Time, Religion and Social Experience in Eural Greece*. Lanham, MD: Rowman and Littlefield.

Hirschon, R. 1983. 'Women, the Aged and Religious Activity: Oppositions and Complementarity in an Urban Locality', *Journal of Modern Greek Studies* 1(1): 113–29.

———. 1989. *Heirs of the Greek Catastrophe: The Social Life of the Asia Minor Refugees in Piraeus*. Oxford: Clarendon.

Jepson, A. 2006. 'Gardens and the Nature of Rootedness in Cyprus', in Y. Papadakis, N. Peristianis, and G. Welz (eds.), *Divided Cyprus: Modernity and an Island in Conflict*. Bloomington: Indiana University Press.

Loizos, P. 1981. *The Heart Grown Bitter. A Chronicle of Cypriot War Refugees.* Cambridge: Cambridge University Press.
———. 2003. *Grace in Exile.* Nicosia: Moufflon.
———. [1975] 2004. *The Greek Gift: Politics in a Cypriot Village.* Mannheim: Bibliopolis.
———. 2006. 'My Visit to Argaki, Saturday, May 17th 2003', *Thetis* 11: 215-218.
———. 2008. 'The Loss of Home: From Passion to Pragmatism in Cyprus', in S. Jansen and S. Lofving (eds.), *Struggles for Home. Violence, Hope and the Movement of People.* Oxford: Berghahn Books.
Papadakis, Y. 2005. *Echoes from the Dead Zone: Across the Cyprus Divide.* London: I.B. Tauris.
Rushton, L. 1983. 'Doves and Magpies: Village Women in the Greek Orthodox Church', in P. Holden (ed.), *Women's Religious Experience.* London: Croom Helm.
Sarris, M. 1995. 'Death, Gender and Social Change in Greek Society', *Journal of Mediterranean Studies* 5(1): 14–32.
Stewart, C. 1991. *Demons and the Devil.* Princeton: Princeton University Press.
Turner, V. 1974. *Dramas, Fields, and Metaphors: Symbolic Action in Human Society.* Ithaca: Cornell University Press.
Turner, V. and E. Turner. 1978. *Image and Pilgrimage in Christian Culture.* New York: Columbia University Press.
Zetter, R. 1982. 'Housing Policy in Cyprus: a Review', *Habitat International*, 6(4) 471–86.
———. 1987. 'Rehousing the Greek Cypriot Refugees from 1974: Assimilation, Dependency and Politicisation', in J. Koumoulides (ed.), *Cyprus in Transition, 1960–1985.* London: Trigraph, pp. 106-25.
———. 1994. 'The Greek-Cypriot Refugees: Perceptions of Return Under Conditions of Protracted Exile', *International Migration Review* 28(2): 307–22.

PART FOUR
IMPACT OF MODERNITY

READING THE CITY RELIGIOUS: URBAN TRANSFORMATIONS AND SOCIAL RECONSTRUCTION IN RECIFE, BRAZIL

Marjo de Theije

The urban landscape is the stage on which many significant religious transformations took place in recent decades. Urbanisation and religious diversification went hand in hand, and the researchers on religion and religious movements accredited the migration to the cities of millions of poor peasants in Latin America as an important contribution to the growth of new religious groups and identities in the urban environment.[1] The same process occurred in Africa and Asia, where the religious realm has rapidly diversified in recent decades, accompanying the process of modernisation and industrialisation. Nevertheless, in the burgeoning field of urban anthropology, which focuses on the anthropology of the modern city, urban space and place, the physical presence of religious manifestations and expressions generally do not receive much attention (Low 1996, 1999; Sanjek 1990). This is notable, because religious buildings and expressions are both quite visible and quite audible in contemporary urban life.

A brief trip through the city of Recife reveals the dominant role religious buildings play in occupying urban space, as a result of the process of religious diversification. The main square of the working-class neighbourhood Alto José do Pino on an ordinary Monday evening is a good illustration of this: while buses shuttle to and from the terminal of the Alto bus line, men play dominos on the street within earshot of the music produced by the Charismatic Catholics in the chapel of José Operário (Josef the Worker) on the upper side of the square and the *crentes* (believers) of Deus é Amor in a building right in front of the Catholic chapel. Added to this cacophony is the music coming from the small bars around the square, some of which are famous for the local version of reggae music. But it is not only in the popular neighbourhoods that the presence of religion is so dominant. Every Saturday night in the nearby middle-class neighbourhood of Casa Forte, the Catholic Mass in the old church on the main square causes traffic jams, and usually some of the churchgoers have to follow the celebration from the sidewalk because there are not enough seats. From the beautiful square, one can see the recently constructed Church of Jesus Christ of Latter-day Saints – another of the neighbourhood's characteristic edifices. If one wanders through the streets of Casa Forte, one encounters many other, though more modest, religious buildings.

The reason for the lack of academic attention to the religious aspects of the city in urban anthropology might be the misplaced presupposition that modernity entails a secularising process, and that urbanisation is the path leading to the end of religion. The demolition of churches in many European towns and cities in recent decades shows that the citizens in Western society have a decreasing interest in institutionalised Christianity. This hidden assumption is, of course, a theoretical flaw, as shown by studies on North American society (see Warner 1993). In many societies, modernity seems to have had other religious consequences. The urbanisation of Brazil was accompanied by the founding of many new religious groups, the increasing emancipation of old religions and a diversification of the religious field as a whole. Like other Brazilian cities, Recife has witnessed many processes of religious meaning making and religiously inspired identity formation. Where Roman Catholicism once predominated, there is now a rich variety of religions, ranging from Anglicanism through Pentecostalism to Mormonism, whereas the previously hidden urban indigenous and Afro-Brazilian cults – such as Catimbó and Xangó – have now emerged into the open. Such religious transformations are worth including in analyses of contemporary urban life.

How, then, can we explain the marginalised position of religion in urban anthropology? Could it be the secularised researcher? Given the prominence of religion in the urban landscape, the bias of urban anthropological research may be the only convincing explanation for the underestimated role of religion in urban anthropology. The religious buildings, festivals and symbols were there, but for many decades the researchers simply did not consider them interesting. By the end of the twentieth century, the construction of new religious meeting places, mosques and Hindu temples, which is partly a result of contemporary global migrations and subsequent settlement patterns in metropolitan Europe and North America, has brought about the understanding that religion is an important feature of the city (Guest 2003; Hervieu-Léger 2002).

Attention to the religious lives of the inhabitants of the city, the symbols and social relations manifest in the religious activities of the urban population, the meanings they attach to religion and to the urban spaces that serve as its context, provides an insight into processes of contestation, identification and symbolisation in the urban landscape. This chapter shows that the religious construction of urban place and space is an important element in the lives of the inhabitants of Recife – Brazil's fourth largest city with a population of around one and a half million.[2] In the urban context of increasing cultural pluralisation, religion plays multiple roles. I explore these roles and the development of religion in this city, by recounting three different episodes of the connection between the urban landscape, urban lives and the religious meaning making and practices of different urban populations. In doing so, the focus is on the visual aspects of the religious presence in the urban landscape, which is related to processes of identity construction and religious group formation.

Religion and the City

To a large extent, religion owes its public visibility in the city to its buildings. In Recife, the Catholic monuments in the old city centre testify to a long and rich history of devotion and domination. Today some of these churches arouse the same awe and wonder they must have provoked three centuries ago. But churches, temples and other religious places are constantly being constructed in the city. Although there is no data on the foundation of churches in Recife, we may assume that the situation is similar to that in Rio de Janeiro, where in the 1990s five new Pentecostal churches were founded each week.[3] The result is highly visible: wherever one goes, one sees religious buildings, the places where religious communities gather, where the divine is near to the human, where worshipping and life rituals take place. In this respect, religious buildings can be seen as markers of a specific realm of urban life; these markers are much more important than is often thought, because they also have a symbolic value. Religious buildings can also be perceived as works of art that can be admired for their architectural majesty or the beauty of their adornments.

Religious constructions are recognisable places in the city, standing out from other places. This conspicuousness need not be especially exotic or revered. In the daily life in the city, temples and churches may serve as landmarks people use to orient themselves and others when moving about the city (e.g. 'When you get to the church behind the traffic lights, turn left, go straight ahead and then turn right after the Igreja Universal do Reino de Deus'). Catholic as well as Protestant churches, both traditional and Pentecostal, can be used for orientation purposes. However, there are exceptions; for example, Afro-Brazilian temples generally are not so visible. This is due to the different character of Xangó, Umbanda and Candomblé as compared to the Christian religions. The absence of Afro-Brazilian landmarks in the urban landscape of most Brazilian cities indicates that these religions are more private, secret and much less public than Catholicism or Protestantism.[4] This is related to the historical development of these religions in Brazilian society: Afro-Brazilian religions were formed under repression and did not try to compete with Catholicism as the country's dominant religion. Until the 1950s, their *terreiros* (temples) were subject to persecution and police control. Now that prohibition is over, they continue in the usually simple edifices often located in the more remote lower-class neighbourhoods of Recife where they had been kept hidden for so long. Even the famous Pai Edu temple in the old part of the city of Olinda is a modest building, recognisable only to those who know it is there. It is nothing compared to the many baroque Catholic churches on the same hills overlooking the city.

Thus, religion was a primary divider of space and place well into the twentieth-century city, with Catholicism monopolising the religious marking of urban space. In the course of the twentieth century, however, this monopoly was broken by the Protestant churches built in the middle-class neighbourhoods, and later by the small temples of Pentecostal groups, like the 'Assembly of God' and 'Brazil for Christ' in the working-class neighbourhoods. Of course, the mere economic power of the elites influenced the urban space much more than the poor people did: the former constructed Catholic churches from colonial times on, and are still predominantly connected to Catholicism. The upcoming middle class in the Brazilian cities in the first half of the twentieth century allied itself to Catholicism (Owensby 1999), and from the 1930s on the Church sought the participation of the middle and higher classes in the Catholic Action movement, and organised such events as the Eucharistic Congresses (de Theije 1999a, 1999b, 2002). Religion can be understood as, among many other things, offering identity to people in the city. The buildings and other visible aspects then become representations of that identity.

Increasingly, Catholicism had to relinquish its dominant position, and in contemporary Recife, as in many other Brazilian cities, other religions have constructed churches in prominent places – such as on important thoroughfares, or large buildings – such as cinemas. It is notably the Igreja Universal do Reino de Deus that has thus contested the urban landscape and changed the use of space for religious purposes. It goes without saying that this contestation of space also symbolises the contestation of the followers of the church, and at the same time is a means to attract more believers. Urban landmarks such as temples are not neutral, but structures to which people attach emotions, give meaning and that might play crucial roles in the formation of both individual and group identities. An important element of the use of urban space by religious groups is the competition between them. The construction of an impressive church building is a public statement aimed not only at the followers and the non-believers, but also at the rivals in the religious marketplace. Religion takes an important role in the contestation of urban space.

Not only buildings mark the religious space in the city: wherever one looks, one sees religious texts, ranging from the artistic decorations on trucks seeking the blessing of God, to graffiti proclaiming that there is no life without belief, or a billboard for a shop downtown alluding to popular saints.[5] Whomever one hears talking, one witnesses references to other worldly beings, from the casual *se Deus quiser* (God willing) to the biblical texts recited on street corners by evangelical preachers. References are also to be seen in gestures, for example, when people make the sign of the cross when passing a Catholic church. Yet another manner in which the religious demarcation of urban space is established is through noise. The cacophony to be heard in Alto José do Pino square is in no way exceptional. Often, *carros de som* (vans with large loudspeakers on top) crisscross the city streets, inviting the people to come to a religious gathering, or simply spreading the word of God. Thus, religion leaves its marks on urban space and place in many ways. People use markers – particularly religious markers – to help them order their environment and to locate themselves within a special, sacred space. Religious features, rituals and churches may also become symbols in the construction of social relations between believers and non-believers.

Sacred Places That Organised the City

Until late into the twentieth century, Catholicism dominated the religious demarcation of urban space and monopolised the social markings in people's lives and in public life. Brazilians started constructing sacred places in the early days of colonisation. There is a close link between the religious developments in Brazil and city life. In the historical development of religious life in Brazil, the urban brotherhoods were of great importance, because the institutional Catholic Church was poorly organised in the sixteenth and seventeenth centuries (de Theije 1990). At the time of the Dutch occupation of northeastern Brazil, Catholicism in Recife and many other Brazilian towns was largely organised by religious confraternities that structured not only the calendar with the festivals of their patron saints, but also the urban landscape by building churches (Boxer [1977] 1993; Mello 1987).

Most of the baroque beauty still present in Recife was built by the faithful. The Catholic Church was poorly structured; Catholicism was largely established in the country in a bottom-up rather than a top-down manner. Organised in brotherhoods, confraternities and third orders, in colonial times the laity took care of the religious infrastructure. They built the chapels and churches, organised the religious festivals and performed the funerals of their brothers and sisters. These lay associations ordered not only the religious life of the early Brazilians, but also the social life of the towns. Each social group had its own brotherhood. The Third Order of Saint Francis united the elite, the Irmandade de Nossa Senhora do Rosário united the slaves, and for all statuses between these two extremes there was a particular brotherhood, confraternity, or third order (de Theije 1988, 1990). Citizens adhered to the religious group that represented their social position in the urban context. Although Catholicism was the dominant religion, it had to be internally diverse in order to meet the needs of the faithful and to build an organised society out of the chaos of early colonisation. Thus, Catholicism both represented unity and variety and offered identification for all.

Catholicism continued to be the common ground for many religious activities far into the twentieth century. The seventeenth- and eighteenth-century Catholic churches in Recife are now major tourist attractions; for example, the golden chapel of the Third Order of Saint Francis is a high point of every excursion through the old city centre. However, these churches still serve to demarcate and as a focus of urban religiosity. Tourists may visit the churches, but many locals still go to them to seek healing and miracles. The numerous *ex-votos* and the *pedidos* (petitions for a grace) on the saints' altars evidence this search for religious meaning and extraordinary events.

The feast of the patron saint of Recife – Nossa Senhora do Carmo – illustrates the many aspects of religion in the city. The celebrations begin a week earlier, but the highpoint is on 16 July, when Mass is held every hour, starting at five in the morning. At three in the afternoon, a Mass is held in front of the basilica, after which a large procession bearing the image of the saint makes its way through the streets of the city centre. Tens of thousands *Recifenses* participate in these acts of piety. According to the anthropologist and Carmelite friar, Frei Tito Figuerôa de Medeiros (1990), the festival represents a combination of several celebrations: it is Catholic, in the sense that it is connected to the universal Catholic Church; it is Afro-Brazilian, because it is the feast of Oxum, the goddess of (among other things) fertility and prosperity, who syncretised with Nossa Senhora do Carmo in Recife; it is elitist, because the local and regional political and economic elites participate in it, as do the rich who have financially supported the festivities since the very beginning; it is the feast of the 'owners' of the saint, the friars do Carmo and the Ordem Terceira do Carmo, who are the main organisers of the feast; and it is an urban feast, held in the commercial centre of the city. It brings together the devotees from throughout city, the suburban *favelas*, and even from bordering states. The shops are closed for the day (it is an official local holiday), but the street vendors sell yellow flowers (yellow is the colour of both Nossa Senhora do Carmo and Oxum in Recife), hotdogs, popcorn, fireworks and all kinds of drinks and religious articles. The square in front of the church and the neighbouring streets become a combination of amusement park and fair, and the main avenue is closed to traffic (de Medeiros 1990: 31).

In the past decade, the old centre of Recife has been undergoing 'revitalization' and its meaning and uses in urban life is changing (Leite 2002). Although the festival has altered considerably over the years, it has nevertheless largely maintained its characteristic ritual forms and content. The democratisation of Catholicism marginalised the elitist celebrations for Our Lady of Carmen and allowed the lower classes to participate in church celebrations. The hierarchical view of society inherent in the festivities for centuries was turned upside down as a result of the new ideological interpretations of the Catholic faith, which, based on liberation theology, contested the old customs. The banquet in the convent, which traditionally was held for the elites, was replaced by an *almoço de confraternização* (confraternisation lunch) offered to all those who helped organise the festival, the bishops and priests who celebrated the masses, the friends and sponsors of the convent and the members of the choirs (de Medeiros 1990: 32). Thus, the relation between the city and the Catholic festival has changed; although a large proportion of the residents continue to identify with Nossa Senhora do Carmo and her position as the city's patron saint.

The impact of the festivities on the inhabitants of Recife is less than it used to be. For those who do not go to the town centre, the holy day of Nossa Senhora do Carmo may pass by almost unnoticed. However, the feast continues to be very visible, because on the saint's anniversary businesses, schools, banks and public services close down, and the festivities are extensively covered in the newspapers and by the local television and radio stations. The Catholic feast also refers to a generalised notion of religiosity that seems to be shared by most *Recifenses*, if only because it is this Catholicism that defines part of the calendar of city life. Living in Recife means also identifying with Nossa Senhora do Carmo.

City life has become ever more complex, and the religious options have increased tremendously. Although Catholicism continues to be a major organiser of public life, it is certainly no longer the only one visibly marking the urban landscape and the lives of the *Recifenses*.[6] Other more or less organised religious options are continually becoming available to them. How this process had its counterpart in the urban landscape can be illustrated by the story of a prominent local family and its mansion in Casa Forte.

The Pluralisation of Religious Space

If one arrives in Casa Forte from Madalena (the adjacent neighbourhood) and crosses the bridge of the Carrefour supermarket, one's attention is caught by a huge marble church topped with a golden angel gleaming in the sun.[7] This temple, which was inaugurated in 2001, dominates the skyline not only for those crossing the bridge, but also for many of the inhabitants of the new apartment buildings that have been built in the neighbourhood during the 1990s. The land on which the temple was built has only recently become religious ground.

Casa Forte is a residential neighbourhood built on the site of an abandoned sugar mill dating from the nineteenth and the early twentieth century, when the society that had its roots in slavery and sugar plantations was deteriorating. The sugar mill was founded in the sixteenth century, and the houses and chapel were located on the square that is now called Praça de Casa Forte. Casa Forte refers to a 1645 battle when a battalion of Dutch soldiers that were occupying the principal house of the settlement, and holding several women hostage, were captured by a Portuguese-Brazilian army (Costa 2001). In the nineteenth century, the sugar mills in the neighbourhoods around the centre of Recife were abandoned and replaced by small farms. The urbanisation of the area did not take long as the area was known for its healthy air and the clean water extracted from the Rio Capibaribe, and within a few decades the small farmhouses had been turned into mansions. Now, at the turn of the twenty-first century, Casa Forte is a middle-class neighbourhood, with huge apartment buildings progressively replacing the nineteenth- and early twentieth-century mansions and the green that used to surround them.

My informant's family – I shall call them the 'Cardosos' – has owned one of these mansions since 1926. At that time, the area was hardly considered urban. Most inhabitants of Casa Forte were from traditional sugar plantation families (Reesink 2003). Unlike these traditional families, the Cardosos were more of an intellectual elite: family members were active in politics and taught law at the university. But like their neighbours, the Cardosos had a large house on their *sítio* (estate), and there were several annexes. For a short time, three generations of the family lived in the house, and from the beginning of the 1930s, after the first couple went to Rio de Janeiro, one of the sons with his wife and their four children plus several aggregated family members lived there. The family of a former worker on a plantation outside the city lived in the annexes. There was a huge garden, with many trees and a small vegetable patch. It was like a country house, and it bordered the Rio Capibaribe.[8]

The Cardosos' house had a saint's room, with angels painted on the walls.[9] There was also a 'sanctuary', in which images of saints were guarded. It is still quite common for Catholic families to have a sanctuary in their houses. This is not to say that all the family members were fervent Catholics; for example, it is said that the Cardosos grandmother was, but that the grandfather was not. He was an intellectual who believed more in science than in religion.[10] However, Catholicism dominated the urban landscape and the lives of the middle classes in Casa Forte and the rest of Recife. Grandfather would go to Mass with his wife every Sunday, and the life rituals of Catholicism structured the lives of the Cardosos. All the children were baptised, received their first communion, went to Catholic school and joined Catholic groups, such as the Apostolate of Prayer and the Children of Mary. The family's friends included priests. From the 1940s on, several family members participated in Catholic Action groups.

In the 1960s and 1970s their children received the same upbringing and participated in Catholic youth groups. Several members of the second generation, who retired many years ago, are still active in such groups as Couples for Christ and other Catholic associations. Their children are less involved in Catholicism. Some attend Mass and have their children baptised and participate in other sacraments, but others have turned away from the traditional family religion and are now involved in Kardecist Spiritism, Sufism, or the Anglican Church. This generation is much less Catholic, and these religious choices of the individual family members coincided with the second, third and fourth new 'lives' of the *sítio* where it all began three-quarters of a century ago.

For many years, the family lived in the house, sharing the land with the families of some former workers. Over the years, parts of the *sítio* were sold off, as the city grew and the land had become more valuable. Starting in the 1930s, other parts were allocated to each of the children, so that they could construct a house of their own. What had once been a huge country estate became a cluster of ordinary urban houses, albeit upper middle-class ones.

In 1975, grandfather died and his widow went to live with her daughter in one of the other houses on the *sítio*. Because grandmother did not want the big house to be sold, it was decided to rent it out. The first tenants were followers of Bhagwan Shree Rajneesh (1931–90). These 'Rajneeshees' were a group of psychologists from the same upper middle class as the owners of the house. However, they had some peculiar customs, such as making primal screams at six in the morning – part of the new forms of active meditation taught by the Bhagwan that disturbed the neighbours. It also bothered the Cardosos, because the rumour went through Casa Forte that 'They dance naked in the house of the Cardosos', without mentioning, of course, the fact that the Cardosos were no longer living there. The Rajneeshees were a new presence in the upper middle-class neighbourhood that Casa Forte had become.

After that, new occupants were found in the form of the Hare Krishnas. This group was at least as 'different' as the previous tenants were. They were considered very exotic, and did not integrate much with their neighbours in Casa Forte. However, the Cardosos liked them better: they not only actually paid the rent, but distributed food to the poor in some of Recife's *favelas*, a religious practice similar to that of the Catholics. One of the Krishnas was a dentist and he treated the poor for free, which was something else the Cardosos admired. Nevertheless, the Krishnas remained a 'peculiar' species, with their dancing rituals in the garden and their saffron-coloured robes.

For the Catholic family, the Eastern religious groups were not of course exactly the ideal tenants.[11] However, what could be done? Moreover, by the end of the following decade, things became even worse. In 1995 – after grandmother had passed away – the family sold the land to a construction company that planned to build an apartment building on it. However, the economic recession obliged the company to sell the land. It was again bought by a religious group. This time, although the group was not Eastern, from the Catholic point of view it was at least as strange as the Rajneeshees and the Hare Krishnas: it was the Mormon Church – the Church of Jesus Christ of the Latter-day Saints – that purchased the remains of the once-grand estate. The new owners pulled down all the remaining colonial buildings and built their magnificent temple, which now dominates a large part of the neighbourhood. The conquest of souls was expressed by the conquest of space (cf. Hervieu-Léger 2002).

We thus see, within three generations of a middle-class family, an urban site and its buildings and uses reflecting the increasing diversification of religions. The 'natural' relation between the upper and middle classes and Catholicism has been replaced by a religious pluralism previously unthinkable, individual members of the family have become members of many different religious groups, and the neighbourhood has visibly changed with respect to the religious symbols and buildings it contains. The middle-class quarter of Casa Forte changed from a neighbourhood in which Catholicism monopolised both the urban landscapes and the lives of the people, even those who were not devout Catholics, as in the case of grandfather Cardoso. This monopoly ceased to exist and the seemingly natural bond of the local territory with Catholicism ended.

The Contestation of Space and the Search for Meaning

The increasing complexity of urban life and religious competition in such neighbourhoods as Casa Forte has to be seen against the background of Recife's tremendous population growth: between 1900 and 1980, the population increased more than tenfold (see Assies 1992: 50). The population of the metropolitan region also grew, and this has had manifold consequences. One is the incorporation of the former almost rural *sítio* into the urbanised part of town and its subsequent high population density at the turn of the century. Casa Forte continues to be a predominantly middle-class neighbourhood. The religious renewals in the form of the Eastern religious groups can be linked to the class identity of the inhabitants of Casa Forte. The arrival of the Mormon Church is more ambiguous. There is little information available in Brazilian social science literature about Mormon missionary practice, but I have the impression that it is less linked to a particular class.[12] Although Mormonism is a relatively recent phenomenon in Brazil's religious landscape, this huge building publicly announces its presence in a very bold manner.

However, the diversification of religious practices in Brazilian cities has taken place mainly in the working-class neighbourhoods and *favelas*. The recent religious activities of the lower classes are extensively documented in Brazilian studies. To a large extent, the urban landscape of the poor areas continues to be structured through the religious, as shown by Motta's research on a syncretic regional cult. Motta (2001) asserts that in Recife, the religion of the poorest people is Catimbó. There are Catimbó centres in the areas where 'often illiterate, under- and unemployed recent migrants' live and, interestingly, he observes an association with the 'ecologically peripheral distribution of Catimbó centres in the hills that surround the city, or on low ground that is subject to seasonal flooding' (Motta 2001: 74). In this respect it is also good to recall the festival of the patron saint of Recife in the Basílica Nossa Senhora do Carmo. The Catholic celebrations are held in the centre of town. There are also Xangó (or Candomblé) festivities, but these are not as public or as visible; they are held in the remote poor neighbourhoods, in simply constructed *terreiros* and are much more difficult to find.

With respect to the pluralisation of religion in contemporary Brazil, the most outstanding phenomenon is the extraordinary growth of Pentecostal churches. From the 1940s on, Brazil's rural population began to migrate to the industrialised cities in the southeast of the country, mainly to Rio de Janeiro and São Paulo, but also to Recife.[13] The usual explanation given by scholars is that in the rapidly growing urban centres, the peasants found a world devoid of all the forms of security they were used to in the countryside. This caused a feeling of confusion and helplessness, which made these people look for a religious solution, a solution they found by adhering to Pentecostal religious communities in the shantytowns in which they lived. They turned to these religious options in search of instant solutions to their urban problems (Banck 1998b; Birman and Leite 2000; Greenfield 2001). Most authors see a connection between poverty and the search for religious meaning and miraculous solutions to problems: urbanisation was part and parcel of industrialisation and modernisation, and led to extreme poverty among the new inhabitants, which in turn led to the increasing importance of religions as an adaptive strategy. In other words, poverty causes religiosity. The evidence on religion as an adaptive strategy to cope with poverty is extensive, such as the work of Banck (1998b), Mariz (1992) and Mariz and Machado (1994). These authors, however, do not say that it is the *only* strategy used to cope with poverty, or that religion is *only* a strategy to cope with poverty. The turn to religion is, of course, more than a functional solution to mundane problems. People may get involved in a religion because they are emotionally moved by a preacher, the power of certain rituals, the awe inspired by temples, or the social practices of a community of church members with whom they come into contact.

Nevertheless, Pentecostal growth is interesting because the anthropological interpretations of it are useful for the understanding of religious uses of the urban space. First, the idea of community in the urban space seems to be an important element in the religious meanings attached to the city. In this respect, it is important to observe that most Brazilians were (and still are) Catholics, and that includes the migrants. The Catholicism the migrants were used to was very much a community matter, a natural community in the countryside. In the city at least, Catholicism was no longer so 'natural'; however, nor were Pentecostalism and the Afro-Brazilian religions (Fry 1978). Nevertheless, it is argued that Pentecostal churches, such as the Assembly of God, managed, by going into the poor neighbourhoods and attracting small congregations, to create (or recreate) a sense of community and belonging in the people. It is difficult to assess whether the community is connected to the territory in this case; in other words, whether Pentecostalism establishes a natural bond between the believers and the local territory in the way that Catholicism had done in previous epochs. The construction of community might be based on affinity, rather than on territory, as seems to be the case in the middle-class neighbourhoods. Thus, Pentecostal believers do not necessarily become members of the church that is closest to their house; instead, they affiliate on the basis of ideological persuasion or aesthetic preferences. Consequently, the idea of community becomes less strongly linked to the local territory. Nevertheless, people experience their religious group as a close-knit community. The same applies to the religious manifestations of the Mormons or the Hare Krishnas, which are less strongly connected to the local community because they are gatherings of believers from all over the city, organised more as networks (see Hervieu-Léger 2002).

In contrast to the Pentecostal churches, Catholicism continued to be organised on the basis of shared places. The Catholic Church was slow to develop an institutional infrastructure in the popular neighbourhoods where the migrants lived, and often there were no churches or priests in the new *favelas*. However, the liberationist Catholicism of the 1970s and 1980s emphasised the importance of community, and the Catholic Base Communities (CEBs; *Comunidades Eclesial de Base;*) that were formed in popular neighbourhoods based on the idea that people would organise according to the streets and neighbourhoods in which they lived. In Recife, these CEBs were called *Encontro de Irmãos* (Meeting of brothers and sisters), so as to emphasise the community, almost family-like, aspect.[14] In this Catholic response to the demands of urbanisation, the religious community is thus foremost territorially based. Recent research by Reesink (2003) in two parts of the Casa Amarela neighbourhood, which is adjacent to Casa Forte, shows that there Catholicism continues to be considered 'natural'. The natural community of the countryside has been reconstructed, and religion is a means to create this bond.

Second, religion plays an important role in the contestation of urban space. Religious groups are not only a form of community in the urban jungle, but they also offer a language with which to give voice to the problems one encounters in the city. As Banck (1990, 1997) eloquently explained, the liberationist Catholic teachings of the 1980s, which emphasised the reading of the Bible by the laity, symbolised access to the skills and the knowledge that are very important in the modern world. Banck (1998a) also showed how religious groups were active in occupying land on which the poor could construct their houses and make a living, and defended their action in religious language. The character of the religious meanings that people developed changed, because here they themselves were actively involved in their production. In this way, the relation between the religious community and the urban space becomes an extremely close one.

Third, as with the Mormon Church in Casa Forte, religious buildings arouse feelings of wonder and awe – feelings that are important to the members of the religious community, as well as to passersby and members of other religious groups. The construction of the buildings can be understood as a manner in which religious groups try to impose their religious authority and to mark their presence in the urban space. As works of art, temples can be interpreted as constructions intended to seduce others, the non-believers (Mafra 2003). Churches also symbolise the knowledge, the ideals and the proximity of the sacred. In the context of religious competition, religious buildings are also statements of these principles of religiousness. The pluralisation of religion increases competition and produces more visible results.

Many other cases could be added to these. In religious group formation and the presentation of religious identities in contemporary urban Recife, buildings continue to play an important role, just as festivals and smaller expressions of religiosity do. The relation between the buildings and the urban surroundings, however, is no longer natural; they should be evaluated for their symbolic meaning, as ideological statements. In the contemporary context of religious competition, this is an important element of religious expression, in which the aesthetic aspect of religious construction might be as important as it was in colonial times (Low 1999).

Concluding Remarks

Urban anthropology and the anthropology of religion usually do not cross paths. Considering the distinctive presence of religious buildings in the urban space and the important role of festivals and other religious activities in urban life, the lack of anthropological attention to religion in the urban landscape is remarkable.

This chapter shows that religion is more than a coincidental happening in the city, and that the city is more than a neutral context for religious phenomena. A look at the intertwining of urban space and religious organisations and meaning making shows that religion is a forceful element in processes of identification and contestation in the urban landscape. 'Reading Recife Religious' reveals many forms of contestation of urban space, and of meaning making through religious rituals, the construction of buildings and the creation of new religious groups.

Thus, the urbanisation that took place in the twentieth century coincided with a growing diversification of religions, as well as the increasing visibility of these diverse religions in the urban landscape. The search for religious meaning, and for religious solutions to mundane problems, seems to be a constant motivation for the urban population in the construction of the religious city.[15] New religions enter the scene; relations between different religions change, and within various religious traditions new interpretations and movements develop, with Catholicism as a leader in this process of religious production. A recent study on religiousness in Recife showed the great variation in beliefs held by Catholics (Souza 2002), and the different versions all have with their demands in respect to the urban space. The growing Catholic Charismatic movement organises mass meetings in the local sports stadium (Geraldão Stadium), the devotees of Frei Damião (a very popular preacher who died in 1998 and whose grave is becoming a place of pilgrimage) need a centre in which to venerate their 'almost saint' and to perform their devotional acts, and the mainstream Catholics need a church building that is respected by Catholics and non-believers alike. The location of these religious places is no longer totally dependent on a fixed territory, as in recent years religious groups have become more organised as networks. This type of religious community formation is common among religious groups that are not dominant in a local situation – a condition that is perhaps valid for an increasing number of different religions in contemporary urban Brazil.

Judging by the conspicuous presence and visibility of religion, the urban context in fact seems to have heightened religious fervour in Brazil. Other scholars support this view: not only has the number of religious options increased over the past few decades, but so too has the Brazilians' adherence to religion (Greenfield 2001: 56). However, the precise role of urbanisation in this process is not clear, apart from the migration and poverty explanation mentioned earlier. The ethnographic data presented in this chapter show that it is not only the poor who participate in the diversification of the urban religious landscape. Such groups as the Rajneeshees and the Hare Krishnas do not usually attract the inhabitants of *favelas*. Furthermore, the preferences of certain parts of the population for certain religions are not fixed, but may change over time, as happened with the Catholic Charismatic Renewal, which arose in middle-class parishes but soon acquired followers in the poorer neighbourhoods (de Theije 1998). Furthermore, I would like to suggest that the availability of religion in the urban context also generates the search for religious meaning, healing and participation in general. Especially when religion becomes very visible – through buildings, texts, public rituals and other acts – this may create curiosity and engender a search for religious involvement. So the circle is completed: the increased religious production and diversification modifies the urban landscape, and the prominent availability of religion in this modified cityscape creates the search for religious meaning and participation.[16] The publications based on statistical data with respect to religious affiliation in 1980, 1991 and 2000 confirms this idea. The data clearly show that Recife, like most Brazilian cities, has become religiously diversified in recent decades. The researchers point to the rapid urbanisation 'that favors the surging of new religions, or the diffusion of religions coming from foreign countries' as an important cause of this diversification (Jacob et Al. 2003: 34).

While waiting at a traffic light on Avenida Rui Barbosa, the seventy-five-year-old father of my interviewee was handed an invitation by a group of Mormons, inviting him to visit the new temple they had built on the land where his wife's family had once lived. He accepted the invitation but told me he would never go there again: 'It's a beautiful temple, but it's very different and they have strange beliefs.'

Notes

1. The first version of this chapter was presented at the international conference 'Shifting Cityscapes: Urban Transformation and Social Reconstruction in Brazil' (Utrecht, 23–24 May 2002). I want to thank the conference participants and Cecília Loreto Mariz and Ton Salman for their helpful comments.
2. The metropolitan area has some 4 million inhabitants.
3. ISER (Instituto de Estudos da Religião [Institute for Studies on Religion]) research cited in *Epoca* 1 October 2000.
4. The notable exception, of course, is the city of Salvador, the state capital of Bahia.
5. An interesting interpretation of this type of expression of religious ideas can be found in Droogers (1988).
6. It should be noted that the veneration of Nossa Senhora da Conceição, in the popular neighbourhood of Casa Amarela, is more important in today's Recife. See Nagle 1997.
7. My thanks to Leopoldina Mariz Lócio and Manuela Lócio for checking this last detail for me after I had returned to the Netherlands.
8. It was also near enough to the centre of Recife to be convenient for those who had servants to do their shopping and drivers to drive them to their *fazenda* in the countryside and to the centre of town. In the 1940s, a *maxabomba* (steam tram) passed the house, connecting the area with the centre of town and the rural university in Apipucos.
9. The family member I interviewed did not know whether her grandparents or great-grandparents had decorated the room, or whether the angels were already there when they acquired the house.
10. Previous generations of his family had been devout Catholics. The family had a special devotion to a saint. At a nearby beach village, they had constructed a chapel for the saint who had helped them in the nineteenth century. Since then, the saint's name has been a part of the family name.
11. The Krishnas left in 1993. The house was then rented to an 'ordinary' family for a short period.
12. With 300,000 members, São Paulo is the largest Mormon community outside Utah (Goering 1999). In Brazil as a whole, there are 650,000 members. Until the opening of the temple in Recife (in 2001, another one was open in Porto Alegre that same year), there was only one in São Paulo.
13. For many Pernambucanos from the interior of the state, Recife is 'south', even though geographically it may be to the north or the east. See de Theije (1999a).

14. See Castro 1987. The successes and failures of CEBs have been extensively studied by, for example, Mariz (1994), whose work has been important for the comparing various religious groups in the poor neighbourhoods with respect to the relation with poverty, and more specifically, with the way they helped the faithful cope with poverty.
15. I, however, hesitate to say that Brazilians have become more religious or more involved in religious activity. The type of activity might have changed as well. New forms of religion (e.g. the CEBs) have received much attention from both scholars and the media. Although this gives the impression that there is 'more religion', it might simply be a result of our increased attention to it. Furthermore, many religious groups started to use mass media to communicate with their followers and to facilitate their missionary activities.
16. There is an additional problem with the poverty thesis. Some authors (e.g. Greenfield 2001) see the link between poverty and religion solely through urban poverty. However, poverty is more severe in the Brazilian countryside than in the country's cities.

References

Assies, W. 1992. *To Get out of the Mud. Neighborhood Associativism in Recife, 1964–1988*. Amsterdam: CEDLA.
Banck, G.A. 1990. 'Cultural Dilemmas Behind Strategy: Brazilian Neighbourhood Movements and Catholic Discourse', *European Journal of Development Research* 2(1): 65–88.
———. 1997. 'Brazilian Christian Base Communities: Organising Rituals for Democracy', in T. van Naerssen, M. Rutten, and A. Zoomers (eds.), *The Diversity of Development. Essays in Honour of Jan Kleinpenning*. Assen: Van Gorcum, pp. 291–301.
———. 1998a. 'Personalism in the Brazilian Body Politic: Political Rallies and Public Ceremonies in the Era of Mass Democracy', *European Review of Latin American and Caribbean Studies* 65: 25–43.
———. 1998b. 'Pobreza, política e a formação do espaço urbano: uma favela de Vitória, 1977–1984', in G.A. Banck (ed.), *Dilemas e Símbolos. Estudos sobre a cultura política de Espírito Santo*.Vitória: Instituto Histórico e Geográfico do Espírito Santo, pp. 157–80.
Birman, P. and M.P. Leite. 2000. 'Whatever Happened to What Used to Be the Largest Catholic Country in the World?' *Daedalus* 129(2): 271–90.
Boxer, C.R. [1977] 1993. *De Nederlanders in Brazilië, 1624–1654*, 2nd ed. Amsterdam: Uitgeverij Atlas.
Castro, G. 1987. *As Comunidades do Dom. Um estudo de CEB's no Recife*. Serie Estudos e Pesquisas, 47. Recife: Fundação Joaquim Nabuco/Massangana.
Costa, F.A. Pereira da. 2001. *Arredores do Recife*. Recife: Fundação Joaquim Nabuco/Massangana.
Droogers, A.F. 1988. 'Brazilian Minimal Religiosity', in G.A. Banck and K. Koonings, (eds.). *Social Change in Contemporary Brazil: Politics, Class and Culture in a Decade of Transition*. Latin America Studies, no. 43. Amsterdam: Cedla, pp. 165–76.
Fry, P.H. 1978. 'Manchester e São Paulo: Industrialização e Religiosidade Popular', *Religião e Sociedade*, 3: 25–52.
Goering, Laurie. 1999. 'Straight-Laced LDS Win Souls in Sensual Brazil', *Salt Lake Tribune*, 7 August 1999. Retrieved 14 August 1999 from http://www.adherents.com/adhloc/indexWhere.html.
Greenfield, S.M. 2001. 'Population Growth, Industrialization and the Proliferation of Syncretized Religions in Brazil', in S.M. Greenfield and A. Droogers (eds.),

Reinventing Religions. Syncretism and Transformation in Africa and the Americas. Lanham, MD: Rowman and Littlefield, pp. 55–70.

Guest, K.J. 2003. *God in Chinatown. Religion and Survival in New York's Evolving Immigrant Community*. New York: New York University Press.

Hervieu-Léger, D. 2002. 'Space and religion: new approaches to religious spatiality in modernity', *International Journal of Urban and Regional Research* 26(1): 99-105.

Jacob, C.R. et al. (eds.). 2003. *Atlas da filiação religiosa e indicadores sociais no Brasil*. Rio de Janeiro: Editora PUC Rio/Edições Loyola/CNBB.

Leite, R.P. 2002. 'Contra-usos e espaço público: notas sobre a construção social dos lugares na Manguetown', *Revista Brasileira de Ciências Sociais* 17(49): 115–34.

Low, S.M. 1996. 'The Anthropology of Cities: Imagining and Theorizing the City', *Annual Review of Anthropology* 25: 383–409.

———. 1999. 'Spatializing Culture: The Social Production and Social Construction of Public Space in Costa Rica', in S.M. Low (ed.), *Theorizing the City: The New Urban Anthropology Reader*. Piscataway, NJ: Rutgers University Press, pp. 111–37.

Mafra, Clara. 2003. 'A sedução em tempo de abundância: análise das igrejas pentecostais como objetos de arte', in O.Velho (ed.), *Circuitos Infinitos*. São Paulo. Attar Editorial/CNPq/PRONEX, pp. 95–127.

Mariz, C.L. 1992. 'Religion and Poverty in Brazil: A Comparison of Catholic and Pentecostal Communities', *Sociological Analysis* 53 (s): 63–70.

———. 1994. *Coping with Poverty. Pentecostals and Christian Base Communities in Brazil*. Philadelphia: Temple University Press.

Mariz, C.L. and M.C. Machado. 1994. 'Sincretismo e trânsito religioso: comparando carismáticos e pentecostais', *Comunicações do ISER* 12(45): 24–34.

de Medeiros, Frei T.F. 1990. 'Nossa Senhora do Carmo do Recife: A brilhante Senhora dos muitos rostos e sua festa', *Comunicações do ISER* 9(35): 30–34.

Mello, J. 1987. *Tempo dos Flamengos. Influência da ocupação holandesa na ida e na cultura do norte do Brasil*. Recife: Fundação Joaquim Nabuco/Editora Massangana.

Motta, R. 2001. 'Ethnicity, Purity, the Market and Syncretism in Afro-Brazilian Cults', in S.M. Greenfield and A. Droogers (eds.), *Reinventing Religions. Syncretism and Transformation in Africa and the Americas*. Lanham, MD: Rowman and Littlefield, pp. 87–98.

Nagle, R. 1997. *Claiming the Virgin. The Broken Promise of Liberation Theology in Brazil*. London: Routledge.

Owensby, B.P. 1999. *Intimate Ironies. Modernity and the Making of Middle-Class Lives in Brazil*. Stanford: Stanford University Press.

Reesink, M.L. 2003. 'Les Passages Obligatoires. Cosmologie Catholique et Mort dans le Quartiers de Casa Amarela, A Recife (Pernambuco-Bresil)', Ph.D. dissertation. Paris: Ecole des hautes études en sciences sociales.

Sanjek, R. 1990. 'Urban Anthropology in the 1980s: A World View', *Annual Review of Anthropology* 19: 151–86.

Souza, Luiz Alberto Gómez de and Sílvia Regina Alves Fernandes (ed.). 2002. *Desafios do catolicismo na cidade: pesquisa em regiões metropolitanas brasileiras*. São Paulo: Paulus.

de Theije, M. 1988. 'De broederschappen en het lokale katholicisme. De confraria de São Gonçalo Garcia en groepsidentiteiten in São João Del-Rei, Brazilië', MA thesis. Utrecht: Rijksuniversiteit Utrecht.

———. 1990. 'Brotherhoods Throw More Weight Around Than the Pope: Catholic Traditionalism and the Lay Brotherhoods of Brazil', *Sociological Analysis* 51(2): 189–204.

———. 1998. 'Charismatic Renewal and Base Communities: The Religious Participation of Women in a Brazilian Parish', in B. Boudewijnse, A. Droogers, and F. Kamsteeg (eds.), *More Than Opium. An Anthropological Approach to Latin American and Caribbean Pentecostal Praxis*. Lanham, MD: Scarecrow Press, pp. 225–48.

———. 1999a. *All That Is God's Is Good. An Anthropology of Liberationist Catholicism in Garanhuns, Brazil*. Utrecht: CERES.

———. 1999b. 'Cebs and Catholic Charismatics in Brazil', in C. Smith and J. Prokopy (eds.), *Latin American Religion in Motion*. London: Routledge, pp. 111–24.

———. 2002. *Tudo o que é de Deus é bom. Uma antropologia do catolicismo liberacionista em Garanhuns, Brasil*. Recife: Fundação Joaquim Nabuco/Massangana.

Warner, R.S. 1993. 'Work in Progress Toward a New Paradigm for the Sociological Study of Religion in the United-States', *American Journal of Sociology* 98(5): 1044–93.

MODERNITY CONTRA TRADITION? *TAIJIQUAN*'S STRUGGLE FOR SURVIVAL: A CHINESE CASE STUDY

Dan Vercammen

❖

It is a spring dawn. Merchant ships and ferries slip through the smog over the dark water of Pujiang River. Horns urge the smaller boats to move on quickly. A humming human river of colourful crowds flows fluently over Shanghai's bund. A chilly wind breathes the foul smell of the city's artery over the already polluted streets. Islands of onlookers form around solitary figures performing slow, waving motion. Some spectators become engaged in the attractive ritual and small numbers of participants grow into larger groups following a silent master. Further down the sidewalk graceful duets evolve when two people move as one in a never-ending repetition of self-defence movements. Still others seem to create flashes of lightning when their ancient looking swords catch the sunlight and cut the early morning air and the fascinated bystanders' breath. This is China's famous martial art. This is modern *taijiquan*.

Taijiquan (literally: the fist of the Great Ultimate) may be one of the images that stick to one's mind when watching documentaries about daily life in China. They are so brave these Chinese, rising early and defying hot and cold weather and bad air to go out and engage in a daily ritual of traditional exercises. Mostly sexagenarian and even older males and females are seen to be doing their Chinese gymnastics in the early hours of the day. It does not seem to do them much harm. On the contrary, they seem to be quite fit for their age. Their strange morning workout is the result of a curious mixture of both ancient and modern habits. The whole world has learnt about this Chinese way to keep fit, and many a Westerner proclaims herself/himself a master of this oriental art.

This chapter presents a case study of *taijiquan* within the boundaries of a study of identity, conflict, evolution and modernity in an urban environment. Urban societies have gone through tremendous changes in the People's Republic of China during the twentieth and the early twenty-first centuries and continue to develop and change rapidly. Especially Shanghai, which is the location I have selected for this case study, may be the best and most extreme example of urban evolution in the last twenty years. As far as I can tell, nowhere on earth has change been so strikingly obvious (most of this city's buildings were removed and replaced by skyscrapers and its territory has been vastly increased). By taking a look at how Westerners use *taijiquan* and how the Chinese export their *taijiquan* systems, I also want to draw the attention to the intercultural communication context. The case of *taijiquan* is a typical example of how the Chinese deal with overwhelming foreign (Western) influence on their traditions and how these traditions try to survive, repositioning themselves in a world of conflicting 'feudal' and modern 'scientific' attitudes and practices. In my opinion, the evolution of *taijiquan* reflects a somewhat general pattern of development in Chinese urban society (changes are more slow and often less obvious in the countryside). As we follow the expanding influence – economic, political and so on – of the Chinese giant in the twenty-first century, it might prove interesting to study how the Chinese tackle the problems of cultural diversity, modernisation and identity conflicts. Although this chapter is based on factual historical material, it is not intended to be the definitive historical account of *taijiquan*'s evolution. It can give us the means to compare, to reflect and learn. I sincerely hope that this modest contribution will help anthropologists and others to create better mutual understanding and communication.

The Basics: China at the End of the Qing Dynasty and the Development of *Taijiquan* During the Twentieth Century

Contrary to what many practitioners and even historians of *taijiquan* believe, it is not an age-old system. Recent investigations (Vercammen 2002) reveal that it was created at the end of the Qing dynasty (1644–1911). It originated as a quite effective martial art and gradually took on the looks of a simple, slow type of Chinese gymnastics.

Before describing its characteristics, it is necessary to take a look at China of the end of the nineteenth and beginning of the twentieth century. Just about everything in China underwent serious identity conflicts and changes during this period. *Taijiquan* presents a grateful example to illustrate this general characteristic.

The nineteenth century was a very difficult time for the Qing regime. Being a foreign regime of Manchu origin,[1] the Qing were not particularly liked by their Chinese subjects, and many a revolt broke out towards the end of their rule. Internal conflicts and protracted rebellions that had to be put down by force led to heavy strains on the financial resources and caused the spreading of the armies all over the country. Especially the Taiping Rebellion (which lasted for more than a decade)[2] cost millions in lives and money, and temporarily deprived the Qing of about half of China (and its tax income) (Michael 1966; Spence 1996). It also spread Western (Christian) ideas more rapidly than the missionaries had been able to do for centuries. Furthermore, foreign powers were banging (violently) on China's doors, trying to unlock this great empire for trade, colonisation and the spreading of Christian ideas. Several wars with the small but superior modernised armies of industrialising Britain, France, Japan and other nations ended with China's defeat and led to the so-called unequal treaties.[3] Chinese society had hardly been moving on, oppressed and confused by Confucianist political and cultural conservatism and Qing instability. China was believed to be 'sick', powerless and in decline, and the continuing wars ending in disastrous results reinforced this view.

Chinese intellectuals and politicians (mandarins) started to look towards their enemies for new impulses and by the end of the nineteenth century some resourceful Chinese went abroad to get a modern education. Several high-ranking military and civil officials tried to learn from their military and political mistakes and spoke openly for modernisation. Generals had watched foreigners (British, French and Americans; see Carr 1991; Wilson [1868] 1991) create small but effective, modern Chinese armies to battle against or with the rebellious movements) and started building their own modernised legions.[4] At the same time, traditional Chinese religious and secret movements started preaching against Western, and especially Christian, influences and praised native Chinese religions and concepts. Missionaries and their Chinese converts were attacked and massacred, and eventually a large rising against the foreigners came about in the north of China towards the end of the nineteenth century. The Qing thought it quite opportune to get revenge on the intruders and openly manipulated and supported the uprising that came to be known as the Boxer Rebellion (1899–1900, see Keown-Boyd 1991). Again the foreign powers united their forces and destroyed the Chinese militia. It only made things worse for the Qing, who were trying to change sides now, by turning against the Boxers and trying to appease the greedy invaders. All these events opened up the road to modernity even more quickly. The first decade of the twentieth century witnessed the total collapse of the Qing and the Chinese empire.

In 1912, after years of unrest and social movement, the Chinese Republic was founded in Nanjing (southern half of China). Its propagator was a foreign educated Chinese physician, Sun Yat-sen, who professed modern ideas and distrusted ancient Chinese culture and practices. His *Sanminzhuyi* (Doctrine of the Three [Principles] of the People) stated his political ideas about the new Chinese society. They were based on a new belief in the power of the Chinese as a strong nation, in the democratic influence (of Western origin) and in caring for the life of the people in general. In a way they reflected a Chinese interpretation of the principles of the French Revolution. *Liberté* was being translated as abolishing both the Manchu rule and the supremacy of this other race over the majority of Chinese. Sun called this the *minzuzhuyi* (the race/nationality principle). *Egalité* was present in his *minquanzhuyi* (the principle of the people's power), which aimed at a more democratic government. *Fraternité* was expressed through the principle of caring for the people's life, *minshengzhuyi*. All of the principles centred in nationalist feelings and the wish to be proud of being Chinese again. These were truly revolutionary principles for imperial China, but putting them into practice proved to be a tough nut to crack: a new would-be emperor, civil wars between Nationalist and Communist forces, a prolonged struggle against the Japanese were to be the explosive ingredients for China in the first half of the twentieth century.

On the political level, things went wrong rather quickly. Political stability was still lacking in this new China. Getting rid of the Manchu rulers created opportunities for powerful local warmongers to aim for higher power, with warlords contending violently for local and national power. Sun Yat-sen was forced to leave his new Republic and fled to Japan in 1913. The introduction of basic concepts of democracy opened up the road to multiparty rule and several political parties were organised. For example, the Chinese Communist Party was founded in 1921. Yuan Shikai – a powerful general under the Qing, who later brought the Qing to abdication and negotiated with the Republicans – was chosen to the presidency of the Chinese Republic. Once in power, he tried to establish a new imperial regime, but finally failed. The most influential and most cunning parties, the Guomindang (Nationalists of Sun Yat-sen) and the Gongchandang (Communists) were not willing to share power and commenced cruel and lasting civil wars, which helped expansionist Japan to get a grip on China, first by creating a new Manchu puppet regime in Manchuria in 1931 and in 1937 by invading China and conquering many parts of it. As it happened, this brought the Chinese together against the foreign aggressor for a while, and brought them foreign military support (mainly USSR and US), but once this threat was dealt with (1945), the civil war and political struggle flamed up once more.

The Communists finally won the war in 1949 and the Nationalists fled to Taiwan. The remnants of the 1912 Republic were resurrected on this island of Formosa, as the 'rebellious' province of Taiwan was once called. The new regime on the mainland went to a lot of trouble to infiltrate in each village and family and spread its ideas. Many traditional social structures (see Fei 1992 for the Nationalist ideas about the social structures) were abolished and disrupted and new ones were created. The basic system became the so-called *danwei* or politically controlled work unit. Power was again one-sided; the people were again being dictated what to do. During the last decade of the twentieth century, a new political wind started to blow. Economic reforms under Deng Xiaoping and the death of most veteran revolutionaries gave unforeseen prosperity to many Chinese and got rid of age-old curses such as famine and mass poverty. This had never been the case before. Political diversity and more freedom were being introduced gradually, and stability seemed to grow.

On the cultural level, we can see nationalist and racist ideas, universalism and missionary policies, cultural, political and ethnic diversity, traditionalism, modernity and standardisation or monopolisation in constant struggle during the twentieth century. In many ways, this struggle mirrors the political and social reforms and illustrates the often-failing attempts to create stable progress. It is present in the arts, in literature, in medicine and so many other aspects of Chinese culture. I am using the evolution of *taijiquan* as an example.

Summarising this all but quiet era of Chinese history, one can detect some important features and characteristics. The Chinese had been suffering from loss of identity during the Manchu dynastic rule; they were now ready to regain their own country and rights. Nationalism and racism (especially against the detested Manchu) were driving forces for politicians and the people's movements alike. Foreign trade and intrusion led to foreign influence on ideologies, politics, military, society and culture. This instigated new identity conflicts: should China stick to its own cultural background and develop in a Chinese way or should it get rid of its ancient, feudal inheritance and become a modern, but westernised country? Was there a third way? Could one stress being more Chinese while undergoing Western influences at the same time? What possibilities were available to safeguard cultural diversities when China was to take on a modern identity? How could the Chinese deal with releasing the people from millennia of 'slavery'[5] and teaching them to accept democratic values? Would they be able to maintain freedom of thought?[6]

If we are to get to grips with these questions at the cultural level, we cannot but look at individual cases. Chinese culture is a very vast and very complex matter, and certainly not a unified system, and therefore, even introducing a certain aspect or field of studies presents a number of difficulties because of this omnipresent complexity. My goal is to make the complex case of *taijiquan* as clear as possible.

Chinese martial arts (now called *wushu*) have been around for many centuries. As in other parts of the world a climate of wars and conflicts stimulates the rise of warriors and soldiers. The early dynastic histories of China are full of stories about political conflicts and wars. It is hard to tell when the first specific systems developed, but about two thousand years ago they already existed (see Xi 1985 for a history of Chinese martial arts). Typical of Chinese types of self-defence (but imitated later on by Japanese systems) is the training of fighting routines in sets of successive movements. These are done either solo or with partners, and may be barehanded or armed. They make one think of choreography, and in fact they are choreographies, because they may have come from or at least may have been influenced by popular dances (Xi 1985: 78 ff.).[7] They were considered a form of performing arts. Often movements and habits of animals such as birds, tigers, monkeys or dragons inspired the movements of the martial artists. Some systems became very famous. The Buddhist *Chan* (the Chinese ancestor of Japanese zen) monastery of Shaolin developed a system that was called *shaolinquan* (boxing of Shaolin) and the fighting monks stood out among the crowd and the emperor sometimes solicited their help. From the Ming dynasty (1368–1644) on, highly sophisticated systems were being practised. Some were of Buddhist origin, and some were not. Some were taught in public places, while others were transmitted secretly within one family or clan or in a secret society. The army also practised routines that were developed out of specific systems of armed and unarmed combat. The martial arts had specific features that characterised Chinese traditions: a specific name was chosen for the tradition (as important as a clan name); a certain (historical or legendary) ancestor or patriarch was chosen as founder and honoured in a local temple or within the house of the elders of the tradition; the transmission of the art was only possible after the disciple had gone through an initiation ritual; the tradition was transmitted orally and by imitation, but also by the study of fundamental texts and the commentaries to these texts written or explained by the teacher and his predecessors; the members of a boxing society became a clan or family: they used titles 'brother', 'father' and others to address each other (even if there were no blood ties involved) and rivalled with other such families (see Vercammen 2000: 64–79 for a description of the Chinese idea of 'tradition'). By transmitting the art, a genealogy developed and lists of official members of the tradition were kept by the clan elders, who also safeguarded the textual transmission and other valuables, and provided the (new) names for the members.

All of these characteristics apply to *taijiquan*. It was founded in the last decades of the Qing dynasty in a family called Yang. The family elder, Yang Luchan (1799–1872), had served with the Chen, an ancient clan of literati and local officials in the first half of the nineteenth century. Being illiterate, he would have been doomed to remain just one of the many millions of labourers-farmers were it not that he showed an unusual talent for martial arts. Chen Changxing (1771–1853), a famous teacher of the Chen tradition, made him his disciple and taught him for many years. After leaving his master's house for the capital (present day Beijing), he started demonstrating his skills and teaching. His reputation grew, as he was never beaten. The Qing court became interested and hired him to instruct a prince and his surrounding, and some members of the imperial bodyguard. His sons continued to teach martial arts for a living and, along with their students, started developing the techniques into a new system. Others learnt of their special methods and wanted to learn from them. Important for the historical development of these techniques into the tradition of *taijiquan* were the contacts between the Yang family and the Wu family. Wu Yuxiang (1812–1880) became a disciple of Yang Luchan's and later studied the Chen tradition for a brief period. The Wu were officials, who brought philosophy, culture, written material, and other fundamentals into the developing system. By the end of the Qing rule and the beginning of the Republic, the martial arts of the Yang and their students had become a true tradition, bearing the name of *taijiquan*. Transmission was possible by being accepted and participating in a ritual; written texts and commentaries were being discussed by the teachers and copied by the disciples; an ancestor was found in the person of a Taoist hermit of the Ming period (1368–1644) Zhang Sanfeng (see Seidel 1970), who was honoured as the patron saint of Taoist martial arts (a detailed history of *taijiquan* can be found in Vercammen 2002).

Taijiquan differed from its ancestor, the Chen martial arts: it contained other techniques and technical names; it had been influenced by Taoist rituals and indeed retained some ritualistic movements (see Vercammen 2000: 44–63); it referred to different fundamental texts; went under a different name, claimed a different founder (the Chen designated one of their Ming ancestors as their founding patriarch). It was also quite different from most other martial arts in method: instead of using the usual repertoire of blocking, resisting punches and kicking, hitting hard, speed, it stressed evasion, bending, yielding, softness, applying subtle psychological influence and the borrowing of the opponent's energy without wasting one's own force. The results when applied in combat were stunning: no one could beat them. In fact, all the principles they used were close to Taoist ideas and practices. They probably chose the name of *taijiquan* because of them. *Taiji* is an ancient name for the supreme cosmic unity, a concept demonstrating that all cosmic forms of being are in fact one (Vercammen 1990: 255–77). *Tai* means 'great', but is only used for something or someone of a supreme nature. *Ji* is the beam of a roof or a pole (both as the 'pole' in, e.g. the North Pole, and as a round pole, to which a door panel is connected and which, in Chinese architecture, replaces the hinges found in Western architecture). These meanings all imply a circular, cyclic movement: on a roof the light of the sun seems to circle during the day and this is repeated every new day in about the same way; the poles form an axis, which forms the centre of the earth's continuous daily rotation; the door pole makes the door rotate over and over. The *Ji* here is in fact the unity of *yin* and *yang*,[8] often represented as a circle divided into a white and a black half. This is the Chinese representation of the view of cosmic evolution as cyclic never-ending changes (represented for the first time in the *Zhouyi* [*Yijing*] or *Book of Changes*, dating from more than two thousand years ago; see Shaughnessy 1998: 1–29). The *Taiji* (Great Pole or Ultimate) is the model of movement in *taijiquan*: the human body is the means of representing and imitating the Great Ultimate for the Taoists, who wrote and developed many theories and practices based on this principle. In *taijiquan* it is applied to martial practice and each and every part of the human *taiji* body is seen as a miniature representative of the Great Ultimate, and all movement in *taijiquan* should reflect this (Dong [1948] 1989: 69). The very facts that the Yang family was never beaten (and therefore stood on top of the martial world) and that this new martial art contained the true essence of ancient Chinese philosophy and cosmology made the founders chose the not very modest and ambiguous name of *taijiquan* (the ultimate [and Ultimate] fist/martial art [*quan*]). The future looked bright for this art, which, at the start of its evolution, was already considered to be number one. In a way, the future became bright, but in other respects *taijiquan* failed to keep up its high standards.

Modernity and Tradition in Interaction: The Case of *Taijiquan*

With the arrival of a modernising society in China, especially in the cities, conflicts arose between tradition and modernity. As mentioned before, China was suffering from an identity crisis. China had been dominated by non-Chinese rulers and beaten by Westerners for several centuries. The self-respect of the Chinese was hard to find. This brave new world, created by the revolution, was to bring salvage. But could this be done without touching the traditions and ancient culture of China?[9] Or were these ancient customs to blame for the backward state China was in? The new Chinese rulers seemed to think they were (at least in some degree). The Republicans were, however, not very interested in communicating with the representatives of the traditions, as may be seen from how they continued to dictate their rules and confronted practitioners and teachers of ancient traditions with new regulations or even the abolishment of their practices. This was the case, for instance, with Chinese medical traditions, where modernisation came about by first abolishing the old medical college system and the replacement of Chinese medical traditions by 'modern' Western medicine (see Kong 1988: 237 ff.).[10] One might say that Chinese medicine went through somewhat similar kinds of evolution as *taijiquan* did, and in this way we will be able to offer a view of these general changes from a different perspective, which will help the readers to compare the same type of reforms within different surroundings. Our conclusions (applicable both for the evolution of Chinese medicine and for *taijiquan*), however, are more pessimistic and therefore quite different from what other researchers may have found.

In contrast with many other traditions (e.g. those of Chinese medicine) the *taijiquan* tradition was still very young during the early revolutionary period, and such developing systems are often more capable of resisting attacks. The martial arts were also linked with the revived martial prowess of China, which made them less suspicious to reformers. Age-old systems tended to lack flexibility and died out with the death of their clan or tradition elders. *Taijiquan* fared differently in the first decade of revolutionary China. It was still shaping its transmission and building its system. The link with Taoism, already present in the textual tradition discovered and/or written by the Wu family, was getting stronger. The other traditional cultural elements present in the texts (neo-Confucianism and some Buddhist elements) became less prominent, at least in Yang, Wu, and Wu traditions.[11] Taoist ideas about how to train the body and how to preserve one's health began to dominate the practice. By the time of the Republic the notion that *taijiquan* originated with the Taoists (and Zhang Sanfeng in particular) had become widespread among its practitioners.[12] *Taijiquan* practitioners made contact with other martial artists, who claimed to practise techniques of similar origin: *xingyiquan* ('fist of body and imaginative capacities') and *baguazhang* ('palms of the eight trigrams'). These schools used the same Taoist and neo-Confucianist concepts to complement their practices. The masters of the different systems met in the larger cities (mainly Beijing and Shanghai), learnt from each other and refined their knowledge through frequent meetings.[13] More texts and commentaries were being produced and published. Here are the first indications of innovation: the contacts between practitioners of different styles were of a peaceful nature, and the secrets of the arts were (partly) published. This would have been almost unthinkable during the old regime. If, in the past, practitioners of contending schools met, they would usually try to fight (and defeat) each other. Secrets and fundamental texts of the tradition were not supposed to be published, but kept by the elders and only the best disciples were allowed to see them, and maybe copy them by hand. But this was a new century. Things were becoming different. Sun Yat-sen had stressed the importance of the people and the equality of everyone. The secrets of the art could be of benefit to all the people. Education was changing, making it possible for all to get some schooling. Science was developing: clearly separated departments of history, physiology, psychology, medicine, etc. were being created at universities, modelled after Western scientific institutions and universities. *Taijiquan* picked up these new ideas and went along. Several practitioners published texts, drawings of the exercises, even photographs of the famous masters posing in the most fashionable photogenic way.[14]

An important shift in mentality has taken place as well as an important change in individual and national identity. The Chinese wanted to break free from their isolation and aversion against the rest of the world and started opening up. It is still a limited opening up, because what may seem quite a revolutionary step (publishing the texts and photographing the secret movements) is, at the same time, reflecting the old idea of keeping things behind: only those who can read (still very few) will be able to know about it and much of the knowledge and the actual tricks of the trade are not divulged. Non-Chinese (except the non-Han, such as Mongols, Manchu, etc.) are not aware of this new martial art, because they cannot read Chinese, nor would they be allowed to study it. The position of the Han Chinese towards the Manchu citizens, who belonged to the race of the formerly detested ruling class, seems to have been mainly dictated by personal relationships, as far as *taijiquan* practitioners are concerned. We see the Yang family at the turn of the nineteenth century keeping up a good relationship with Manchu students, such as Wu Jianquan – founder of the Wu Jianquan style of *taijiquan* (see Chen Zhenmin and Ma Yueliang 1935), whereas a descendant of the Yang tradition, Wang Yannian, refers to this Wu tradition as not having had access to the true secrets of the Yang because they were of Manchu race (Wang 1980: 7).

At the general cultural level, the Republic was responsible for language reforms: the classical written Chinese was abolished and a new literary Chinese language based on the spoken language was introduced. The *taijiquan* published texts reflected both classical written language and the new language (the commentaries and descriptions). An educated Chinese would have had little problems adapting to the new system, a newly educated Chinese might experience difficulties reading the old written documents.[15] The opening up is irreversible, and can only continue, because, once the material is published, it cannot be undone and others will have to go even further if they want to make a reputation for themselves. It is indeed a true first step towards the world. Whereas the foreign world has no easy access to the Chinese secrets, the Chinese do have a way to figure out foreign secrets. Many intellectuals either leave China to study abroad or try to get hold of foreign literature. They learn modern Western science and combine it with Chinese knowledge or replace Chinese knowledge with Western science. The figures in Xu ([1927] 1984: 44 and 47) are perfect examples of the application of Western physics (dynamics and the effect of forces) to the study of *taijiquan*. These drawings are very un-Chinese and the texts accompanying them reveal profound Western influence. They explain the use of *taijiquan* from the point of view of physics (or dynamics to be specific). Xu ([1927] 1984: 34) stresses the importance of dynamics for understanding *taijiquan*. In his view the study of *taijiquan* is very much linked with that of (Western) physics, and especially with the study of forces. They are two of a kind. I want to stress that this way of commenting on an original Chinese phenomenon with a foundation in ancient Chinese civilisation such as *taijiquan* is typical of this new era. Also typical of China is that there are others who do not go that far and stick to ancient Chinese views. The figures in Chen ([1933] 1986: 72 and 82) are drawings of the patterns of energy circulation inside the body when doing the exercises and the patterns of *qi* (the breath, and vapours of the body, actually the source of life)[16] and body fluids movements, accompanied by traditional verses intended for learning by heart. This book was published six years after Xu's and shows that in the 1930s the struggle between Chinese science and concepts and their Western counterparts was still going on. The drawings of the *qi* circulations are based on representations dating back to (at least) Song time (960–1279).[17] The discussion of these drawings and the principles behind them are explained from a purely Chinese point of view, using ancient medical and physiological knowledge. There is no Western influence. Chen's book reveals his background: he comes from an old family of (local) government officials and literati, who take pride in Chinese civilisation and probably prefer it to the modern mixed theories. When explaining the philosophical *taiji* principles he reverts to neo-Confucianist images and concepts, since neo-Confucianism was the orthodoxy of the Chinese officials after the Song dynasty (Chen [1933] 1986: 11–71).[18] This example shows us that some propagators of a traditional Chinese practice were quickly absorbing Western science to form a new Chinese modernity, whereas others were not willing to move into westernised modernity, at the same time engaging in limited modernisation by publishing hitherto secret knowledge. Modernity was (and still is) better expressed as 'modernities' in China.

As mentioned before, the 'clan' elders kept the genealogies of practitioners belonging to their school. The elders and their disciples performed rituals for the deceased predecessors in a special room, hall or temple dedicated to the founder and/or ancestors of the system. From interviews with informants in Shanghai and Hangzhou I learnt that this was still being done during the Republican period and for some time into the communist era (the Cultural Revolution of 1966–76 made these practices extremely difficult). Acceptance of a disciple by a master was also officially 'performed' in the ancestral hall, in the presence of not only the master and the elder disciples, but also of the founder, predecessors and former teachers. During Qing times, the teaching took place in a special hall inside the teacher's house, preferably near the ancestral hall or in a field or garden nearby (if circumstances demanded so). With the new China taking shape, some of these customs changed drastically. Genealogies were sometimes published (cf. Yang [1931] 1984: 1–3), making it possible to check whether a so-called master was accepted by the orthodox tradition. The situation definitely changed: *taijiquan* was being taught by several masters in several places; it was spread publicly, not secretly in the ancestral house, and it spread more rapidly than ever, making it necessary to make the genealogical lists available to the general public through publication. Again we see different approaches to these changing circumstances. Whereas Yang Chengfu, one of the earliest and certainly the most important public teacher of Yang *taijiquan*, offers (traditional Chinese) explanation, full sets of photographs illustrating all positions or movements, classical texts and commentaries, and a genealogy in his book, moderniser Xu only offers the classical texts and his commentaries on the principles found there from a practical and (Western) scientific point of view, but almost no photographs (those included in his book are there to explain basic principles). He does not stress the teacher's or clan member's point of view: to guard against 'illegal' transmission by people not connected with the clan. His interest is focussed on the scientific value of his text, his concern being whether it would be sufficiently acceptable to the modern educated Chinese readership.

From the 1920s on there is evidence to prove that teaching *taijiquan* (and other martial arts) was being organised in a different way. The old practice of accepting disciples was still used (it again became customary to do so in the 1980s and might still be the case with some masters today) (Vercammen 2000: 64–79). In general, however, teachers founded the so-called Boxing Societies (*quanshe*) or went to teach in modern sports centres, where martial arts were just one of many possible sports courses that students could take. One of Yang Chengfu's disciples offers a fine example of how things progressed by describing his own experience of learning and teaching *taijiquan* (Chen 1925: 5). In 1915 he moved to the capital where he started learning *xingyiquan* and *baguazhang*, two kinds of internal martial arts (*neijiaquan* or *neijia wushu*) from a famous master Sun Lutang. Then he heard from a friend that there existed a third type of internal training called *taijiquan*, which was taught by the Yang family. In the autumn of 1917 Chen had the opportunity to visit Yang Chengfu and asked him: 'People say that the Yang tradition of *taiji* is most refined, but that you do not transmit it to others lightly. Is this right or is this wrong?' Yang replied: 'That I do not transmit it to others is not the case; I wish it to be the right person, and then I transmit . . . If you like it, sir, I will not keep it as a secret treasure'. Chen studied for seven years with Yang Chengfu and learnt all the postures of Yang *taijiquan*. He and Yang became friends and it could be assumed that what Chen Weiming writes is in accord with the official Yang version of the facts. In 1925 he founded the Zhi Rou Quanshe (Society for the Boxing That Brings About Softness)[19] in Shanghai, which in the 1920s and the 1930s was the most advanced city in the East. He publicly instructed *taijiquan* in Shanghai and used his book as teaching material for his students, whom he considered to be *wenyazhi shi* (cultured gentle[wo]men). Obviously he was taught in the traditional way (oral instruction in private) by Yang Chengfu, but modernised the teaching by instructing his students publicly and by offering them copies of his book, which contains photographs of the postures, explanations of the principles, some of the classical texts of the tradition, and questions (from his students) and answers (he offered them) concerning all kinds of *taijiquan* issues. Traditionally educated Chen makes use of modern means to reach more students and provides them with written material that they would have to copy by hand otherwise (as was customary before). This is the start of a new evolution: the popularisation of *taijiquan*. As we shall see below, Yang Chengfu himself followed suit. It is not only an example of changing the way of teaching, it also had a profound effect on the contents of the teaching, as is discussed later in the chapter. In any case, the teachers who took up this method of instruction were less careful in accepting students: they did not select them on the base of character, talents, perseverance, or other traditionally required characteristics, but accepted them if they paid their fees and behaved in a civilised way (*wenyazhi shi*). This was the beginning of public teaching for all – in sports clubs, streets and parks, but one can be sure that private transmission was still customary for a few selected disciples.

The most striking change on the practical level was the aim for standardisation. Possibly this was caused by the need to have some teaching material that could be used everywhere. Having photographs published in handbooks and starting courses based on the material contained in the book probably helped the standardisation process. Just about every style of Chinese martial arts had sets of movements, which were developed according to certain patterns (very often these patterns were inspired by the shape of Chinese characters). They were mainly mnemonic means to make it possible to remember tens or hundreds of different movements. These routines or sets (*tao*) were transmitted to all within the tradition, but often they were altered or adapted or even replaced with others by some teachers. *Taijiquan's* immediate predecessor, the martial art of Chen Changxing,[20] contained several routines, both unarmed and armed (see Gu 1983: 26–27), but other *tao* (routines) were practised by other members of the Chen clan (Vercammen 2002: 35–51).

It is evident from what we know about Chen Weiming's concept of the Zhi Rou Quanshe, that what he taught was a standardised set of movements, which is illustrated in his book. We can assume that it was what he learnt from Yang Chengfu. It resembles the movements shown in Yang's books a lot, but it is not exactly the same. Being only a disciple of Yang's Chen Weiming did not have the authority to create a universally accepted, uniform set. Yang Chengfu was the main representative by the end of the 1920s,[21] but he was illiterate and maybe originally did not have such a well-developed commercial mind as that possessed by Chen.

Yang Chengfu had common sense and a wish to see his tradition grow. It did not take long before he started teaching publicly himself and eventually the capital became too small for his plans and he took to travelling all over the country to teach *taijiquan*. He took several of his disciples with him. His friend and disciple Dong Yingjie (1888–1961) finally took over the difficult and hazardous task of travelling and instructing pupils in the South of China and in Southeast Asia.[22]

In the winter of 1929 several *taijiquan* experts, including Yang Chengfu (who was undoubtedly the most important among them), worked on the creation of a Yang *taijiquan* set of movements. The initiative presumably came from the vice head of the Zhongyang Guoshuguan (Central Hall for National Martial Arts), Li Jinglin (1884–1931), who had studied *taijiquan* and was a master of the swordsmanship of the Wudang tradition.[23] The Zhongyang Guoshuguan was the product of modern China: it was a centralised institute, located in the very heart of revolutionary China – Nanjing, where Sun Yat-sen had organised the Republic. It was created with the help and blessings of the government and was intended for (scientific or modern) researching and teaching martial arts. The main goal was to train talented martial artists and researchers, who could raise the standards of new revolutionary China in this field of studies, in a standardised way (standardised training, centralised exams, etc.). Many a famous martial arts master was invited to teach there (Yang Chengfu was among them) and graduates from this prestigious national institute would spread the new standardised arts over the rest of China (Yu 1999: 261). The organisation and goals of this institute reflect the new spirit: standardisation, popularisation, modern research and (re-organised) tradition were the main ingredients. The new famous art of one of the later instructors, Yang Chengfu, could not escape 'reform'. This curious reform not only reveals something interesting about the evolution of *taijiquan*, but about China in general.

First there is the vice head, Li Jinglin. He is the representative of an ancient martial art, the practise of the Taoist Wudang sword (see Li 1988: 386–37). Yet it is clear from examining his art (fragments are printed and illustrated in Li 1988) that the Wudang sword techniques that he used were a mixture of ancient (Taoist) sword handling[24] and newly developed martial arts (mainly *baguazhang*; see Vercammen 1998: 6–64). His influence on the standardisation was clearly ambiguous: he stressed the (presumed) Taoist origin of *taijiquan* (Zhang Sanfeng) while at the same time aiming at the new goal of standardisation for uniform teaching. The result of the standardisation can be seen in the book *Taijiquan Jiangyi* (*Talking About the Meaning of Taijiquan* [1930] 1988).[25] Comparison between this set and the sets of the Chen clan's martial arts shows big differences in execution of originally the same movements, different names for the positions or the same names for different positions, and, not without importance, it has eighty-one movements.

Eighty-one is an important number for Taoists: the main text of Taoism, the *Daodejing* or the book of Laozi, contains eighty-one chapters, and so do other Taoist (and medical) classics, such as the *Suwen* (Plain Questions) and *Lingshu* (Spiritual Pivot) parts of the *Huangdi Neijing* (The Yellow Emperor's Inner Canon) and the *Nanjing* (The Canon on Difficult Issues). The Taoist alchemists paid great attention to number eighty-one, because it is equal to nine times nine, being the highest of *yang* numbers and reflecting the purest of the pure. In his preface Li Li mentions the alchemical traditions. Upon closer inspection this set contains (hidden) Taoist rituals. It could be said that this made *taijiquan* both more ancient, by linking it more closely to ancient Taoist traditions, and more modern, because it was standardised and infiltration of modern (Western) research was made possible and was indeed already going on.[26] It was usual in the traditional methods of teaching *taijiquan* and martial arts in general to stress the practise of postures: remaining in immobile stances for a long period of time (sometimes for hours). This is very hard training and therefore it is not suitable for all. By putting more stress on the set(s) of movements the wide spreading of *taijiquan* became more feasible.

The *rushi* students (those that have entered [*ru*] the room [*shi*]), that is, the real disciples (Vercammen 2000: 64–79), were still being trained the old-fashioned way. There was a change in attitude towards the goals of the practice in general, too: the stress was not so much on the martial aspects alone, it was now stressed that this exercise could be used for improving one's health. Yang Chengfu, being the head of the orthodox Yang tradition played an important role in propagating this. In his influential *Taijiquan Shiyongfa* (*Practical Methods of Taijiquan*) Yang Chengfu explains: 'If one is able to cultivate one's body (person) but not to beat adversaries, this is civil skill; if one is able to beat other persons but cannot cultivate one's body, this is martial skill ([original] note: only soft *taiji* methods are true practical *taiji* methods). If one is able to make people cultivate the body and also resist adversaries and develop practical use at the same time, this is totally civil and martial complete *taiji*' ([1931] 1984: 143).[27] Yang Chengfu added another modern-ancient feature, by publishing his 'Essentials of *Taijiquan*', a short text that lists essential points of the practice: it presents ancient Taoist principles of health preservation applied in *taijiquan*, and also the principles that can pass for modern common sense advice, especially if one is aware of the commentaries that are implied (see Despeux 1981: 109–13 for a French translation of the abridged version of the principles; and Vercammen 1999 for an annotated Dutch translation of the text).

This episode of *taijiquan*'s evolution tell us something about the struggle between modernity and tradition in *taijiquan* (and in Chinese society): the Chinese want to modernise, but they also want to be proud of their traditions and do not see a problem in mixing modern and ancient ingredients. Their interest is in progress, but they do not want total capitulation in favour of Western views and ways. Yet they do not refuse Westernisation to a certain extent. It is a similar process as that which is taking place at this time in other areas of Chinese (urban) society and in other elements of Chinese cultural heritage, such as Chinese medicine (Hsu 1999; 2001). Survival and co-existence of different types of *taijiquan* are the central theme.

During the next few decades China was thrown into turmoil: the 1930s, for instance, witnessed the fighting between the Nationalists and the Communists in a bloody and cruel civil war. Moreover, the Chinese continuously had to fight off Japanese attacks on their territory. Some books on *taijiquan* were still being published during this period and the spreading of the practice was continuously enhanced.[28]

The next big event in the modernisation of *taijiquan* came when, after the Communists had finally defeated the Nationalists, the new Chinese government saw some opportunities in the martial arts for guiding the people towards better health by daily exercise. A central national association for sports and physical education had been founded in the capital (Zhonghua Renmin Gongheguo Tiyu Yundong Weiyuanhui) and in 1956 they produced a simplified set of twenty-four movements (*jianhua taijiquan*) based on the older Yang standardised set. It had been thoroughly investigated and tuned to fit the purpose of popularising *taijiquan*. The original order of the movements had been rearranged, the many repetitious movements in the Yang set had been omitted, and everything was now divided in eight groups of three movements, making it easy to teach and easy to learn, remember and perform both for beginners and advanced age people. Nothing was left of the Taoist ritual contents, except for some names of positions, and by disrupting the structure of this exercise a lot of its main essence had disappeared. The 'purpose' of Taoist rituals[29] is to make the person executing them enter into contact with the 'ingredients' of the whole universe and communicate with it to transfer and generate 'essence' or essential power.[30] This practice was completely lost. But then, by this time most of the teachers (who had modernised their art) and practitioners (who were not 'real' disciples anyway) were probably unaware of this hidden secret of *taijiquan*, so, it was no big deal to them. The name *taijiquan* was altered: it became *taijicao* (the gymnastics of *taiji*). This reflects the fact that the officials wanted to create a new 'tradition', identified by a new name (they actually wanted to abolish the ancient or 'feudal' traditions).

In this stage of modern Chinese history, we see the government trying to make culture available to all the people. To be able to do so, culture needs to be simplified. One of the most striking examples of this policy is the simplification of the language. This time it is not simply about adapting the written language to the spoken one, as described before. This time the Chinese characters are under attack. Through consecutive campaigns several groups of characters were simplified into easier to write and remember characters (they have less strokes). Furthermore, a Chinese system of romanisation or transliteration was developed (based on the old Anglo-Saxon Wade-Giles system), which is introduced in schools, on signs in the streets, and so on. The possibility of changing Chinese characters into Western writing was under consideration, but finally cancelled, because of the impossibility to differentiate between the many homophonous characters.[31]

The same process of simplification was applied to the martial arts and *taijiquan* in particular, where complex movements and long routines (eighty-one or sometimes more than hundred movements were the habit) were replaced by simpler ones and were made easily 'digestible'. It had effects that were similar to the language simplifications: more people were moved to learn or use it, but the variation and beauty had suffered a lot and the lack of movements and repetitions made it a poor exercise for training one's memory.[32] The most fundamental problem is not the change of pattern or movements, but the fact that doing the routines does not teach the student the skills of *taijiquan*. Unless one practices the stances (fixed positions through which internal motion and transformation is stirred) for many years and many hours per day, nothing much changes.[33] The daily performance of the simplified (and even complex) set of movements may cause some improvement in cardiovascular activity and flexibility, but this is also the case with other types of exercise such as running and is not particular of the practice of *taijiquan*.[34] It was, however, quite suitable for beginners and people who lacked time and capacities and the suppleness to perform the original complex movements.

In a China that was recovering from half a century of violence the authorities did not want to support martial skills (unless they were used for defending the country). Martial arts were transformed into acrobatic or gymnastic routines with little practical use as far as self-defence was concerned. *Taijiquan* underwent the same reconstruction. Partner exercises were allowed and promoted, but officially had to become some kind of choreographic duet. All of this changed again in the 1980s, when contests again allowed for real martial applications and free fighting.[35] Political influence ruled over individual ideas in this modernisation of *taijiquan*. It is therefore of a totally different nature than the modernisations of the 1920s and 1930s. It mirrored the communist policy of getting a hold on each individual and aiming for common and not individual goals. This is rather strange for a country that was based on individualistic philosophy and political rule during its dynastic history and until the Republican period (Fei 1992). The grip on the people was firm, but the influence of individual orientated lifestyles and views was not broken, not even by rigid measures and teachers of *taijiquan* kept on teaching their methods, secretly if necessary, to protect themselves and their tradition.

The individualistic nature of *taijiquan* should be stressed (it is after all an exercise for personal development) by referring to the work of a Chinese sociologist/anthropologist of the revolutionary period, Fei Xiaotong (1992), to discuss Chinese characteristics of individuality and modernity and create a broader perspective of the peculiar situation of Chinese society in this period and throughout the twentieth century in the last section of this chapter. Again it was Yang Chengfu who had mentioned the individual training and development of a student of *taijiquan*:

> Some people ask how many years it takes to learn *taijiquan* well. I say that even if [people] practice this boxing with the same intentions, we cannot speak about [them] in general terms. If a teacher transmits the boxing in the same way, each person's disposition and temperament are different. There are those who learn it well in one or two years, there are those who learn to understand it in three to five months, and there are also those who study for ten or twenty years and still don't understand. Good boxing doesn't depend on the height of the body, nor on one's age; it depends completely on one's capabilities to grasp it. ([1931] 1984: 141)

He added that he studied for fifteen years and still wanted to look for teachers. When teaching large classes of students, as was the case with the new boxing schools of Yang's time, little attention could be paid to each individual's progress. The accent had shifted from a more individual orientated method of teaching towards the instruction of large groups and under the communist rule of the 1950s through the 1980s the focus was on the masses. The approach of many *taijiquan* teachers and the official sports associations or organisations reflected this focus. In a way it helped them to gain social status and influence over large groups of people. Most of them probably enjoyed teaching masses as it created ways to feed their egos in times of wiping out of individualism and personal or family tradition.[36] It was the curious Chinese combination of serving the people and the state while at the same time serving one's own purposes.

After Deng Xiaoping's 1980s reforms, which stressed modernising and rendering Chinese culture more scientific, the individual's liberties were tolerated much more than before. The individuals did, however, need organisations to procure information and security. This led to the establishment of national, regional and local associations for the (scientific) research and instruction of *taijiquan* or some personal style of *taijiquan*. These associations gathered knowledge and material wherever they could get it, creating libraries and/or practical and theoretical information centres. They are modern day images of age-old guilds of people from the same line of trade that existed in imperial China and are still present in more traditional Chinese societies.

It is necessary to go back in time to explain the need for the creation of such associations. In the Ten Years of Great Chaos, as the Chinese used to call the period of the Cultural Revolution (1966–76),[37] China was disrupted in its traditional social structures, relations, education, traditions, knowledge, and so on. For *taijiquan*, which partly belonged to the 'feudal' world, this meant that traditional teaching was made impossible and that many books were destroyed and handwritten sources were burnt or had to be hidden underground. Taoism, which advocates freedom, was under severe suspicion and this definitely damaged the transmission of Taoist elements of the teaching. The associations that started to appear during the 1980s and 1990s provided relatively safe havens for practitioners, traditions and written and oral material. Through them some of the material that was unavailable during and after the Cultural Revolution has reappeared and investigations (organised by the association members) into different traditions has saved some from extinction. Some of the older material has been dug up (often to be taken literally) by individual masters and handed down to individual disciples. In some cases they have started teaching openly again.

The final phase of *taijiquan* evolution to be taken into consideration is the universal popularisation, which started in the 1970s. International politics played an indirect role in this event, with the US role proving to be crucial. As is commonly known, after the retreat from the mainland, the Guomindang established a republican government on Taiwan. They were aided by the Americans, who feared Red China and forged the rebellious, from the communist point of view, island into a major military stronghold. US advisers went to Taiwan to help stop the Red Danger. One of the advisers, a former marine and then CIA informant Robert Smith, developed an interest in Chinese martial arts. He befriended several traditional masters (i.e. modernised, Republican era type, teachers) of different traditions and studied with them. One of his friends was Zheng Manqing (1900–1975), who had been a student of Yang Chengfu. Through Smith's writings[38] and translations of Zheng's works, interest in *taijiquan* began to grow in the United States. Zheng finally went to the United States to teach. And as history tends to repeat itself he changed the teaching: he created a personal simplified set of movements (thirty-seven movements this time), which retained more of the original characteristics of Yang's set, but nevertheless was tailored to fit the Westerners' mentality.

The growing popularity of other martial arts such as karate and the Hong Kong kung fu movie industry certainly helped to sell *taijiquan* to the public. As a 'soft and easy' martial art it especially appealed to the participants in the

Flower Power movement. It further lost its martial characteristics and became a Chinese gymnastics and ecstatic exercise, beneficial to young and old, and promising prospects of fine health and bliss with little investment. When the power seemed to leave the flower, the New Age took over and we can now find a prospering New Age *taijiquan* society, whose members are only interested in forgetting their daily worries by doing *taiji* gymnastics. While *taijiquan* (or *taijicao* to be more precise) was spreading in the United States and US- based teachers started conquering the world of potential *taijiquan* clients, China was trying to get out of its isolation. Once it had opened up, Mainland China began to participate in cultural missionary activities throughout the world. *Taijiquan* and *shaolinquan* became the main export products emerging from the martial arts storehouse.

Meanwhile, serious Western practice and scientific research was stimulated first by the publication of the work of French sinologist Catherine Despeux on *taijiquan* (mainly based on information from Taiwan), and the author's pioneering fieldwork in Mainland China and his PhD thesis on the internal school of Chinese martial arts, of which *taijiquan* is the most famous representative. Several researchers (mostly anthropologists and a few sinologists) are working on studies about different aspects of *taijiquan* now, and we may expect some publications in this field of studies soon. Popular literature is already easily available, but most of the time the contents have little to offer to the serious student.

Yang *taijiquan* profited most from the spreading and it has become the most widely practised form of *taijiquan* around the world. The other styles try to follow in its steps but they are less successful. The simplification process of *taijiquan* seems to have stopped, but not only the Yang style has lent itself to simplification, because simplifications of other styles have emerged since the 1980s (Kan 1984 and Men 1984). Chinese and international contests are being organised with the purposes of further awakening interest in the practice and creating opportunities for practitioners to meet and learn from each other. These contests offer possibilities to demonstrate one's skill at executing *taijiquan* sets or at beating an opponent in *tuishou* ('pushing hands') and *sanshou* ('scattering hands') competitions.[39]

From its founding at the end of the Qing rule, *taijiquan* has been struggling through several attempts at modernisation. The first, at the end of the 1920s, managed to standardise movements but also left the complexity of the hidden Taoist rituals intact. It introduced new ways of teaching that co-existed with the old ones. The second aimed at massive popularisation and became a thorough simplification, ending in loss of contents and effects and disruption of the traditional teaching methods. The third allowed for the emergence of new kinds of associations, with the survival of some almost destructed material and traditions as a direct effect, while at the same time aiming at internationalisation, with loss of cultural characteristics and disrespect with many (especially Western) people as the immediate result and possibilities to investigate and rediscover as an indirect consequence. The description of this evolution should make it clear to the reader that modernity, identity, diversity and culture are complex matters, especially in China, but it also offers perspectives for their investigation in a comparative way.

Modern Traditionalists and Reformers

In order to enable the reader to get a clear picture of *taijiquan* evolution and transmission in China in the past twenty-five years, I recount here some of the experiences I had when practising with and interviewing some *taijiquan* masters. My main focus is on my fieldwork in Shanghai in 1985 and 1986. My informants were well-known teachers in Shanghai and China (and in the case of Cai even abroad). I did not study *taijiquan* with Cai, but while he was teaching me *xingyiquan* (the boxing of the body and the imaginative capacities), he was also supervising (Chinese) *taijiquan* students, and I could observe his similar approach. It is customary for disciples to express one's gratitude to one's teachers by publishing one's experiences with them. By writing this, I am partially fulfiling this obligation. As a scientist, however, I feel I should write about them not in the usual praising way, but in a critical way. I have used their real names without alterations.

The first teacher I met was Zhou. He was a short, strong man with a temper, probably in his forties, who liked fighting. He taught *xinyiliuhequan*,[40] *sanda*[41] and *taijiquan* at the Jingwu Tiyuhui (Essential Martial Arts Physical Education Association, a physical education centre founded in 1910 as Jingwu Ticao Xuexiao, Essential Martial Arts Gymnastics School) on Sichuan Road in Central Shanghai (Xi 1985: 180–81). I went to look for him after seeing an ad for *xingyiquan* courses in a local newspaper.[42] The thing to do if one wanted to take courses was *baoming* (to register), which I did, as a student of *xinyiliuhequan* at the office of the Jingwu Tiyuhui. When I later met the teacher and asked him to become his student, he probably felt both honoured (accepting his first Western student would bring him the respect and jealousy of his colleagues and fame in China and abroad) and suspicious about how this westerner had found out about him. I had to come again before he let me participate. The courses started at six in the morning and took about an hour and a half. His teaching was a mixture of traditional training and modern methods, spiced by his own character. My fellow students and I were taught stances, single repetitious movements, and applications first (after doing warm-up exercises, which were left to the design of the students). This is a traditional method. I frequently asked him to tell me the names of the movements we did, but he was reluctant to do so (but finally did tell me). His comments on the movements were brief, to the point, and aided by the repositioning of our stances. Most of the time he would talk Shanghainese, with some selected remarks in southernised *putonghua* (standard Chinese speech) in my direction. Sometimes he would use explanations of a physiological nature, in which he mixed modern Chinese medical views[43] and Westernised physical education knowledge. He wanted us to become tough fighters, being able to put up with punches and kicks, and therefore included applications in his courses. We were urged to spend a lot of time practising and taking other courses he taught. During a private interview he proudly showed me photographs of his feats and skills, and assumed I would follow suit.[44] After some time he found me talented enough to learn other techniques as well and invited me to his evening courses. In the morning he stayed on to teach me special fighting techniques and *shaolinquan* (which he also introduced in his morning courses of *xinyiliuhequan*), and the Chen and Wu styles of *taijiquan*. Sometimes he sparred with me (the sparring was mainly based on Western boxing and Chinese kicking and wrestling techniques).

In return he wanted to learn English from me and started dreaming of a career in the West for me (I would be the 'great king of Chinese martial arts' in the West) and for himself as my teacher. Our sessions lasted long after the Chinese students had gone (some days until ten in the morning). I brought another Western student along and indirectly opened up the road towards the Jingwu Tiyuhui for other foreign students. When I told Zhou I had also found other teachers, he started to look for them (without my knowing) and when he had found them, discussed their teaching me. In his view, they were not well suited. One day another teacher was teaching *xinyiliuhequan* at the Jingwu Tiyuhui, when Zhou was teaching us. He made remarks on the other teacher's style as being not 'traditional' or 'original', and referred to his own teacher as an official representative of the *xinyiliuhequan* tradition. Zhou's *taijiquan* was modernised. It was standardised much more than his *xinyiliuhequan* was: he taught the standardised sets of movements and *tuishou*, but these techniques were not about learning the essence, but about learning how to participate in the new contests. It was crucial to be able to dislodge the opponent from his place with just any means available, and this meant that traditional techniques were sometimes replaced with new effective inventions. Zhou seemed to have little knowledge of the internal work and the classical texts (he never referred to them). His demonstrations of *taijiquan* did not strike me with awe, nor did they resemble the image of *taijiquan* described in the classics. However, as a former champion of all China, he was a good fighter.

Shen (born 1939) was another type of person. He was a more cultivated man than Zhou. His father had worked for the French, when they had ruled one of Shanghai's foreign concessions, and he was living with part of his family in his paternal house in this former foreign area. He had started but not finished studies in chemistry, but boasted knowledge of Western science. His knowledge of *taijiquan* was profound. He knew some of the classics and did demonstrate special skills mentioned in these classics in a way I had never seen. The internal work was clearly there. His main teacher was Yue Huanzhi, a professor at Shanghai's Zhendan University[45] and a disciple of Dong Yingjie, the friend and disciple of Yang Chengfu. He must have been talented because he did not study long with this teacher (there was some major distrust towards Shen it seems among his fellow students).[46] Shen said that he had improved his teacher's style in some respects[47] and created a *qigong* (Chinese health and meditation exercises) method based on *taijiquan* and a mixture of Taoist and Lamaist exercises, oral teachings and his Western scientific knowledge.[48] He mainly perceived himself as a Chinese physician (he used his *qigong* knowledge to treat patients)[49] and a Buddhist, but was also proud of his Taoist backgrounds (his grandfather belonged to the famous *Longmen* tradition, he told me) (Esposito 1993). He had forgotten some of the movements of the sets of his Yang *taijiquan*, but was a pure traditionalist in the way he taught me and had had a complete training, including *tuishou*, *sanshou*, and traditional weapons training.[50]

None of my other *taijiquan* teachers were able to perform *taijiquan* as well (i.e. reflecting the ideal presented in the classics) as Shen did. Therefore, I spent a lot of time with him during my fieldwork in China and afterwards invited him to stay with me in Belgium and provide me with further instruction. He called himself a scholar but was, however, unable to separate fact from fiction (also a traditional Chinese problem), and enjoyed manipulating his students to a high degree for the purpose of enhancing his prestige. In this he reflected (and consciously imitated) a traditional Taoist boxing master, who gathered students in public places and through trance induction made them demonstrate his manipulative skills. His teaching was extremely intensive (stance practice lasted hours) and quick to deliver spectaculars results (I could use the same manipulative powers after a few months). In general he taught public courses in schools and sports centres, and instructed me in the privacy of his room. When he thought I had enough skill to demonstrate he took me to public parks where he used me to show off. Shen's teaching a foreigner and having been able to instruct him with the most refined skills of *taijiquan* gave him a lot of prestige and attracted large crowds of spectators and new patients for his practice. Often we read classical Taoist texts and he gave me his commentaries and explications of dark passages, a traditional way of teaching the theory of practices. The peculiarity of his type of *taijiquan* transmission was the rigid adherence to traditional teaching methods while at the same time explaining physical and internal effects by means of traditional methods (through reading texts and presenting commentaries) and (his own interpretation) of Western biochemistry. He did not like the official modernisations and standardisations, but frequently stressed the revolutionary nature of his own improvements on the tradition. He was both critical and admiring in his attitude towards his teacher and the Yang tradition in general and I learnt a lot of 'secret' gossiping from him.

My third teacher was Cai (born 1928). I nicknamed him 'Mr. Millimetre'. He had inherited a family tradition of martial arts, called *huaquan*, which is a northern style of *waijia* (external school), but he also learnt the internal school's *xingyiquan* and *taijiquan*. A Chinese friend of mine organised my private courses of *xingyiquan* with him. These took place in the big practising hall of the Shanghai Tiyu Xueyuan (Academy of Physical Education).[51] He was a professor of *wushu* (martial arts) at this academy and quite famous because of his defeating a Russian and an American boxer in the 1940s. He had been involved in the official revisions of *wushu* in the People's Republic and was quite an influential figure in official circles. Besides teaching his students he also published several books on the practice of *wushu*.[52] I could only study for a few months with him, because he was called back to Beijing in 1986, to become the vice head of the newly established Zhongguo Wushu Yanjiuyuan (Chinese Wushu Research Institute).

To me, Cai was the epitome of a sports teacher: having a somewhat military body posture, instructing his students in a direct manner, using little words and little praise and spending relatively almost no attention to the philosophical or other backgrounds. The practise had to be precise, in his opinion, and he kept correcting my positions until they were right up to one millimetre. He only taught standard sets and repetitions of single movements, which I had to repeat for an hour and a half until my legs felt like those of an elephant. They were private sessions, but sometimes there would simultaneously be one other student under his guidance for personal instruction of *taijiquan*. His lessons showed me how the modernised and standardised *taijiquan* (and in my case *xingyiquan*) was transmitted. It recalled memories of physical education lessons at my secondary school. Whereas I had a close personal contact with the previous two teachers, my contacts with Cai were of a reserved nature. I did not get the time to discuss things with him or ask many questions. He did not seem to think highly of foreigners and was full of national pride. One day he saw me talk to a fellow Chinese American student at Fudan University, who also had private courses (I think they were tennis lessons) at the Tiyu Xueyuan, he told him that he should have been the one who practised this gem of Chinese martial culture. I do not think he felt sorry to leave me on my own when he was called away. This is representative for courses and teachers educated or teaching at official state institutes of high reputation. There is a constant atmosphere of distance (teachers and students were of a different 'nature'), nationalism and politics, which I never experienced with my other teachers, who considered me more of a friend than a student.[53]

The last teacher I want to mention is my *taijiquan* teacher at Fudan University. To my regret I cannot recall his name, but he was an amiable and well-trained sports teacher. *Taijiquan* (*taijicao*) was just one of the sports he taught, and while he executed the movements as they should be executed according to the official standardisation, he was honest enough to admit that he actually did not really know *taijiquan* that well. His job was to teach *taijiquan* morning courses to foreign students at Fudan. At the beginning we were probably about twenty or more to attend his classes, but numbers dwindled quickly (probably because of the early hour). The first thing he taught us was the simplified set of twenty-four movements. When this was finished, he had very few students left, but still agreed on teaching the longer standardised set of eighty-eight movements.[54] I tried to get some information about *taijiquan* from him, but he said he was not really into it, and could only comment on my progress. In the end only a handful of students were left and he asked me to continue teaching the others, as I was obviously well acquainted with the matter. Finally there were just two of us students practising the sets that he had taught us. I never saw him again.

Some of them I met again later on to study some more or interview them, but the most intensive period was during my stay at Fudan University. These four people seem to me representative for the different types of teachers one can find in Shanghai, and maybe the whole of Mainland China. I did have other teachers but did not spend enough time with them to merit a discussion here.

I did not study with teachers from Taiwan, but from conversations with some Taiwanese teachers and with Taiwanese people in general I am convinced that there would have been differences between mainland masters and their supposedly more traditional counterparts on Taiwan (see Despeux 1981 for information on Taiwanese *taijiquan*).

Modernity, Identity, Culture, Diversity and Context: A Famous Collection of Fragile Chinaware

From what we have seen so far it should be obvious that modernity, identity and culture are quite diverse and should be read as plurals. During the tumultuous history of the twentieth century in China several types of *taijiquan* traditions were continued or discontinued. As far as teachers are concerned, I think they make individual choices and once they have made up their mind stick to it. Few are left who defend their tradition against and prevent corruption from what contaminating source you may have. Most of the time they are hiding their inheritance from society or they are careful in letting others in on their secrets. Some do not care much for the others within the tradition and prefer to make up their own school. They are generally not much appreciated by the other teachers, especially not by those belonging to a clan or rigid tradition. Then there are those who do not care about tradition because they find these things to be evil, old-fashioned and even dangerous and a threat to modern Chinese society. They prefer to stick to a gymnastics type of *taijiquan*, which is supported by scientific research evidence of the benefits of such a standardised practice and by the physiological effects of the practice. Then there are some who seem to be balancing between all of these methods and who try to be eclectic (i.e. they take useful stuff from all).

Taijiquan itself went through several modernisations and standardisations. The main result is that incredible numbers of people all over the world know about *taijiquan* (usually it is actually some kind of *taijicao*) or practise something their teachers call *taiji* (most of the time wrongly spelt as 'tai chi'). As far as the contents of the original traditions are concerned, most of those were lost during the standardisations and modernisations. What we are dealing with now is, most of the time, very different from what was being practised at the beginning of the twentieth century.

The case of *taijiquan* presents us with a 'miniature model' of Chinese urban society. It also provides food for thought about Chinese culture and how to understand it. Westerners do not know much about China and often have difficulties in getting into contact with Chinese people. Taking *taijiquan* as an example, the Chinese seem to be able to get through to Westerners, especially if we consider the success of such a practice as *taijiquan* in the West and the amount of uncritical attention Chinese teachers of *taijiquan* get from Western students.[55] The main communication problem seems to lie with the West, not with China and may well have to do with our colonial attitude versus other cultures, and may be even our decolonialised but uninformed attitude of admiration, respect, and wonder. I share the opinion of Rik Pinxten that we, social scientists, ought to 'be fully aware of the theory- and culture-ladenness and of the interactional nature of research' and that any culture 'stands for a fully developed autonomous perspective on the world and should be studied accordingly' (1997: 88). Pinxten introduced the concept of 'root principles' (or 'cultural intuition') as a means to reach the goals of description of cultures and, utterly, comparison of cultures. He holds the belief that 'any . . . type of knowledge is based on, and is to a large extent unified by deeper and vaguer insights' (Pinxten 1997: 89). For Chinese culture he refers to the *yinyang* philosophy, which indeed is a very fundamental characteristic of the mind and actions of the Chinese. I fear, however, that this root principle is often not well understood. It should be understood to grasp the ideas behind *taijiquan*, which is the practice of this principle, and to be able to dig into different forms of society and culture in China throughout the ages.

The full extent of the *yinyang* 'concept' is complicated. To the Chinese it is not really a 'concept'; it is a fundamental observation of Nature's doings. Its meaning shows us a natural phenomenon: a mountain slope. When the sun shines on one side of the mountain, it is called *yang*. When clouds gather above the mountain or when it gets dark, this is called *yin*. These are not stable conditions, they change all the time and have characteristics that are called cyclic 'repetition' and 'exchange'. Every day and night things seem to happen in somewhat similar ways, but yet they are never exactly the same. This is the very essence of this view on the world: never-ending cyclic repetition with manifold variations caused by sun- and moonlike actors (this is the very meaning of what the Chinese call *yi* or change).[56] Action in this perspective is what the Chinese consider evident. Stagnation is problematic. And yet we in the West have this idea about Chinese culture as if it has remained the same during thousands of years. Research and fieldwork by mainly anthropologists or anthropologically inspired sinologists start to change this erroneous view. The Westerners also have an idea that Chinese society under the communist rule did not allow for personal freedom and caused only repression of the individual. As has been demonstrated through the case of *taijiquan* this is not true. In other cases I have investigated (such as Chinese medicine) this also proves not to be true.

Fei Xiaotong (1992) discusses a 'diversified way of association' as a characteristic of Chinese society. He stresses the combination of an individual orientated society and networks organised by social relationships. But Fei is a Republican period writer, whose view of China reflects Guomindang, Confucianist, and Christian/Western influences. He does not write about the disruption during the communist rule of social relationships. Nevertheless, I find his view fundamentally right, in as much as it shows the cohabitation of 'opposites' or what in a Western dualistic view would be seen as conflicting ideas or circumstances. It shows the unity of *yinyang* (I use *yinyang* as one word to reflect this)[57] as being present in Chinese society. As this chapter demonstrates, throughout the evolution of *taijiquan* and its masters, these 'conflicting' situations are always present: the individualists, the communists, the reformers, the traditionalists, the modernisers, the contra revolutionaries and so on. They are all present at all the time, living together and creating the power of transformation of Chinese society. This power is the exteriorisation of the *yinyang* root principle. Looking at China from this perspective we get a better view, or at least a more complete view. It can, in the end, maybe make us understand that it is the multitude of seemingly conflicting ideas and individuals that make our lives and societies so interesting. In *taijiquan* the essence is the co-operation of opposing components and the resolving of conflicts by preventing them to move to their extremes through rightly timed adjustment to the forces that are already there. We cannot but live with different views, beliefs, cultures and personalities. Seen from the *taiji* point of view, we should not accentuate the differences in people and societies or cultures, but look for the one principle that like a string runs through all.[58] I advocate that understanding the root principles of different cultures should bring us to understanding the very root principles of mankind. It is a very fragile world of chinaware we live in, but then, if we take good care of it, the chinaware can last for a very long time.

Notes

1. The Manchu people were 'invited in' by Chinese contesters of the Ming regime (1368–1644) to help them overthrow the ruling house. Once they were in, they liked it so much that they decided to stay and took over the power themselves. They kept some of their own traditions and customs and forced the Chinese to comply, but, in general, they became more Chinese in their ways as they continued to undergo the strong Chinese cultural influence.
2. The Taiping (Great Peace) Rebellion found its roots in the teaching of Hong Xiuquan (1814–1864) during the 1840s. Hong had studied Christianity and proclaimed himself 'the second son of God' and 'Jesus Christ's younger brother'. He was a Hakka (a Chinese minority group in the South of China) and created a doctrine based on ancient Chinese ingredients (such as peasant movements, secret societies, the universal peace [messianic] message of ancient Taoist origin, etc.) and simplified Christian religious concepts. After taking on the role of a political leader and establishing the Taiping Tianguo (the Heavenly Nation of Great Peace), he launched his followers on a path to civil war (from about 1852 to about 1868) and eventually destruction, when openly defying the Qing Dynasty.
3. These wars led to opening up Chinese 'treaty' ports for foreign investment, trade, and even (local) rule, as the Western powers and Japan, the already modernised Asian power, forced treaties on the Qing, who lost land concessions to their enemies in these ports and the capital.
4. They became forebodes of the warlords and their armies that were typical of post-revolutionary and pre-communist China.
5. By 'slavery' I refer to not being able to express one's will or to benefit from political rule. The Chinese peasants were in a certain way still able to influence political rule. In many cases the fall of a certain dynasty and the rise of another one was the result of peasant uprisings (frequently caused by famine or other more or less natural disasters). Often the leader of the revolt became the first emperor of the new dynasty. The peasants were usually let down, once the leader had obtained his goals.
6. It should be made clear here that I do not think that modernity started with the end of the Qing or that revolutionary thought or action in China only started in the nineteenth century. We can find enough proof of modernisation, technological (r)evolutions, and philosophical revolutionary thought and so on through China's history. Needham's gigantic *Science and Civilisation in China* provides enough proof of China's inventions, modernisations and so on. To keep things simple I focus in this chapter on the evolution of *taijiquan* and the revolutionary

period of the nineteenth to the twenty-first century. I also tend to disagree with those who consider the latter half of the Qing rule to be a period of only standstill or fallback. This may be true in general for Chinese culture and technology, but is certainly not the case in some respects, such as the revolution caused by growing Western influence on different fields of science. Martial arts also kept on developing during the nineteenth century and maybe reached their zenith with the fall of the Qing.

7. The word *wu*, meaning 'martial', is a homophone of the word for dancing. One of the older words for martial arts is *wuyi*, which literally translates as martial arts, whereas the modern *wushu* refers to martial techniques (Xi 1985: 59 ff.).
8. For an explanation of the basic meaning of *yin* and *yang*, and their associative meanings, see Vercammen 1995: 166–67 in Van Alphen and Aris and the last chapter of this article.
9. Instead of viewing Chinese culture as one monolithic mass, one should look at China and its culture as one whole with different cultures in its diverse parts. The cultural heritage of Southern China is very different from that of the North. The different climates and geographies created different evolutions. People used to have different physiognomy (before the age of modern communication and travelling infrastructure) and they used to speak different languages (the Chinese language and dialects of the North are maybe even more different from those of the South than English is from German) in different regions (the official standardisation of the Chinese language solves this 'problem'). Traditions of any kind show many local characteristics or may only exist locally.
10. Modernisation and innovation in Chinese medicine has been studied by several scholars such as E. Hsu's *Innovation in Chinese Medicine* (2001). Hsu (1999) had also written on the transmission of Chinese medicine, which deals with the transmission of *qigong* (a general name for a multitude of Chinese systems to promote health through physical and psychological exercises). *Taijiquan* incorporates a lot of *qigong* practice and is therefore also linked with Chinese Medicine and its transmission (see Vercammen 2000: 64–79). In 1985–86 I engaged in the same kind of fieldwork as Hsu, but came to somewhat different results, as far as *qigong* is concerned. I made comparable observations for modern *taijiquan* transmission, discussed in this chapter.
11. There are two Wu traditions. The characters of the family names are different in Chinese, but spelt in the same way in transcription.
12. This was mainly due to the publication of some 'evidence', which upon closer inspection does not stand. See Vercammen 2002.
13. See Vercammen 1990 for a description of the three systems.
14. As was customary in the West, China also introduced modern photography and photographer's studios. Famous *taijiquan* master Yang Chengfu (1883–1936) had photographs of movements, performed by his students, made for his books in a studio against the then popular background of a painted forest scene (Yang, C. [1931] 1984: 69–70). He demonstrates the movements of his *taijiquan* himself against a curtain as the background in the same book.
15. The problem became even bigger later on, when the Communists introduced simplification of the written characters, and classical Chinese was reserved for very few experts. Most young Chinese now are unable to read the classical literature (but translations into modern written language and simplified characters are sometimes being made), especially if it is written in complex characters (texts in classical Chinese are sometimes republished in simplified characters). I recall an anecdote in 1985 when I was studying at Shanghai Fudan University, when my Chinese roommate called in all of his classmates to watch this strange foreigner read classical Chinese texts, something which they were unable to do.
16. For a clear picture of the *qi* concepts, see Vercammen 2000.
17. We know of two-dimensional charts, inscribed drawings on stone or wood, and paintings on paper or silk, dating from earlier periods than the Song, and three-dimensional representations of the body (usually models of a man in bronze) from the Song on. Examples of these types of representations can be found in Vercammen 1995: 156–96.
18. A description and translation of some of the contents of Chen's book may be found in Despeux 1981: 217–66.

19. *Taijiquan* is meant here. It used the Taoist idea of becoming as soft (and as powerful) as water as a principle of its martial art.
20. Chen Changxing (1771–1853) was Yang Luchan's main teacher. Luchan was Yang Chengfu's grandfather. *Taijiquan* was partly based on Chen Changxing's sets of movements.
21. His elder brother, Yang Shaohou, died in 1930.
22. Yang Chengfu became ill when he was travelling in the southern parts of China. He could not take the food and humid climate. He died in 1936. I thank the Dong family for providing me with information on this matter.
23. Wudang is the name of a famous mountain range in Hunan province. It is a Taoist mountain: many Taoist masters resided there, and it has several Taoist monasteries and temples. The legendary founder of *taijiquan*, Zhang Sanfeng, stayed there, and is said to have 'discovered' *taijiquan* by watching the fight between a bird and a snake. He then took the evading movements of these animals as the basis of his new martial art and defeated many bandits with it the very next day. Another story tells us that a mythological Taoist emperor, Xuanwu, taught him *taijiquan* in a dream. The results were the same: the bandits were all killed. Zhang Sanfeng is the patron saint of the Taoist school of martial arts (Vercammen 1990).
24. This type of sword (with a straight edge) is used in many Taoist rituals. It is probably the oldest kind of sword in China (figurines representing military officers from the tomb of the first emperor and of the later Han dynasty carry this type).
25. It contains explanations of the movements, but no photographs, only drawings, written by Yao Fuchun and Jiang Rongqiao and published in Shanghai in 1930. It contains a foreword by Li Jinglin, dated 1929 (Yao and Jiang [1930] 1988, 'Li Jinglin's Preface,' 1), and another preface by Li Li, who seems to have been a Taoist and therefore refers to the Taoist principles of *taijiquan* in his text (Yao and Jiang, 'Li Li's Preface,' 1–2).
26. In the first quarter of the twentieth century a Chinese historian named Tang Hao started a modern investigation of the origin and development of *taijiquan*. He was joined by some later on, and contested by others. See Vercammen 2002.
27. The book of Yang Chengfu was actually written by Dong Yingjie, his literate friend and student.
28. Some Japanese travelled in China during this period and gathered knowledge and techniques from the Chinese. This was also the case for the martial arts. Japanese forms of *budo* (ways of the warriors) such as judo and aikido were developed by people who had learnt Chinese techniques (*shuaijiao* or Chinese wrestling and *taijiquan* respectively).
29. It can be argued whether rituals do have a 'purpose'. See Pinxten 2000: 115–19 and Staal 1989. The result of doing Taoist rituals is the realisation of communication with the universe, quite often by 'walking on stars'. This ritualistic way of moving is a very ancient practice, and is originally ascribed to Yu the Great, a so-called Culture Hero, who is considered to be the 'inventor' of the Chinese systems of water control (e.g. building dikes and irrigation channels). The Taoist Canon (Daozang), a most important collection of Taoist texts (published in 1445), and many other Taoist texts or text collections contain descriptions and/or drawings of ritual walking patterns. For certain Taoist rituals, see Lagerwey 1987.
30. 'Essence' refers to the pure and refined essential powers stored in each part of the universe and in the universe as a whole. The performer of the rituals and her/his universe become one in her/his own body.
31. When observing Chinese in conversation, one frequently sees them write something with their index finger on the palm of their hand. This happens when the other person does not understand to which word s/he is referring. The most obvious way is to 'write' it on one's hand to make the other read it. Without referring to the characters (if they had been abolished) the only other way would be to use sign language, which takes much more time and often does not necessarily lead to the other understanding what one means.
32. Practising the long sets of *taijiquan* requires a steady concentration, not only because of the amount of movements to remember, but especially because of the repetition of some sequences of movements. Because after such repetitions other movements follow, it is easy to 'get lost' if one does not pay attention to the right order. One may end up getting stuck in doing the same movements over and over again until one remembers the following steps.

33. A lot can change if one practices the stances diligently. In *taijiquan* terminology this is called '*qi* being stored in the bones'. It shows externally by making rapid and extreme changes of muscle tension possible (one can be as soft as a newborn baby and hard as a rock), by being able to absorb the energy of a kick or punch without suffering pain or injury. Internally all functions are working more economically and the body's resistance to pathogenic influences is greatly increased (this author's own experience and his investigation of masters and students of Yang style taught in traditional ways).
34. Experiments in China and the United States show several (minor) changes in the body's functioning (see, e.g. *Journal of Psychosomatic Research* 1989 33[(2]): 197–206). We may, however, seriously doubt the use of this kind of experiments for several reasons. I can sum up some of the problems: the way *taijiquan* is done in different experiments is not standard, almost everyone does it differently, and therefore, it is very hard to come to scientifically acceptable results; the amount of research is limited and does not suffice to lead to conclusive results; the way *taijiquan* is practised in general is very different from the way it was intended to be practised and people sticking to the prescribed essentials (such as those recorded by Yang Chengfu and others) are rarely seen.
35. Before going to China for the first time in 1985, I had been practising Chinese martial arts with Yu Guanxiu (Jie Kon-sieuw), a traditional Chinese teacher originating from Surinam, who taught southern Chinese martial arts. This training involved practical applications and full and semi-contact fighting. When I studied with Zhou Minde, once a *taijiquan* champion, in Shanghai's famous Jingwu Tiyuhui his students were still inexperienced in contact fighting compared with me, as this type of training had just been opened up.
36. Several of my *taijiquan* teachers/informants were very proud to teach large groups. One even boastingly told me that in the 1960s he taught over 1,000 people in a public park in Shanghai and that his audience was larger than that of a famous Buddhist teacher. To him it was a matter of quantity and not so much of quality.
37. These are the traditional dates, but the influence of this chaotic phase of the Chinese revolution lasted at least until the early 1980s and some disastrous results can still be seen today (teenagers in this period did not get education and lack certain acquired skills necessary to survive in a modern information technology world).
38. Smith wrote about Japanese, Chinese, and oriental martial arts. On Chinese martial arts he published, among other works, *Chinese Boxing, Masters and Methods* (1980) and, together with Zheng Manqing, *T'ai-Chi, the 'Supreme Ultimate' Exercise for Health, Sport and Self-Defense*. Some information on *taijiquan* is included in Donn F. Draeger and Smith, *Asian Fighting Arts* (1969). A recent interview by R. Mason with Smith was published in the *Journal of Asian Martial Arts* (Mason 2001).
39. *Tuishou* uses fixed and free patterns of four basic *taijiquan* techniques; *sanshou* allows for free application of any *taijiquan* technique.
40. *Xinyiliuhequan* (the six co-ordinates boxing of the mind and the imaginative capacities) is a tradition of *xingyiquan* (the boxing of the body and the imaginative capacities) that originated in Henan province and was mainly practised by Chinese Muslims. *Xingyiquan* is one of the three forms of the so-called internal school of Chinese martial arts. See Vercammen 1990 for a history and analysis of *xingyiquan*.
41. *Sanda* is a kind of free fighting, which includes ingredients from different kinds of Chinese martial arts and Western boxing. As such it is also a good example of modernisation in the martial arts.
42. I have described my first visits to the Jingwu Tiyuhui in 'Transmitting the Way of Qi', Vercammen 2000: 68 n. 2.
43. Modern Chinese medical knowledge is based on Western medical knowledge, much more than on traditional Chinese knowledge. See Vercammen 1995: 157 and Hsu 1999.
44. Some pictures showed him bare-chested as he was absorbing kicks and punches from other people. During the lessons he frequently demonstrated his skill to absorb the power of a punch by hitting his own face (a funny sight, but no marks were left).
45. Later renamed Fudan University.

46. Interviews with other *taijiquan* informants and with master Li, an older student of Yue's made it clear that Shen was considered an outcast and that he was therefore not particularly liked.
47. He probably did so openly and this is something that is not done in a traditional environment.
48. A younger colleague and former student in martial arts of mine wrote an MA thesis on Shen's style. See Esposito 1995.
49. See Hsu 1999 for her similar experience with *qigong* practitioners.
50. He tried to recover some of his knowledge through my collection of books and by watching me doing my sets training.
51. The Tiyu Xueyuan can be compared to a Western university's physical education department.
52. He published a series of books on *huaquan* (Cai [1957] 1983) and some of his books were translated into English. A short biography can be found in Fang et al. 1987: 224.
53. They did make political remarks and were proud of their Chinese heritage, but expressed these feelings in warm, personal discussions, not in a reserved and distant manner.
54. This set was developed as the standardised set of Yang style *taijiquan* during the Communist rule, and was the main one that was used at the so-called form-contests (demonstrating one's skill in performing this and other sets).
55. On several occasions I witnessed small-scale 'experiments'. I remember one Dutch Chinese teacher of martial arts, who when I came to know him first, did not like *taijiquan* and preferred to teach other more spectacular styles. When *taijiquan* became popular, I found out that he participated in massive demonstrations as master X from Shanghai, expert of *taijiquan*. Very few people doubted this.
56. Thesis defended by this author at his PhD defence (Vercammen 1990).
57. Chinese dictionaries of the dialectics orientated toward People's Republic usually write it as *yin-yang*.
58. Vercammen (1989: 51). 'Taiji Quanjing' (The Canon of Taijiquan). This passage quotes from Confucian doctrine.

References

Cai, L. 1957 [1983]. *Yilu Huaquan* (First Routine of *Huaquan*). Beijing: Renmin Tiyu Chubanshe.
Carr, C. 1991. *The Devil Soldier*. New York: Random House.
Chen, W. 1925. *Taijiquanshu* in Yang, C., in C. Yang et al. [1931] 1984. *Taijiquan Xuan Bian*, Beijing: Zhongguo shudian.
Chen, X. [1933] 1986 (facsimile). *Chenshi Taijiquan Tushuo* (An Illustrated Explanation of Chen Clan *Taijiquan*). Shanghai: Shanghai Shudian.
Chen, Z. and Ma, Y. (eds.) 1935 (facsimile s.d.). *Wu Jianquan Shide Taijiquan* (The *Taijiquan* of Wu Jianquan). Hong Kong: Jinhua Chubanshe.
Cheng, M. and R.W. Smith. 1967. *T'ai-Chi*. Rutland: Charles E. Tuttle.
Despeux, C. 1981. *Taiji Quan, art martial, technique de longue vie*. Paris: Guy Trédaniel.
Dong, Y. [1948] 1989. *Taijiquan Shiyi* (The Meaning of *Taijiquan* Explained), 9th ed. Hong Kong: Private publishing.
Draeger, D.F. and R.W. Smith. 1969. *Asian Fighting Arts*. Tokyo: Kodansha International.
Esposito, M. 1993. 'La porte du Dragon: L'école Longmen du Mont Jingai et ses pratiques alchimiques d'après le Daozang xubian (suite au canon taoïste)', Ph.D. dissertation. Paris: Université Paris VII.
———. 1995. *Il qigong: La nuova scuola taoista delle cinque respirazioni*. Padova: Muzzio
Fang, J. et al. 1987. *Zhonghua Wushu Cidian* (Lexicon of Chinese Wushu). Anhui: Anhui Renmin Chubanshe.

Fei, X. 1992. *From the Soil, the Foundations of Chinese Society (a Translation of Fei Xiaotong's Xiangtu Zhongguo)*. London: University of California Press.
Gu, L. 1983. *Pao Chui* (Cannon Blow). Hong Kong: Haifeng Chubanshe.
Hsu, E. 1999. *The Transmission of Chinese Medicine*. Cambridge: Cambridge University Press.
—— (ed.). 2001. *Innovation in Chinese Medicine*. Cambridge: Cambridge University Press.
Kan, G. 1984. *Chenshi Jianhua Taijiquan Rumen* (Introduction to the Simplified Taijiquan of the Chen Clan). Hefei: Anhui Kexue Jishu Chubanshe.
Keown-Boyd, H. 1991. *The Fists of Righteous Harmony, a History of the Boxer Uprising in China in the Year 1900*. London: Leo Cooper.
Kong, J. 1988. *Zhongguo Yixue Shigang* (Outlines of the History of Chinese Medicine). Beijing: Renmin Weisheng Chubanshe.
Lagerwey, J. 1987. *Taoist Ritual in Chinese Society and History*. London: Collier Macmillan.
Li, T. (ed.). 1988. *Wudang Jueji—Miben Zhenben Huibian* (The Superb Skills of Wudang—A Compilation of the Secret and Authentic Books). Jilin: Jilin Kexue Jishu Chubanshe.
Mason, R. 2001. 'Fifty Years in the Fighting Arts: An Interview with Robert W. Smith', *Journal of Asian Martial Arts* 10(1): 36–73.
Men, H. 1984. *Sishibashi Taijiquan Rumen* (Introduction to the Forty-Eight Positions Taijiquan). Hefei: Anhui Kexue Jishu Chubanshe.
Michael, F. 1966. *The Taiping Rebellion, History and Documents*. Seattle and London: University of Washington Press.
Pinxten, R. 1997. *When the Day Breaks, Essays in Anthropology and Philosophy*. Frankfurt: Peter Lang.
——. 2000. *Goddelijke Fantasie*. Antwerp: Houtekiet.
Seidel, A. 1970. *A Taoist Immortal of the Ming Dynasty: Chang San-feng* in De Bary, W.T. et al. (eds.), *Self and Society in Ming Thought*. London: Columbia University Press, pp. 483–531.
Shaughnessy, E.L. 1998. *I Ching, the Classic of Changes*. New York: Ballantine Books.
Smith, R.W. 1980. *Chinese Boxing, Masters and Methods*. New York: Kodansha International.
Spence, J. 1996. *God's Chinese Son, the Taiping Heavenly Kingdom of Hong Xiuquan*. London: HarperCollins.
Staal, F. 1989. *Rules Without Meaning. Ritual, Mantras and the Human Sciences*. New York: Peter Lang.
Vercammen, D. 1982. 'Het in-het-geheim overgeleverde taijiquan van de Yang Familie', M.A. thesis. Ghent: Ghent University.
——. 1989. *Neijia Wushu, the Internal School of Chinese Martial Arts*, vol. 1, Ghent: Ghent University.
——. 1990. 'Neijia Wushu', Ph.D. dissertation. Ghent: Ghent University.
——. 1991. *The History of Taijiquan*. Antwerp: Dao.
——. 1995. 'Theory and Practice of Chinese Medicine', in J. Van Alphen and A. Aris (eds.), *Oriental Medicine*. London: Serindia, pp. 156–96.
——. 1998. *De handpalmtechnieken der acht trigrammen: geschiedenis, teksttraditie en geheimen der innerlijke Chinese vechtkunst*. Antwerp: Belgian Taoist Association.
——. 1999. *Taijiquan, de klassieke teksttraditie*. Antwerp: Dao.
——. 2000. 'Transmitting the Way of Qi', in D. Vercammen (ed.), *The Way of Qi*. Antwerp: Dao, pp. 64–79.

———. 2002. *The Mystery of* Taijiquan. Antwerp: Dao

Wang, Y. 1980. *Yangjia Michuan Taijiquan Tujie* (Illustrated Explanation of the Secretly Transmitted *Taijiquan* of the Yang Family), 2nd ed. Taibei: Private publishing.

Wilson, A. [1868] 1991. *The 'Ever-Victorious Army', a History of the Chinese Campaign under Lt.-Col. C. G. Gordon, C.B. R.E. and of the Suppression of the Tai-Ping Rebellion*. London: Lionel Leventhal Limited.

Xi, Y. 1985. *Zhongguo Wushu Shi* (History of Chinese Wushu). Beijing: Renmin Tiyu Chubanshe.

Xu, Z. [1927] 1984 (facsimile). *Taijiquan Qian Shuo* (A Superficial Explanation of *Taijiquan*), in C. Yang et al., *Taijiquan Xuan Bian*. Beijing: Zhongguo Shudian.

Yang, C. [1931] 1984 (facsimile). *Taijiquan Shiyong Fa* (Practical Methods of *Taijiquan*), in C. Yang et al., *Taijiquan Xuan Bian*, Beijing: Zhongguo Shudian.

Yao, F. and R. Jiang. [1930] 1988 (facsimile). *Taijiquan Jiangyi* (Talking about the Meaning of *Taijiquan*). Shanghai: Tianjinshi Guji Shudian.

Yu, G. 1999. *Jingxuan Taijiquan Cidian* (A Selective Lexicon of *Taijiquan*). Beijing: Renmin Tiyu Chubanshe.

Notes on Contributors

Simon Coleman is Jackman Chair at the Department of Religion, University of Toronto. His research interests include Pentecostalism, pilgrimage, material culture, hospital chaplaincy and the aesthetics of hospital space. His books include *The Globalisation of Charismatic Christianity* (2000), *Locating the Field: Space, Place and Context in Anthropology* (edited with Peter Collins, 2006) and *Multi-sited Ethnography: Problems and Possibilities in the Translocation of Research Methods* (edited with Pauline von Hellermann, 2011). He has conducted fieldwork in Sweden, Nigeria, the United Kingdom and the United States.

Peter Collins is Senior Lecturer in Anthropology at Durham University. His main interests are in religion, ritual and symbolism, Quakerism, aesthetics, space and place, historical anthropology and narrative analysis. His recent publications include: *Dislocating Anthropology? Bases of Longing and Belonging in the Analysis of Contemporary Societies* (edited with Simon Coleman, 2011), *The Ethnographic Self As Resource: Writing Memory And Experience Into Ethnography* (edited with A. Gallinat, 2010) and *Locating the Field: Space, Place and Context in Anthropology* (edited with Simon Coleman, 2006).

Lisa Dikomitis is Researcher at the Hull York Medical School. In 2010 she gained her PhD in Comparative Sciences of Cultures (i.e. social anthropology) at Ghent University (Belgium). Lisa Dikomitis has published widely about Greek and Turkish Cypriot refugees and is the author of *Cyprus and Its Places of Desire. Cultures of Displacement Among Greek and Turkish Cypriot Refugees* (IB Tauris, 2012). For her postdoctoral research Lisa Dikomitis ventured into medical anthropology with a special interest in primary care and mental health issues.

Bruno Drweski is Researcher and Lecturer at the Institut National en Langues et Cultures Orientales at Paris (France). His main focus is Polish language and political history. He published in different European languages on these issues and on the recent developments in former eastern Europe, especially those states which entered the European Union recently.

Renée Hirschon was educated at the Universities of Cape Town, Chicago, and Oxford. She was Senior Lecturer at Oxford Brookes University before becoming Professor and Chair of the Department of Social Anthropology and History at the University of the Aegean, Greece (1987-98). She is now Senior Research Fellow at St Peter's College, University of Oxford. She is also Senior Member of St Antony's College where she serves on the Advisory Committee of the European Studies Centre, and a long time Research Associate of the Refugee Studies Centre, Oxford University. Her many publications include *Heirs of the Greek Catastrophe* (2nd ed 1998), *Crossing the Aegean: An Appraisal of the 1923 Population Exchange between Greece and Turkey* (2003) and *Women and Property, Women as Property* (1984).

Rik Pinxten is Professor and Senior Researcher in Anthropology and Head of Department of Comparative Sciences of Culture at Ghent University (Belgium). His current research focus is on identity as a central mechanism in cultural and religious learning processes. He has published widely on the anthropology of knowledge and the comparative study of religion.

Marjo de Theije is Associate Professor at VU University and CEDLA. Recent publications include *Local Battles, Global Stakes. The Globalization of Local Conflicts and the Localization of Global Interests* (VU University Press, 2011).

Dan Vercammen is Professor of Chinese Culture, Arts and Medicine at China Arts College in Antwerp (Belgium) and researcher at the Taoist Alchemical Studies Center (Antwerp). He holds a PhD from Ghent University in Oriental Languages and History. His research focuses on Taoist alchemical and medical traditions and traditional Chinese arts. He has published widely on Chinese Medicine, Martial Arts and Taoism and frequently organizes conferences and seminars on these subjects.

Giorgos Vozikas is Researcher at the Hellenic Folklore Research Centre of the Academy of Athens. He received his PhD from the University of Athens in Folklore. His research focus is on symbolic systems, pilgrimage and local identity. He has participated in a number of international conferences and has published several articles including 'Miracle narrative and our Lady of Proussos' (*Narratives Across Space and Time: Transmissions and Adaptations,* forthcoming). He is a member of the Hellenic Folklore Society and of the American Folklore Society.

INDEX

A
Afro-Brazilian cults/religions, 98, 99, 102, 107
Aghia Marina. See St Marina
Agios Fanourios, 86-88
Anglicans, 56
architecture, 45, 48-50, 56, 60
Argyrou, V., 82, 93
Assembly of God, 100
associations, 66
Astyphilia. See Urbanisation
Athens, 4, 5, 8, 66
Augustine, vii

B
baptism, 7, 8, 10
baptismal certificate, 7, 8
baptismal name, 8
Bhagwan Shree Rajneesh, 104
birthday, 70, 73,
border, 80, 83
  crossings, 83-93
Bourdieu, P., 48, 50
Boxer Rebellion, 116
bride, 71, 74-76
Britain, 45-6, 51-5, 57-60
brotherhood, 101
buildings, 48-9, 51-2, 54-5, 60, 98, 99, 100, 105, 108, 109, 110
built environment, 45, 48-9
Byzantine, 5, 9

C
Cai (teacher), 132, 134-135
Candomblé, 99, 106
Castells, M., vii, 47
Catholicism, 99, 100, 101, 102, 103, 104, 105, 106, 107, 108, 109
Catimbó, 98, 106
Charismatic Catholics, 97, 109
Chen, Weiming, 124-125
Chicago School, 45-7
Chinese Republic, 116-117, 121-123, 129, 137
church, viii, ix, 4, 5, 6, 7, 8, 11, 13
  and community, 67
  and city, 67
  dedication of, 67-68
  and experience of space, 67-69
  foundation of, 67-68
  local, 69, 73, 75, 76
Church of Jesus Christ and the Later-day Saints, 98, 105
Church of Greece, 6, 7, 8, 13
city, vii-ix, 46-9, 55,
civil marriage/divorce, 7, 8
civil registration, 8, 14
civil registry office, 7, 8
communion, 70
Communism, 27, 117, 123, 127, 129-30, 137
Communitas, 77
community, 65, 67, 68, 69, 70, 72, 75, 76

culture, 66
  differences, 9
  folk, 67
  identity, 7
  literate, 65
  patterns, 7
  popular, 65
  resistance, 6
  rural, 75
  traditional, 67, 72
Cyprus, 79-93

D
dance, 72
Data Protection Act, 11, 14
death
  as birthday (for true life), 72-73
  as marriage (to Christ), 74-76
  See also marriage
decoration, 69, 70, 71, 75
Delaney, C., 80, 85, 93
Deus é Amor, 97
Dong, Yingjie, 125, 133
Dubisch, J., 82, 85-87, 93
Du Boulay, J., 87, 93
Dutch, 103
Dutch occupation, 101

E
eighteenth century, 45, 47, 50, 53, 55, 57, 60
emancipation of old religions, 98
Enlightenment, x
European integration, 4, 6, 13

F
Fei, Xiaotong, 137
festival, religious, 70-72
  cultural heritage, 72
  identity, 76
  interpretation of, 76
  local identity, 72
  national identity, 72
  official religion, 72-73
  popular religion, 72-73
  social function of, 76
  symbolic meaning of, 76
  See also panegyri

flag, 70, 71
Fudan University, 135

G
globalisation, 4, 6
God, 25
Graham, B., 36, 38, 42
Greece, 3-15, 65-77
Greek Civil code 7, 8

H
habitus, 50
Hart, L., 87-88, 93
Health and Wealth Movement, 34
Hellenic League for Human and Citizen rights, 8, 13
Hirschon, R., 81-82, 86, 88, 93
Holy Synod, 11, 12
homogeneity, 3
homogeneous, 3, 10
house
  refugee, 81
  symbolic, 87

I
icon, 5, 10, 73-74, 76
  processing of, 71-72, 74
icon stand, 68
identity
  cards, 10, 11, 12, 13, 14
  church building, 68-69
  cultural, 66
  formation, 98, 99, 100, 106, 108
  local, 67
  national, 3, 4, 8, 9, 10, 13, 14
  personal, 9, 12, 14
  religious, 3, 4, 8, 9, 10, 14,
    See also festival, religious; saint; locality; name
Igreja Universal do Reino de Deus, 99, 100
Ilioupoli, 66, 76
immigration, 3, 13
industrialization, 106
Islam, 7

J
Jews, 7, 8, 13
Jingwu Tiyuhui (Essential Martial Arts Physical Education Association), 132-133
John Paul II, x, 18, 25
Judaism, 7

L
Lausanne
   Convention, 3
   Treaty of, 9
Lent, 6
Li, Jinglin, 125-126
life stance, vii-x
Loizos, P., 80, 81, 83, 93-94

M
marriage as death, 75
martial arts, 114, 118-121, 124-134
martyrdom, 66, 71, 74-75
   festival, 72-73
   as rite of passage, 72-73, 75
   See also death
meaning, 48, 50, 53, 60
memory
   narrative, 66
   of rural past, 66
metaphor, 66, 74-76
Methodists, 55-6
migration, 65
modernisation, 4, 7, 14
modernity, x, 13, 22, 98, 106, 116-117, 120, 123, 127, 136
Moody, D.L., 38
Muslim, 3, 7, 8, 13
Muslims of Thrace, 9

N
name
   dedication, 68, 69-70
   identity, 67, 68, 69-70
   name day, 70
naos. *See* church
narrative
   as means of forming concepts, 66
   reality, 66
Nicosia, 80
nineteenth century, 45, 47, 53-57, 60
non-place, 36
Nossa senhora do Carmo e Oxum in Recife, 102

O
Olinda, 99
Ordem Terceira do Carmo, 102
Orthodox, 11, 14, 67
   Christians, 3, 7, 9, 10, 13
   Church, 8, 11, 12, 71, 73, 77, 82
   material culture, 85-90
   miracles, 82, 89
   religion, 65
   rituals, 82, 85-90, 93
   saint, 69, 76
   sites, 85-90
Ottoman
   Empire, 10
   millet system, 9
   rule, 9
   state, 3
Our Lady of Carmen, 102

P
Panagia ton Katharon, 82, 86-87
Panegyri, 65, 72, 73, 76, 89. *See also* festival; religious
PASOK government, 4, 7, 11
Pentecostal, 99, 100, 106, 107
pilgrimage, 80, 85, 88-89, 92
Pinxten, R., 137
pluralisation, 99, 103, 106, 108
private/public, 4, 10, 11, 12, 13
procession, 71-72, 74-76
Prosforo, 70, 76
Proskynisi, 73-74, 77
Protestantism, 99
public visibility, 99, 109

Q
Qigong (health and meditation exercises), 133
Qing (dynasty), 115-117, 119, 123, 130
Quaker meeting house, 45, 48-60
Quakerism, 47, 53, 55-6, 58-60

R
Recife, 97, 98, 99, 100, 101, 102, 103, 104, 105, 106, 108, 109, 110
refugees, 79-93
  urban, 81-83, 86-87, 91
religion, vii-x, 6, 9, 10, 11, 12, 13, 18-19, 22, 26
  official, 65, 66
  popular, 66
religiosity, 3, 5, 13
religious, 4, 5, 7, 12, 13, 14
religious practice, 6, 10
religious rites, 8, 9
Religious Society of Friends. *See* Quakerism
religious space, 103, 109
religious vitality, 5
ritual, 49-50, 71, 72, 74-75, 85-93
Roman Catholicism, 98
rural
  background, 65, 75
  capital, 65
  communities, 72
  culture, 75
  festival, 72
  immigrants, 65
  past, 66
  tradition, 75

S
sacred, the, 4, 49-50
Saint
  feast, 69-70, 72
  identity, 76
  locality, 68, 76
  names, 69-70
  patron, 67-68, 76
Sarris, M., 88, 94
Schuller, R., 36
secularisation, 4, 5, 8, 12, 13, 14
semiology, 48
seventeenth century, 50-1, 53, 55, 57
Seymour, W., 33
Shanghai, 114, 121-124, 132-135
Shanghai Tiyu Xueyuan (Shanghai Academy of Physical Education), 134
Shaolinquan, 118, 131, 133
Shen (teacher), 133-134

socialism, 18-29
space, 65, 67, 68, 73
  religious 45-6, 48-50, 53, 60
Stewart, C., 87, 94
St Marina, 87
  dimensions of the, 68, 74
  localisation, 68, 76
  locality, 66, 87
  See also Saint
street market, 72
Sun Yat-sen, 116-117, 121, 126
Synaxari, 74, 75

T
Taiji, 120, 123, 127-128, 131, 138
Taijiquan (Fist of the Great Ultimate), 114-138
Taiwan, 136
tama. See vow
Taoist, 119-121, 126-128, 130-131, 133-134
Third Order of Saint Francis, The, 101
time, 69-70
  feasts of saints, 69
Toronto Blessing, 40
town, vii-x, 45-6, 53, 55-7, 59
tradition(alism), 117-121, 123-131, 133-134, 136

U
Umbanda, 99
Universal Church of the Kingdom of God, 41, 42
urban ecology, 45, 47-8
urbanisation, vii-xii, 45-8, 55, 65-66, 97, 98, 103, 106, 107, 109, 110
urbanism, 45-6, 48, 55
urbanite, vii, xi, 21

V
vernacular building, 51, 53-4, 56
village community, 81, 93
vow, 67, 68, 69-70

W
warehouse, 38, 39, 41, 42

Weber, M., 46, 48
Willow Creek Community Church, 38
Wirth, L., 46-7, 55
Word of Life, 39, 40, 41

X
Xangó, 98, 99, 106

Y
Yang, Chengfu, 124-127, 129-130, 133
Yi (change), 137
Yinyang (or *yin* and *yang*), 120, 126, 137-138
Yue, Huanzhi, 133

Z
Zheng, Manqing, 130
Zhou (teacher), 132-133